For Jacob Pandian
Isabelle Nabokov

RELIGION AGAINST THE SELF

RELIGION AGAINST THE SELF

An Ethnography of Tamil Rituals

Isabelle Nabokov

OXFORD
UNIVERSITY PRESS
2000

OXFORD
UNIVERSITY PRESS

Oxford New York
Athens Auckland Bangkok Bogotá Buenos Aires Calcutta
Cape Town Chennai Dar es Salaam Delhi Florence Hong Kong Istanbul
Karachi Kuala Lumpur Madrid Melbourne Mexico City Mumbai
Nairobi Paris São Paulo Singapore Taipei Tokyo Toronto Warsaw

and associated companies in
Berlin Ibadan

Published by Oxford University Press, Inc.
198 Madison Avenue, New York, New York 10016

Library of Congress Cataloging-in-Publication Data
Nabokov, Isabelle.
Religion against the self : an ethnography of Tamil Rituals /
Isabelle Nabokov.
p. cm.
ISBN 0-19-511364-0; ISBN 0-19-511365-9 (pbk.)
1. Hinduism—India—Tamil Nadu—Customs and practices. 2. Tamils
(Indic people)—Customs and practices. 3. Tamil Nadu (India)—
Religious life and customs. 4. Spirit possession—India—Tamil
Nadu. I. Title.
BL1226.15.T36N33 2000
306.6'0954'82—dc21 99-34727

1 3 5 7 9 8 6 4 2

Printed in the United States of America
on acid-free paper

For Penelope

PREFACE

This book is a documentation and analysis of a spectrum of practices by means of which congregations of suffering and congregations of kinship in the South Arcot district of Tamilnadu, South India, deal with crises of inclusion and exclusion. It emphasizes that these practices are so strongly similar to one another that anthropological categories like "initiation," "divination," "sorcery," "countersorcery," "demonic possession," "exorcism," "investiture," and "sacrifice" do not gloss their common symbolic structures, processual dynamics, and underlying resonances. It also contends that anthropological dualist or triadic models of the ritual process fail to describe Tamil rituals. Participants, for instance, are not separated from society, put in the realm of liminality, and then put back in society as is assumed in most of these models, but are continuously drawn into an "innermost" space. Finally, the book distinguishes between two kinds of ritual structures: "prescriptive" rituals, which pressure people to incorporate an outer or public image of themselves, and "performative" rituals, which let them author their own transformations; but it argues that both kinds ultimately do violence to the self. At its broadest level, this book is about how religion coerces the Tamil person into becoming someone at odds with his or her self.

ACKNOWLEDGMENTS

I thank all the Tamil women and men who accepted my garbled questions, invited me into their homes and shrines, tolerated my intrusions at family rituals, and made my ethnographic project possible. My debt to them is enormous. No words could express the gratitude I feel for their patience and hospitality.

Ethnographic research was funded by the American Institute of Indian Studies to which I extend my deepest appreciation. Throughout fieldwork, the AIIS directors and administrators in India and in the United States, Ms. Kaye Hill, Joseph W. Elder, P. Venugopala Rao, and especially Pradeep Mehendiratta, assisted me in every possible way and I thank them all for their support.

Without the help of my five field assistants this work would not exist. I single out M. Savarana Kumar from Madurai, whose good-humor and courtesy won me the sympathy of many South Arcot villagers and contributed to the success of the entire field project. Saravana was recommended to me by Ulrike Niklas and introduced to me by Eveline Masilamani-Meyer, so my thanks to them as well. P. Srida from Alampoondi offered English translations and valuable commentaries of many interviews. From Madurai, P. Velraj, and D. M. Saravanan also worked with me on interviews, transcriptions, and translations of many tapes. Finally M. Thavamani of Gingee, who joined me halfway through my fieldwork, came closer than any to becoming a true intellectual collaborator in this research

Other established scholars provided mentorship and assistance in India. Alf Hiltebeitel's lecture on the cult of the goddess Draupadī at the Kamaraj University of Madurai inspired me to settle nearby Gingee where he had documented her festival. T. Murugarathanam, professor and head of the Department of Tamil Studies at Madurai Kamaraj University, served as my academic mentor in India. J. Rajasekaran, coordinator for the University of Wisconsin Language Program Abroad, always made my stays in Madurai productive and fun, offering not only experienced advice, but, perhaps more importantly, his friendship. The same goes for Swami Sevananda, who always opened his door and his mind to my research. In Madras C. Arunachalam searched the city's libraries and bookstores for publications relevant to this project. Two French-speaking Petits Frères des Pauvres, Shanti and Anand, who resided in a nearby village, greatly facilitated my entry in the field. Their long familiarity with South Arcot was extremely beneficial to me, and I am grateful for the many delightful evenings we spent together. From L'École Française d'Extrême-Orient in Pondichery, the late Francoise L'Hernault lent me access to her detailed maps of Tamilnadu, while Jacques Pouchepadass from the Institut Francais also extended kind assistance. I also wish to remember the collegial feedbacks from other scholars who were conducting research in Tamilnadu during the time of my fieldwork: Lee Weissman and his wife Linda Levine, Marie-Louise Reiniche, Nick Dirks, Martha Ann Selby, Lyn Bigelow, and Paul Shepherd.

My colleagues and students in the Department of Anthropology of Princeton University provided the most important intellectual base for the development of this book. Vincanne Adams, Jim Boon, Abdellah Hammoudi, Rena Lederman, Ranjini Obeyesekere, Larry Rosen, Alison Lake, and Sarah Pinto all contributed in a variety of direct and indirect ways to refine analyses. I owe most to Hildred Geertz who patiently saw and encouraged many directions of thought and to Emily Martin for much kindness and encouragement over the years. Gannanath Obeyesekere's critique of a preliminary version of the introduction gave me much to think about. I hope this book expresses how much I am indebted to his critical approach to "personal symbols" and ethnography of Sinhalese religion.

Others have been generous with their time and criticisms. I am indebted to Kausalya Hart, George Hart, and the late K. Paramasivam, for their language instruction. I learned a lot from conversations with David Knipe, Narayan Rao, and Peter Claus. Walter Lippencott, Ray Fogelson, Soraya Tlatli, Elizabeth Oram, Lucia Melgar, Kirin Narayan, and especially Rand Valentine saved me from sinking into despair many times. Margaret Trawick's insightful reading of my dissertation for the University of California Press encouraged me to turn it into this book. Gerald Berreman's commitment to write against images of radical otherness that pervade much ethnographic writing has been a constant source of inspiration since graduate school. I am most grateful to David Shulman, for his recommendation that I publish this book and for gently helping me "see" what it says. His analyses of Tamil devotion inform this work from beginning to end.

Some passages and sections of this book have been published elsewhere. I thank the editors and publishers of the following journals for permission to reprint materials:

Deadly Power: a Funeral to Counter Sorcery in South India. *American Ethnologist* (in press).

Expel the Lover, Recover the Wife: Symbolic Analysis of a South Indian Exorcism. *The Journal of the Royal Anthropological Institute* (N.S.) 3(2): 297–316.

When the Dead Become Brides, Gods, and Gold: Marriage Symbolism in a Tamil Household Ritual. *Journal of Ritual Studies* 10(1):113–133.

In preparing this book I had a good deal of editorial assistance. I would like to mention Nicolas Knipe and Margaret Case for respectively helping me with chapter 7 and the Introduction. I also want to thank Cynthia Read, MaryBeth Branigan, and others at Oxford University Press for taking interest in this book and giving it their outstanding care. Last, Peter Nabokov cheerfully read the entire manuscript and provided many insightful comments and suggestions. Peter has always been my harshest and most valued critic; for his candid feedback, I am deeply grateful.

The strength behind the words is from my mother; the rest is for Penny.

CONTENTS

RELIGION AGAINST THE SELF

INTRODUCTION

Religion was not on my agenda when I first went to South India. My plan was to investigate the meanings with which Tamil people invested their pasts, and the area around the trading town of Gingee (*Ceñci* in Tamil) 180 kilometers southwest of Madras seemed a promising fieldsite for this project. This parched wasteland of granite boulders and thorny plants once sustained a sequence of medieval kingdoms with large armies and legendary heroes. I rented a one-time grocery shop in a multicaste village about an hour's walk from Gingee. Dutifully, I began visiting the fort in Gingee, inquiring about local narratives of its rulers. I collected genealogies, court cases, residential patterns, and agricultural cycles. But after I had pursued this subject for about three months, the direction of my fieldwork changed dramatically.

The morning of December's new moon, 1990, some of my new friends urged me to visit the highly popular temple at Mēl Malaiyaṉūr, a few kilometers away from my residence. Although described by scholar Eveline Meyer as "the most important source of the cult" of the goddess Aṅkāḷaparamēcuvari, who is renowned throughout Tamilnadu for making "her power available to devotees" (1986: 66), the temple was seen by my new acquaintances simply as a place that should be visited so that I could better know the neighborhood.

So around dusk I parked my scooter outside the temple's unassuming main gate, shed my sandals, and halted at a small, open-air shrine where a female medium had set up shop. I quickly regretted my curiosity. The heavy-set woman, in her early forties, began yelling at me to employ her services. When I pleaded with a strained smile that I just wanted to watch, she acted insulted: "You think I don't have any *cakti* [female divine power]?" she huffed at me in a theatrically loud voice. Bystanders laughed, I was mortified, it took apologies and a tip to persuade her that I was not doubting her spiritual gifts. Then I watched her enter a state of trance and encountered another world. Over those long hours I got an inkling that her transactions with the spirits of her clients' deceased relatives embodied existential meanings that were far more urgent and relevant to the living than any predetermined inquiry into their legendary past.

It is no exaggeration to say that I spent the remaining eleven months of my research trying to understand the seances I witnessed that night. To my disappointment I did not see the female medium who had accosted me for several weeks afterward. But I followed leads and traced out connections regarding the sort of traffic she conducted between human beings and supernaturals. In pursuing others with the expertise or predilection to cross into other dimensions of existence, I was also led to transgress boundaries. For my ethnographic field now spread beyond the customary, fixed sites and particular scenarios of village temple worship into a spectrum of "religious" expressions and symbolic manipulations which, until very recently, have gone largely undocumented in India's anthropological literature.

Entering This "Tamil World"

At first I gravitated toward locations with a local reputation for containing *cakti*, spiritual energy and healing power. At the more modest end they included homemade shrines, involving no more than a shrouded anthill or a grouping of dung-plastered bricks, that were erected by the shamanlike independent practitioners known in Tamil as *cāmis*. But I also kept visiting the Mēl Malaiyan̲ūr temple, which served as a free market for all sorts of spiritual operations, including sorcery removals and exorcisms. There I first developed consultant relationships among the troupes of ritual musicians, the *pampaikkārar*, who vied with free-lance healers for a piece of the temple's thriving spiritual action.

Generally these sanctuaries came alive twice a week, Tuesdays and Fridays, with especially intense sessions during the lunar junctures of new (*amāvācai*) and full (*paurṇami*) moon nights. Then people thronged to discover the causes of persistent illnesses, to resolve personal problems, to be relieved of sorcery spells and possessing demons.[1] They were drawn from all non-Brahmin sectors of Tamil society, and included high-ranking, so called "Sanskritized"[2] castes (*Ceṭṭiyār, Mutaliyār, Ācāri*) who publicly stigmatize such practices as "superstitious" and "inferior" to the ritualized exchanges with deities conducted by Brahmin priests in orthodox temples. But most were rural villagers belonging to low-to-middle castes who owned little or no land and survived as day-laborers in local agricultural fields. Some also fit the social category called by Sara Dickey the "urban poor" (1993), working in factories, owning small peddling businesses, or toiling in menial jobs.

What all had in common, however, and often in distressing abundance, was profound personal affliction. Many were at the lowest points in their lives: incessantly arguing with loved ones or running away from domestic quarrels and becoming deeply dispirited over the ruptures. I also heard stories of death, sickness, abandonment, and all manner of unwelcome suffering. This common experience and consequent sharing of misfortune produced, in turn, the sort of bonding phenomenon that Victor Turner (1969) called "temporary communitas," and that has been compared to the solidarity of devotees in more orthodox pilgrimage centers (Dumont 1986; Herrenschmidt 1981; Assayag 1992). But unlike the large temples, where pilgrims may mingle but do not personally interact, I gained the impression that these lesser-known religious centers yielded a more intimate, face-to-face "congregation of suffering," as strangers from different social, economic, and territorial backgrounds talked for days about their emergencies, traumas, and dreams.

Fieldwork in these sanctuaries was emotionally difficult but logistically easy. Since diagnostic seances and healing rituals united people who were uprooted from familiar settings and social roles, my attendance, although conspicuous, was not structurally out of place. Patients and their families were expected, indeed encouraged, to exchange, quite publicly, their most detailed and private case histories. And because exorcist and countersorcery rituals were already polluted, inauspicious affairs, my note taking was perceived as threatening only to myself. The linkage of introductions and connections that I made evolved from their own internal logic. My bridge from diagnostic seances to countersorcery rituals, for instance, was not merely accidental: the *cāmis* usually prescribed these "removals" for their patients. I entered the living narratives of their "therapies" much as one turns the page of a novel to find out what happens next.

Once the storylines of my investigations came to a close, however, I was left with a plethora of cultural images that lent visual and verbal narrative body to the torn, incoherent emotions of pain, loss, and suffering. Then my job was to retrace those experiences, reelicit participants' memories and commentaries, and recover some awareness of how ritual processes had shifted people to new conditions of confidence, integration, or "health." That ethnographic "extension process" forced me to delve more deeply into local discourses on personal disturbance, patients' biographies, and the sources of healers' powers.

I was very fortunate. Patients usually had no problem with my follow-up interviews at their homes. More than once I felt embarrassed by the ease of our relations, by the plain, uncomplicated way in which they let me record their stories, from initial adversity through degrees of ritualized resolution. As for the articulate, often insightful specialists themselves, Edward Harper's comment that "a reason for the lack of written literature on [South Indian] shamanism is the reticence of informants to volunteer knowledge of the subject" was certainly not my experience (1957: 267). If anything, had I been less inhibited and more willing to simply listen than to "elicit" information, the healers with whom I worked for the better part of a year might have taken me far deeper into their working cosmology.

Another View of This Tamil World

Toward the latter period of my fieldwork I entered this low-visibility arena of direct supernatural communication from the perspective of the musicians whom I had met and profiled as a result of studying exorcist rituals at the Mēl Malaiyaṉūr temple. Observing my work with independent ritual practitioners, they were concerned that people "in America" would get a lopsided view of their culture spiritual operations. "We don't just expel demons from this world," one complained to me. "We also invite family and lineage deities back into it. Come and see!" Since customarily these "invitations" to household and lineage gods were conducted on the agricultural fields privately owned by kin groups, once again I found myself visiting religious grounds located outside the purview of village religion and its pervasive systems of caste and political patronage.

But these kin-centered "invitations" transpired on a different ceremonial schedule. Rather than responses to crises or inauspicious events, they fell at the juncture of positive, planned life-cycle transitions, which mainly meant marriage and children's ear-piercing rites. My inquiries into them were not dictated by the biweekly and bimonthly rhythms of the vernacular exercise of religious power but by the timing of rites of passage, which in the South Arcot district are usually held over the Tamil months of *Vaikāci* (May/June) and *Āṭi* (July-August).

These "invitations" proved more difficult to record than the rituals of affliction. As corporate affairs which, save for the officiating musicians, excluded anyone unrelated to the household or lineage, my presence always stood out. And unlike the "congregations of suffering" who had only their painfully present predicaments in common, these "congregations of kinship" shared a long history whose less harmonious aspects were apt to resurface during these occasions; in fact, it might be said that the former addressed current discord in an efficient, timely fashion while the latter was forced to wade through the accumulated resentments of past discords that had never been resolved. These charged situations could be fraught with old injuries, hurt feelings, and deep family secrets, so fieldwork required constant vigilance.

Furthermore, the symbolic operations that "invited" dead relatives (in the form of tutelary deities) to marriage or lineage gods to ear-piercing ceremonies were considered more precarious than those that expelled demons; some people feared that me and my recording devices might inhibit their successful arrival and blessing. To ease their anxieties I usually kept a low profile, put away my camera and stood some distance from the ritual scene—a complete reversal of my behavior during exorcisms when everyone insisted I stand among them and tape-record every word of dialogue between specialists and spirits. Even those precautions were not always enough at the "invitations," and one spirit had me evicted because my field assistant wore an inauspicious black shirt.

The more I observed these "invitations" the more I was struck by their isomorphic relationships to exorcism and countersorcery. Although their context was auspicious, their spirits incorporated rather than expelled from society, the same processual structure, discursive procedures, and set of symbols were in operation. Through the comparative study of these ritual systems emerged whatever ethnographic insights come from this work; by tacking back and forth between them, this Tamil world, the "field" of my fieldwork, gained focus. The inventive reworking of symbols I had previously noticed in other contexts, the novel way of handling identical images, the different answers to the all-pervasive question addressed to spirits—"Who are you?"—all pointed to the underlying resonances and linkages in this loosely knit fabric of cultural practices that fell beneath the level of village festivals and public ceremonies.

The Core Ritual Process of This Tamil World

This book, then, is a cumulative description and speculative reflection on these practices in Tamilnadu, South India. It grew out of a string of serendipitous and structural connections I made while moving from one consultant to another, more often than I would like to admit following intuitions on the spot and walking in the dark. As this research direction deepened theoretically and branched out spatially, one conviction started to emerge. This multidimensional "Tamil world" that I pursued through a cluster of rural communities and amid the criss-crossing relationships between these technicians, patients, or celebrants and the relevant spirits was somehow unified. Although its emotional tenor and mode of articulation varied here and there, it seemed governed by a similar organizational scheme, social ethos, epistemological framework, and core ritual process.

Of course, I do not pretend to be the first ethnographer to perceive a common pattern behind a range of religious phenomena. As early as 1909, the French folklorist Arnold van Gennep discerned a "wide degree of general similarity" among life-cycle rites from many parts of the world (in Bell 1997: 36). The originality of his scheme lay in his awareness that in most cultures, ceremonies of birth, childhood, social puberty, betrothal, marriage, pregnancy, fatherhood, initiation into religious societies, and funerals effect changes in social states by means of a three-stage sequence that involves changes of spatial locations. First ritual participants are physically removed from their communities and concomitant social identities. After passing through a second stage of no identity or social affiliation, in the third stage they return to society, where they are reincorporated into a new social status and role (also see Victor Turner's reworking of this framework, 1969).

For the rituals presented in this book, the Van Gennep model has limited utility. True, most of them emphasize processual movement through space, such as the entrance into a village or house; the crossing of streets; the passing through doors, arches, and gates; and so on. True, again, most of them exhibit the phases of separation, transition, and reincorporation. But although participants are first officially "warned" to show up at a place "outside" the community, this preamble and subsequent procession to that "outside" location have unique connotations in Tamil symbology.

As the scholar of South Indian classical and folk literature A. K. Ramanujan has pointed out, "outside," identified in Tamil as *puṟam*, is an entrenched South Indian category that is inevitably paired with *akam*, meaning "inside" (1967; 1986; also see Shulman 1993). During the first three centuries of the Christian era, *caṅkams* ("fraternities") of Tamil poets employed these terms to divide their poems into two classes. The *puṟam* variety consisted of "public" poems on war, action, kingdom, community, good and evil, death, and so on, while the *akam* group consisted of "love" poems (1967: 99). Ramanujan also noted that *puṟam* poems are "placed in a real society and given a context of real history," as evidenced by the fact that they often mention the names of kings, heroes, poets, and places (1967: 101). In contrast, "*akam* poetry is directly about experience, not action; it is a poetry of the inner world" (1967: 103). In such poems no personal names are to be mentioned, and the evocative associations of "landscapes" become more important than particular places (1967: 104).

So a Tamil ritual procession to an "outside" place does not exactly correspond to a "passage" out of the community as implied in Van Gennep's (and Turner's) model, nor to a "sacred" place apart from the "profane," as suggested in Durkheim's view of religion (1965). Quite the contrary, it actually announces a movement toward a "public" realm.

But the full significance of such progression remains still more complex. In South Indian religion, as David Shulman discovered in his analysis of a mid-twelfth-century Tamil devotional story, "The always critical boundary between inner and outer is meant to be crossed" (1993: 35). This conflation of categorical domains is also the goal of the ritual and religious experiences presented in this book. They seek to match public and private worlds in order for them to "meet," merge, and fuse. This is not surprising, for the Tamil word for God, *kaṭavuḷ*, means "crossing," "exceeding," or "surpassing," suggesting that the religious experience is always conceived as a form of intersection, a point of contact and coalescence between two domains or more of experience.

In the rituals I have documented, such "crossings" are initiated with the "warning" to "meet" again in an "outside" place. But they gain momentum with the subsequent representation, or sometimes fixation, of a supernatural in an image—an effigy, for example, or a decorated pot—for all to see in that exterior landscape. As many scholars have noted, visual apprehension of the divine constitutes the minimum transaction if not the experiential core of Hindu devotion (Babb 1981; Eck 1981: 7). Devotees yearn to see ("take *darśan*") and to be seen by temple deities whose images are often striking for their large and highlighted eyes. Some explain that this reciprocal eye contact dissolves boundaries that normally prevail between divinity and humanity (Fuller 1992: 73). It is much the same in the rituals presented in this book, seeing is "a kind of touching," a "form of knowing" (Eck 1981: 9). The act of *darśan* (in Tamil *tarica*<u>*n*</u>*am*) also becomes a form of absorbing, so that any objectification of a supernatural is always a form of assimilation as well.

In the Hindu *pūjā*, a basic form of worship in domestic and temple contexts, such assimilation of a deity culminates when a camphor flame is shown (*ārāti*). At this point, Christopher Fuller writes, "The divine and human participants are most fully identified . . . God has become man and a person, transformed, has become god; they have merged" (1992: 73). Scholars have also shown that such fusions are accomplished by other sorts of reciprocal relations (Appadurai and Breckenridge 1976; Wadley 1975; Babb 1975; Inden 1976; Ostor 1980; but see Raheja 1988 and Fuller 1982, 1992). Worshipers make offerings of food, cloth, and incense and receive *prasāda* in exchange, the deity's leftover food that is now imbued with his or her more purified and more powerful "substances." Although these transactions are often said to establish unequal, even hierarchical relations between the parties, they can create powerful ontological transformations (Marriott 1976: 111–12). Since *prasāda* is always consumed, worshipers absorb the deity's essence into their bodily persons. In these models, then, Hindu *pūjā* accomplishes a sensual incorporation of divine "grace" into the person (also see Shulman 1993: 34-47).

All these processes are visible in the folk rituals I have documented. The camphor flame is shown, offerings to deities are returned to, and consumed by, devotees. But many of these rituals do not leave it at that. They add another step: the request that the supernatural subsequently incorporates himself or herself in a human body. Trance-possession often becomes the means by which ritual participants assimilate supernaturals into their persons. "Who are you?" is the question that is then always asked of the possessing power. The question itself belongs to the realm of *pu*<u>*r*</u>*am*, the world of public, external, and fixed identities. And sooner or later possessing supernaturals do reveal who they are and what they know, think, feel, and want. Communicating through the voice of their human mediums, they prove to be "persons" one can know, argue with, and urge to stay or scram.

In Tamil concepts, the "public" acquires its full meaning only in relationship to its opposite, the "private." The *aham* or love poems, for example, evoke the famous five main landscapes of Tamilnadu, each with its specific climate, flora, fauna, habitat, and so on, which also correspond to various phases of love between man and woman (Ramanujan 1967:104). The result is that the exterior landscape has only the characteristics of what Ramanujan called the "interior landscape," and vice versa (1967). It is much the same in the rituals presented in this book: the makings and unmakings of cosmological persons also require personal investments by their relations. For *they* are the ones who truly give form to the ritual cosmology, as they complete what is "publicly" known of supernaturals with highly specific, felt significances created out of their "private" biographies and existential circumstances. This is especially true in the case of the possessed persons who infuse their possessing deities and demons with their own personality and emotional dilemmas.

Supernaturals thus wind up acquiring human identities and subjectivities. But the reverse also becomes true: human beings gain the names and identities of their possessing spirits. These lendings and blendings of personalities, however, are not equivalent. Supernaturals have characteristics that are somewhat crystallized, stereotypical, and often overdrawn. Some even have generic rather than specific or unique attributes. By contrast, human beings have particular, different life experiences. The fusion of cosmology and psychology results in a complexification, or "enlargement" of supernaturals, but a simplification, or reduction, of human beings. In other words, the subjectivization of supernaturals "corresponds" to an objectification of participants, who wind up acquiring fixed or typical, even archetypal, names and identities. Their appropriation of "objective" identities is precisely the goal of all these rituals.

Participants' return to an "inside" place, be it a temple or a household, then, does not announce a reincorporation into society, as in the Van Gennep's model of the ritual process, but rather an interiorization or individuation of the "public" world. This is evident by the fact that the procession back home does not start until participants solemnly "promise" to live up to their newly acquired identities and their concomitant roles and obligations. This commitment is the culmination of the Tamil ritual process, its raison d'être.

Prescribed and Performed Transformations

Because participants are co-creators in the logic and instrumentality of their own transformations, a Tamil ritual is never a representation of society as determining of the individual, as it appears in a Durkheimian interpretation. Yet, many of the practices presented in the following pages still do not corroborate Victor Turner's proposition that ritual is the place where human beings spontaneously discover and experience a deep awareness of society as a shared human need (1969).[3] If anything, many of the Tamil supernaturals profiled in this book arrive at these rituals with a contrary perspective: with the perspective that life with others is simply not worthwhile. As we will see, many of them confess that they untimely took it away by hanging or drowning themselves. And others, more often than not spirits of deceased parents, "do not feel like" accepting their children's invitation to "come home." Kinship relationships and identities are always problematic to Tamil spirits. The goal of many—but not all—of these rituals then consists of persuading them, as well as the human beings who speak on their behalf, to change their minds and "see" things from an "outside" perspective, in which life with others is all there is. But how do rituals move participants to new dispositions and points of view?

Anthropological analyses of ritual have long been preoccupied with this problem of transformation. Until recently, the question of how might ritual actually shift people to new psychological, social, or even ontological states of being was answered by highlighting the communicative properties of what Victor Turner once called "the basic building-blocks" or the "molecules" of ritual, namely symbols (1969: 14). In the case of ritual healing, for example, it was argued that symbols formulated the causes of affliction (be they social, cultural, or psychological) and then reframed understandings so that participants could grasp and resolve their problems (Csordas 1983, Dow 1986). These orientations also drew upon Claude Lévi-Strauss's classic essay "The Effectiveness of Symbols," (1963) which argued that a Cuna shaman's recitation of a birth incantation eased difficult labors because it gave parturient women a "language" to predicate and overcome the physiological processes obstructing their delivery.

But recently anthropologists have taken issue with Victor Turner's central assumption that rituals and their "molecules" inevitably evoke social meanings in participants (1967).[4] Edward Schieffelin, for example, showed that the Kaluli spirit performance in New Guinea was not geared toward highlighting symbolic meanings and that instead the "reality" of such seances "emerged" through nondiscursive, dramaturgical processes (1985, also see 1996). Robert Desjarlais too did not find symbolist perspectives particularly useful in explaining how Meme, a Yolmo shaman from Nepal, healed his patients. As he wrote, "I do not believe that Meme recovers a spirit primarily through the use of metaphors, symbolic transformations, or rhetorical tropes, as recent studies of 'symbolic healing' hold" (1992:208). Because Meme's craft instead involved "a healing of bodies, of sensibilities, of ways of being in this world," Desjarlais called attention to the "sensory" dimensions of these Yolmo rites. For his part, Bruce Kapferer shifted from an analytical focus on semantics to an investigation of forms and procedures, suggesting that the organization of Sinhalese exorcist performances—arrangement of ritual space, positioning of audience and participants in this setting, and manipulation of media such as song and dance (1979a, 1979b, 1983)—was essential to understanding its transformative impact on participants. This was because their subjective metamorphoses were "made to parallel the transformations taking place in the objective structure" of the rite (1983: 180).[5] Maurice Bloch confirmed that ritual did not so much "mean" as "do" things to people. The special use of formulaic speech and song in the ritual language of the Merina people in Madagascar, he argued, actually "restricted" what could be said and "coerced" speaker and audience into accepting its terms and content (1986).

My own contention with symbolic analyses of ritual transformation lies elsewhere. Too often symbolic perspectives focus on the formal characteristics of symbolic structures (Yalman 1963) or cultural associations of symbols

(Turner 1967) instead of exploring how participants might fill them with meanings drawn from and relevant to their own particular experiences. My fieldwork caused me to realize, however, that the symbols manipulated during Tamil rituals have no self-existence—they feed upon personal engagement for their lifeblood. Nor can I account for their "effectiveness" by invoking the peculiar associative ("multivocal" or "ambiguous") properties of symbols (Turner 1967; Laderman 1987). In the Tamil case at least it is not symbols and their formal characteristics which in and of themselves change the ways in which people see, feel, and think about themselves or the world, as is often implied in symbolic analyses of rituals. Rather, it is people who infuse these constructs with highly specific, felt significances created out of their existential predicaments so as to address or resolve them.

This book contends that the playing out of these subjective investments hinges on two variants of the core ritual process just described. Some Tamil rituals are "prescriptive," others are "performative"—to borrow Marshall Sahlins's useful distinction between two kinds of social structures (1985). The former follows explicit rules about who may do what and with whom; in the latter people seem to be making up the rules as they go along. So with Tamil rituals: some give participants no other option but to comply with stated procedures and aims; others permit everyone to make their own performative and interpretative choices. In these processes, at the same time, lie different outcomes. "Prescriptive" rituals work to make people adopt "public" identities. "Performative" rituals leave them free to walk away from social roles and personal relationships.

"Prescriptive" changes of inner dispositions are closely linked with the objective forms of the ritual, as Kapferer contends for Sinhalese exorcisms (1983). This is evident from start to finish: from the "warning" that programs participants for the forthcoming action to their final "pledge" to internalize their transformation. But "prescriptive" rituals often strike me as even more "totalizing" than the exorcisms Kapferer describes from Sri Lanka, for the basic reason that they make nonengagement very difficult, if not virtually impossible. A series of formulaic procedures pressure participants to comply with the demands placed on them, so that the ritual process, as Maurice Bloch argues for the Merina circumcision ceremony, "can become a form of power or coercion" (1989: 24). Moreover, such rituals take full possession not only of the mind but of the body as well, causing deep and irreversible mutations in participants physical persons and, what Robert Desjarlais might call, their "sensory" senses of self (1992, 1996).

"Performative" rituals (and this applies to certain religious experiences discussed in this book as well) also follow a formal logic and coherent sequential organization. The difference is that here the imposition of a relatively consistent frame of reference does not enforce uniform interpretations or transformations on all the participants.What is paradoxical is that such open-ended rituals are encoded with strong imagery of a predominantly aggressive—even destructive—tone. Since they make it possible for participants to "perform" a disengagement from social roles and personal relationships, I suggest that evading the "exterior" realm and its obligations might be just as problematic for the Tamil person as "crossing" over it. In fact, this process may be more traumatic for, as we will see, here the violence is self-"performed."

The Person in This Tamil World

A second body of anthropological theory engaged by this book is somewhat more specific to India. Central to most classical anthropological models of caste society are controversial understandings of just what constitutes "the Hindu person." Since much of my description concerns the ritualized makings and remakings of the Tamil person, let me touch on this debate.

The French anthropologist Louis Dumont (1970) initiated this discussion by expanding on personhood as a cultural category as introduced by his teacher Marcel Mauss (1979 [1938]). Dumont contrasted the social and moral significance of "the individual" in Western societies with the presumed absence of such a concept in "traditional" societies such as India. While not denying that Indian society was composed of physically separated beings, he contended that the "individual as a cultural value" was lacking in India (1970). To him the Indian derived his sense of identity and even reality, not from his autonomous being but only through "relations" (1970: 42).[6] The "particular man" was encompassed by groups such as village, caste, and family. His allegiance lay with such collectivities (Mines 1994: 5). But Dumont did find something akin to the Western concept of individualism in the Hindu ideal of renunciation. As he wrote: "The renouncer leaves the world behind in order to devote himself to his own liberation. Essentially he depends upon no one but himself, he is alone. He thinks as an individual, and this is the distinctive trait which opposes him to the man-in-the-world and brings him closer to the western thinker. But while for us the individual is in the world, here he is found only outside the world, at least in principle" (1970: 45).

The argument that individualism played no role in caste society did not fare any better among anthropologists than Dumont's classification of the Indian person as "homo hierarchicus"—a genus that seemed to exist only to oppose its modern Western antithesis, "homo aequalis" (1980). Indian and American scholars shortly criticized it on grounds that it was "ethnocentric" (Shweder and Bourne 1984), "condescending" (Berreman 1971) and "essentializing" (Appadurai 1986). Moreover, it was plain wrong, as contemporary writers have found that the very people who had been the focus of Dumont's extensive ethnographic research (1986), apparently "*do* recognize individuality as an essential feature of ordinary life" and that in fact "individuality lies at the very crux of a Tamil sense of self, as well as his or her sense of others" (Mines 1994: 2, his emphasis; also see Beteille 1986; but see Barnett 1976).

But even McKim Marriott, an overt opponent of Dumont's binary oppositions, concluded that the Indian person was *not* an individual (1976). However, he and Ronald Inden offered a different line of reasoning (1977). It was not so much that the Indian was less autonomous, less independent, and less equal than the American, but he or she was a different person altogether. According to Indian ways of thinking and behaving, persons are thought to be composite of transferable particles that form their personal "substance" (1977). Thus our Judeo-Christian notion of a unity of body, soul, mind and conscience, thought, and action, which is summed up in the concept of the person that Dumont calls the "individual," does not apply in India. Far from being integrated in a relatively bounded, unitary, and indivisible whole—in short of having individuality in "our" sense of the word—the Hindus are "dividual." They break down when exposed to "incompatible substances."[7]

My research suggests that these views of the "Indian" are not irreconcilable. The actors of this book are something other than "individuals" or "persons" in the Western sense of these categories. But there are problems with both formulations. Dumont assumes that the acquisition of social identities, be they holistic or individualistic, is a straightforward process in which people readily adopt any and all distinctive attributes that constitute a "person" in their society. But Dumont, much like his teacher, is not interested in the subjective realm—in what Marcel Mauss called "the sense of the self" (1979). My fieldwork experiences taught me, however, that one must never dismiss what Meyer Fortes called "the question of the awareness of the self, [the] *moi* of Mauss' analysis" (1987: 250).

Indeed, the attempts to ritually connect (or perhaps better superimpose, inner and outer characteristics) and endow the "me" with personhood is never an automatic process in Tamilnadu. It seems to go against the grain of the particular man and woman. This is particularly evidenced in the verbal transactions of all "prescriptive" rituals, as spirits and their human hosts actively resist being confused or merged with others or taking on the very kinds of relational identities that Dumont takes for granted. Finally, "inner" and "outer" experiences do not seem to blend very well. The pervasive symbolism of decapitation and recapitation that threads through all final phases of "prescriptive" rituals suggests that the end-product is a split person, a "divided self," we may say.

My research seems rather to corroborate Marriott and Inden's "dividual" model of the Hindu person (1977). But if Dumont's "particular man" is too socially determined and too relational, Marriott and Inden's person is not sufficiently either. His or her ontology and mode of being in the world is physical, almost entirely physiological, as evidenced by repetitive references to "bodily processes," "inborn codes for conduct," "genera," and the like (1977). To be sure this person does "transact" with others, but mostly in terms of "matter," "substances," and "particles." Thus, his or her difficulties with boundaries, with merging and differentiation, arise not in terms of personal relationships and their psychological dynamics—in the kinds of situations, in other words, which for most people in the world constitute much of the experienced reality of personhood—but over exchanges of food and bodily fluids.

This book offers a contrary perspective to this "transactional" view of Indian ritual action. It argues that the fundamental subject of Tamil religion is identity. The critical question that it asks, and answers, is: "Who are you?" The bodily manipulations and metamorphoses that it enacts have intensely subjective and existential implications. This is evidenced by the fact that many of the rituals I have documented specifically target the head, which in Tamil culture is the organ that most concretely symbolizes one's personality (also see Beck 1979: 32, 40).

This book also objects to the "transactional theory" of ritual that emerged from the "dividual" model of the person. At the core of the model is a person with a high propensity for breaking down into separate "particles" and mixing with "particles" of different kinds of substances. But such a volatile person still remains within the legacy of Western assumptions about bounded, united, and essentialist selves. For he or she strives to retain a sense of wholeness or absolute idendity by means of ritual action. According to Marriott and Inden, it is the function of ritual to remove, if only temporarily, incompatible or negative substances from Indian persons or, on the contrary, recombine them with more powerful or valuable substances of deities (Wadley 1975, Babb 1975, Inden 1976; Ostor 1980; Daniel 1984; Raheja 1988). I argue instead that far from integrating or reintegrating people, Tamil rituals may fragment them to the point of splitting them apart. The person who emerges from many of the rituals and religious experiences presented in this book is a compound of disparate identities that do not always blend very well.

Entering the Hindu world through such Tamil rituals may better highlight our own similarities to Indian people than Dumont's and Marriott's respective focuses on "holistic" and "dividualistic" identities allow. I am not saying that life in South India is the same as life in the United States; this book emphatically demonstrates that it is not. But I do maintain that the rituals and experiences I am about to recount can teach fundamental truths about social life that transcend cultural barriers. The differences they embody, the conceptions they reflect, the apparent lack of logic they sometimes display, should not mystify us. They raise metaphysical and existential questions which, although expressive of the "coded" worldview of Tamil society, are more broadly human in scope. They ask how we know ourselves to be—or not to be—the persons we are supposed to be, and how our cultural ways of knowing ourselves come to organize and sometimes restrict our "inner" experiences and subjectivity?

The Plan of This Study

The chapters that follow are organized to provide a progressive understanding of a down-to-earth, "working" Tamil cosmology that comes to light in bits and pieces through an analysis of the various ways in which it "intersects" with the "inner" realm of human experiences. Together they traverse a field of connections and disconnections with supernaturals, others, and the self.

Over this century South India has undergone a revival of the devotional fervor (*bhakti*) first popularized by the Tamil poets and saints between the seventh and the ninth centuries (Clothey 1986). Increased participation in practices such as firewalking (Hiltebeitel 1992), flesh piercing (Assayag 1992), and pilgrimage (Kjaerholm 1984) have moved devotees to experience deities directly, intimately, and intensely. Expressions of this "neo-bhakti" religion, as Fred Clothey calls it (1986: 260), implicate the multiple manifestations of the South Indian goddess, whose worship has dramatically expanded since the fourteenth century (Bayly 1989: 30; Stein 1980: 239; 330–31). What has been overlooked, however, is that the goddess does not merely "come on" devotees during festival scenarios. Just as commonly she appears to ordinary men and women in everyday settings, demanding that they serve her forever (but see Trawick 1984).

The first four chapters of this book document this divine selection process, highlighting its violent, sexual undertones, the nature and application of the special gifts received by these "recruits," and the implications of the goddess's interventions into this world. They show how these days the goddess's primary function on earth is to extricate people from troubled relationships. At the heart of these chapters lie fundamental questions: Why does the goddess force herself on her designated initiates? Why do they follow her? Why is their patients' "removal" from overweening or moribund relationships fraught with funeral symbolism?

Over the next four chapters I introduce a category of supernaturals, the spirits of the dead, who are usually located at the very bottom or altogether left out of anthropological models—so-called "genealogies"—of the Tamil pantheon (Moffat 1979, Caplan 1989). What this book demonstrates, however, is that spirits of the dead are no less constitutive of Tamil Hinduism than the goddess or the great god, Lord Śiva. In fact, in my mind, they are the elemental figures of South Indian pantheons.

A major reason for these spirits' prominence in village pantheons is that they are most likely to "cross" your path. In the past Western missionaries watched this happened all the time, recording how spirits of "men and women, boys and girls," as Henri Whitehead put it in 1921 (1988: 20), were prone to possess the living, especially if, as Bishop Robert Caldwell had already noted in 1875, "they had met with a sudden or violent death" (1984: 163; also see Elmore 1984: 155). Although missionary descriptions of such possessions are replete with prejudicial interpretations and factual errors, they still disclose a vibrant, well-established tradition of boundary transgressions between this world and the hereafter (also see Knipe 1990). As for their antiquity, Tamil scholar George Hart maintains that "[In South India] there is evidence that the belief in possession through the spirits of the dead is older than the belief in possession by gods" (1983: 118).

Chapters 5 through 8 turn to the ways in which the dead contact the living. But just using the word *dead* in connection with these spirits levels variations that include untimely, timely, and "cool" deaths. Each category of spirits gains articulation through a particular mode of apparition, a distinct etiology, and a down-to-earth moral ethos. The untimely dead tend to "catch" young married women who consequently suffer from psychic and reproductive disorders. These spirits must therefore be "made to run away." The timely dead may "come on" their living relatives but their possessing manifestations are never so disagreeable that they must be exorcised. Those who have "cooled" may be eligible for the love, affection, and worship of their relatives. The question is what are the personal and social predicaments of human actors that come to light through these spirits' distinctive ways of coming and going or staying in this world?

Chapters 8 through 12 present two rituals: the investiture ceremony of the household deity and a sacrificial complex for a lineage god.[8] These two rituals are structurally related not only to each other, they also bear a strong resemblance to the exorcism in chapters 5 and 6. Yet all are opposed to each other and "prescribe" contrary transformations. What then are these transformations? As we will see, the overlaps and repetitions of Tamil religion are entirely consistent and too obvious to ignore: at every moment its "prescriptive" rituals are in unison with the message that individual and society must be interconnected in mutual regulation. We will have other opportunities to see that in the Tamil world, the medium—in this case a system of binary oppositions—is often the message.

The movement of this book is therefore from intimate to collective "crossings" by human beings over to the supernatural world and back. Because each one of these "crossings" is replete with highly specific and deeply personalized meanings, I present them from the perspective of individual experiences. It is also my hope that through a case-study approach, some of the practices that I will describe may appear less "strange," more culturally plausible, and fraught with all the significance that we accord in our society to personal transformation.

1

PAINFUL CROSSINGS

Suresh was a member of the *Tēnpaḷḷi* caste who cultivated two acres of land that he and his wife owned on the edge of the "forest" (*kāṭu*) near the village of Somatur in the South Arcot district of Tamilnadu. Close to fifty years old when we met, he was a handsome man with long hair, which he tied in a knot that hung low down his neck. He would never allow me to photograph him. The life-changing event that made him a "healer" (*vaittiyar*) took place around 1973.

The Goddess Wounds Suresh

> I was plowing my field when something cut my foot. It began to swell up. Like a trident it pierced my foot, but I did not see the trident. This was the first time that Amma came. She came as a trident and pierced my leg. For a month I was sick and unable to eat properly. I did not know what was happening to me until Amma came in my dream in the form of a little girl and told me, "I am with you. Don't worry, you need not to seek any treatment. I will protect you. Through you I will say *kuṟi*. You must do good things for people."

After this "dream" (*kaṉavu*) Suresh recovered from his injury. From then on he began to receive regular visitations from the goddess. Nor did she only appear in dreams; Suresh explained that she "came on" him, by which he meant that the goddess possessed him. As she promised, during those states he was able to "interpret signs" (*kuṟi collutal*) which are beyond human knowledge.

It took only a few weeks for Suresh to learn to control the onset of these communications with the goddess. Beating a drum and singing her praises, he induced himself into states of trance so as to forecast people's futures and diagnose their sicknesses. Furthermore, he could exorcise the evil spirits that had "caught" them. Word of his powers spread quickly throughout the nearby villages, and the needy and curious came to test his predictions and try his healing powers.

As his reputation grew, he convinced the village authorities (*Panchayat*) of Somatur to let him build a small sanctuary to his goddess, who was named Kaṇṇiyamma ("Virgin Lady"). On the village commons located next to the field where "Amma cut" his foot, he constructed a small enclosure roofed with palm leaves. When I encountered him he had presided over this homemade shrine for more than fifteen years, entering states of trance whenever clients arrived for consultation.

Suresh's experience was similar to that of some other six men and one woman whose work in small Tamil villages I documented.[1] All were similarly initiated by various South Indian goddesses and dispensed their supernatural gifts on a regular basis.[2] Because they could read *kuṟi*, or the invisible "marks" that encode the meaning of the past, present, and future, these recruits of the goddess were sometimes referred to as *kuṟikārihal*, if female, or *kuṟikārar*, if male.[3] But in social interactions, a female initiate was simply addressed as Amma, a term that literally means "mother" but which is also the polite form for every person of the female sex, married or unmarried, including the goddess herself. For his part, a male initiate was normally greeted as *cāmiyar*, the honorific form for *cāmi*. This Tamil contraction of "swami" literally means "God" and by extension is used to address most categories of religious specialists one might encounter in Tamilnadu.

Although the Tamils appear to have no need to specify what is distinctive about these recruits of the goddess, we must remember that their religious authority rests on highly particular experiences. For unlike orthodox priests of major Hindu temples (*pūcāris*) and the so-called "god-dancers" (*cāmiyāṭis*) who "dance" deities at major festivals (Inglis 1985), *cāmis* like Suresh are not handed down their religious role by institutional means, such as inheritance through the male line. And unlike the *canniyācis*, or "renouncers" of Hindu society, these initiates rarely elect a spiritual path. All the *cāmis* I met in the South Arcot district came to their callings during moments of personal crisis or severe illness, through sleeping dreams (*kaṉavu*), or more often through what was usually called *taricaṉam* [from the Sanskrit *darśan*: "seeing"], meaning an "appearance," "vision," or "revelation" of the goddess.[4] Their profiles always underscore the intensity of those initiation experiences.

The Goddess Descends on Nagaji

A forty-five-year-old man, Nagaji was raised in a small village of *Kavuṇṭars* near the bustling town of Gingee. For over a year I visited his compound on a weekly basis, learning gradually how this frail man with clear eyes and a warm smile managed to reenergize his dispirited petitioners. Nagaji obtained his supernatural powers one morning in early 1979. At the time he was a married milk peddler with four young children.

> On that day I left home earlier than usual to sell milk because my wife and I had had a fight. Those days we were often not on speaking terms. On my

> way to Gingee a beautiful lady appeared to me, asking me to follow her to a clump of thorn bushes. I did, but she disappeared. I heard a voice that said "don't stay here" and I fell unconscious. When the villagers found me and woke me up I realized that I had been lying in these thorny bushes for three days.

Returning to the spot a week later Nagaji had a second revelation. The goddess Śakti, creator of the world, disclosed that she had invited him to "follow her." But this time the goddess did not appear in a vision; she "descended" upon his body. Now Nagaji understood that he had been chosen to serve her for his entire life. He broke up with his wife, renounced sexual love altogether, and dedicated himself to his new mistress.

> I began to clear the ground where the goddess had first appeared to me and slept there every night. Śakti kept coming back and instructed me on how to heal people's body aches. Later the people whom I cured provided me with enough money to acquire the things necessary for worship—a lamp, bells, trident, spear. I was able to build this temple for Śakti.

In this sanctuary, tucked away in a grove of trees two kilometers from Gingee, Nagaji identified the causes of persistent sicknesses, prescribed remedial rituals, and exposed the hidden histories of his clientele. Drawn by his growing reputation, his circle of patient-followers eventually extended to the major South Indian city of Madras.

The Goddess Scares Basha

Basha was a forty-six-year-old Muslim man who was raised and still resided in Gingee town. Before I met him, the local rumor mill had alerted me that he employed mantras or "spells" not only to heal but also to perform *pillicūṉiyam*, a word which Reverend Gustave Diehl translated as "black magic" (1956: 229). This echoed a cultural stereotype I often heard from Hindus, which associated Muslim men with powers of sorcery, and made me uneasy, at first, from seeking him out.

But it was he who noticed me one day at the Aṅkāḷaparamēcuvari temple of Mēl Malaiyaṉūr where, I learned, he had been observing me for quite some time. A heavy-set man with piercing eyes, he immediately invited me to record a countersorcery rite that he was to conduct in the temple's eastern, open-air grounds where such free-lancers were expected to practice. When I asked how it happened that the Hindu goddess Aṅkāḷaparamēcuvari guided this Muslim man step by step through his exorcism, he replied that since childhood he had followed both religions, and later, at his home, he explained,

> I was twelve and in fourth grade. I used to get bad marks in school and the teacher beat me. I did not want to go back to class, but my father forced

> me. When bathing with my Hindu friends, I noticed that they saluted the sun. I wondered whether it was not this that enabled them to get good grades. I began to salute the sun. When I told my father, he advised me instead to meditate on a few mantras from the Koran that he taught me. I followed his recommendation and I still recite these mantras. But I never lost my faith in the worship of the sun. I have always been both a Hindu and a Muslim at heart.

At the age of thirty-three, Basha had his initiatory experience,

> I was managing an estate at the time. But I was miserable and wanted to end my life. My wife and I were fighting a lot. One day early in the morning I went to a mango grove on the estate. There I found a couple. They were fighting and the man was beating his pregnant wife. I gave them some money and they went away. I forgot about my own unhappiness and lay down. A woman with long hair appeared. She touched me and told me to get up. I was afraid to be found with her, I did not need any more trouble. I was afraid she might be a bad spirit (*pēy*). I told her to come back the next morning. She was facing West. She walked away but came back once more to wake me up. I remembered that I wanted to die and that there was no point in being afraid. I followed her, I could not see anything, I fell down and fainted. People found me and carried me back to my home. When I woke up much later I felt different. I felt that I acquired some strength. I fasted and did not speak much. I began then to say *kuṟi*.

After this vision, Basha separated from his wife so as to serve Aṅkāḷaparamēcuvari who regularly communicated with him, instructing how to help people with "problems" (*kaṣṭams*). In the compound of his Gingee home, he built her shrine and consulted on a daily basis.

The Goddess Inflicts Smallpox on Raghavan

Finally I became acquainted with a thirty-seven-year-old *cāmi* named Raghavan. A tall, lean man with fluid gestures and high-pitched voice, he had grown up in a small South Arcot village but after the birth of his second child had moved to Madras and joined the wholesale fish business of his *Cempaṭavar* (inland fishermen caste) family. On our first interview he said half-jokingly, "You ought to stop asking questions about Tamil demons—one day one will catch you." When I promised to look him up that day he nodded approvingly, and our relationship was off on its friendly, teasing course.

But he could also be serious, as one afternoon we sat in his courtyard and he recalled his dramatic acquisition of the power to "say *kuṟi*." As a teenager he was suffering from smallpox, a sickness that throughout India is personified as a goddess.[5] Before its eradication from Tamilnadu in the 1970s, the infection was also a common means by which the goddess, widely known as "Māriamma," revealed herself to initiates.[6] In Raghavan's account, however, smallpox prompted his recruitment by a different goddess.

> I was thirteen and had smallpox. One day, the first day of the village festival for our goddess Kālī, I had a vision. I was lying on the Mother's lap. The procession was going by our house. I ran out and stripped the costume from the man who (personified and) danced Kālī. I put on the goddess's clothing and held her weapon and finished the procession as Kālī herself. It was at this festival that I began to say *kuṟi*. That night the son of the *tarmakarttā* (custodian of the temple) suddenly died. His father wanted to know what had caused his death. Amma answered through me. She said that because the *tarmakarttā* had not presented her with the customary blood offering (*kāvu*) she had taken his son's life as the sacrifice that was due to her.

Since then Raghavan was regularly possessed by Kālī and, for the most part, practiced *kuṟi* in his Madrasi home. But twice a month he took consultants suffering from demonic sickness or sorcery spells to the Aṅkāḷaparamēcuvari temple in Mēl Malaiyaṉūr. And since Raghavan was only a diviner, he then referred them to the temple's troupe of ritual musicians (*pampaikkārar*) for treatment, serving as culture broker between ailing urbanites and rural healers.

The Visions Analyzed: When Pain Is in Order

The *cāmis* I met were always willing to talk about their visions of the goddess. Undeniably this was because, as Lionel Caplan notes among Protestant prophets in Madras, "The vision confers and legitimates the charismatic calling" (1988: 14). Yet so far as I could tell, details of the *cāmis'* initiatic experiences were not known to occasional petitioners and regular devotees. Moreover, the *cāmis'* own reactions to my queries about the genesis of their vocation indicated that their recollections never seemed rehearsed or routinized. And while many had much to say about this or that aspect of their practices, when it came to their biographies, they seemed surprisingly coy or even nonchalant.

Perhaps this was because such "mystical states," as the philosopher of religion, William James, characterized them, are essentially "ineffable," that is, they cannot be expressed in words (1961: 299–300). Or perhaps it was because to the *cāmis*, there was no going back, and no need to recapture the painful buildup to their positive transformation. As Anthony Wallace rightly comments, such a climatic vision "functions almost as a funeral ritual: the 'dead' way of life is recognized as dead: interest shifts to a god, the community and a new way" (1956: 270). Indeed, more important to the *cāmis* I met than their past transformations was their reputation and proven effectiveness as diagnosticians or curers. Furthermore, to them the goddess's apparition had been intensely meaningful, but more importantly, utterly real. The spiritual epiphanies I was eliciting in the form of self-conscious, processual, and dramatic narratives were experienced, instead, as lightning bolts. Their ramifications may have unfolded in retrospect and over time, but their psychological or spiritual potential arrived instantaneously.

Despite the brevity of their testimonies, however, and marked differences in their social origins and preferred modes of applying their divine gifts, all the *cāmis*' recollections strike me as encoded with consistent symbolism and dynamics. They also follow the distinctive, revelatory process of Tamil rituals outlined in the Introduction, developing its paradigmatic structure into a narrative form. Our task is to reexamine this revelatory process as we seek to unravel its peculiar configuration and intensity in the *cāmis*' testimonies.

The initial apparition of the goddess occurred when in their everyday lives the *cāmis* were relatively disempowered. By this I mean more than social, economic, or political deprivation. For *cāmis* do tend to be recruited from the ranks of rural or urban poor and do not always hold commensurate status to their clients and sympathizers. Suresh's community was classified in the British Census Report of 1901 "as a semi-Brahmanised forest tribe, who speak a corrupt Tamil" (Thurston 1987 vol 2: 382); at the time of my fieldwork the *Tēnpaḷḷis* of Somatur were still unintegrated into the lives of the agricultural castes.[7] They resided on the margins of villages, on the edge of the "forest," where they foraged for forest products such as bark, roots, wild fruits, beeswax, tamarind seeds, gum, firewood, and especially honey (*tēṉ*), after which their caste was named. But W. Francis's observation that in 1906 the *Tēnpaḷḷis* of South Arcot "are perhaps the poorest and most miserable community in the district," (in Thurston 1987 vol 2: 389) no longer applied in 1991, for at least in Somatur some *Tēnpaḷḷis*, like Suresh himself, did own land.

Two of the other *cāmis* also belonged to fringe communities. Basha was Muslim and therefore in the minority, and a third *cāmi*, Murukaṉ, whom I will introduce in the next chapter, was a *Paṟaiyaṉ* or Untouchable and excluded from caste Hindus due to imputed impurity.

Yet the argument of I. M. Lewis (1971) that "ecstatic" experiences afford marginal or subordinate members of society a means to gain political clout and social status fails, in my view, to adequately explain the specific life experiences that propelled the initiation of the *cāmis*. More important, at the time of their visions our four recruits were suffering from sickness (Suresh, Raghavan) or experiencing marital problems (Nagaji, Basha). And later we will see how the goddess may also appear to those who have just lost beloved kin. These circumstances seem to confirm what anthropologists have noted throughout the world: emotional afflictions or personal crises are critical springboards for life-changing religious experiences (Gibbal 1994; Trawick 1984; Obeyesekere 1981; Kendall 1988).

Each of the four *cāmis*, then, was undergoing some sort of painful physiological or psychological transition at the time. Their liminality was evoked through the symbolic language of their vision accounts; spatial and temporal images of "thorn bushes," "grove," and "festival" conformed to Victor Turner's observation that being in "between and betwixt" is the critical requirement for receiving what he called, the "communication of the *sacra*" (1964: 19).

But such images also suggest that all four *cāmis* first made connection with the goddess in an "outside" place. Suresh was plowing his field, Nagaji was on his way to town, Basha was touring his boss's estate, and Raghavan quickly raced outside to join the temple procession. All these testimonies, then, open with a movement away from an inner, private space, the home, which is depicted as a seat of quarrel and crisis, toward an outer, public domain where the goddess actively asserted herself into her recruits' field of vision. This is consistent with broader representations of the oft-described importance of *darśan* in Hindu ritual practice. According to Diana Eck, " 'seeing' in this religious sense is not an act which is initiated by the worshiper. Rather, the deity presents itself to be seen in its image" (1981: 6).

Both Basha and Nagaji came in full view of a "beautiful" woman "with long hair." Their descriptions are not unusual; in the initiatic dreams of Telugu initiates in the nearby state of Andhra Pradesh, "the goddess appeared in her most benign form, as a beautiful woman of light complexion standing in the midst of a garden and beckoning with her hand" (Nuckolls 1991c: 69).

Nuckolls himself interprets such "benign" representations as expressions of, and solutions to, problematic "psychodynamics" (1991c: 63). His informants were initiated during childhood bouts of smallpox, a disease that in northeastern coastal Andhra is also personified as the goddess, so he suggests that "to be attacked by the 'great mother' in a culture where mothers are viewed ambivalently as sources of nurturance and annihilation may have been a frightening and confusing experience for [these two men]. . . . To reconcile their conflicting feelings, Baskarao and Ramareddy may have adopted identification as a defense against the 'great mother' and against the conflicting maternal images she represented" (1991c: 69).

Nuckolls is not alone in translating South Asian religious experiences into Western, psychological mechanisms (Roland 1988; Kurtz 1992; Vitebsky 1993; Ewing 1997; also see Nuckolls 1996). Indeed, it is Gananath Obeyesekere, from nearby Sri Lanka, who has most eloquently defended the Freudian thesis that "a certain class of experiences are so painful, complicated, and out of the reach of conscious awareness that the individual must express them in indirect representations and symbol formation" (1981: 33). This seems to be what Obeyesekere means by the "work of culture" which by means of what he calls "personal symbols" allows for the expression of and relief from such unconscious conflicts (Obeyesekere 1977; 1981; 1990).

I suspect that the *cāmis'* visions that were recounted to me were invested with similar "personal" or private significances. The presence of the goddess as a desirable woman or divine lover could easily have appealed to Basha and Nagaji, who were experiencing marital difficulties at the time. And as a teenager suffering from smallpox, it is not hard to imagine Raghavan transferring his complicated feelings for his mother onto his nurturing (she held him "on her lap") but pathogenic goddess. Finally, Suresh's dream of a little girl was not without personal resonance, for he was married to a woman at least twenty years younger than him and who remained childless. Quite likely these *cāmis* did indeed "see" in the goddess the missing wives, mothers, and daughters of their lives.

But there are problems with such psychological interpretations. I am not speaking of the familiar objection that they are ethnocentric because they derive from Western personality theories. It is true that the goal of the ethnographic enterprise is not to impose our own conceptions of the self on other peoples but to explore what *they* assume about personhood, how they symbolize it, on what bases they formulate a sense of self, and how they interpret what we would term emotional behavior. It is also true that when we conduct such inquiries we discover important differences between Freudian and South Asian religious perspectives. The Indian psychoanalyst, Sudhir Kakar, for example, is quick to remind us that "according to the Hindus, the disturbances in the order of the self . . . are not seen to have their genesis in early family connections, but are related to the notion of the workings of karma over the whole of the individual's life cycle as well as across the cycle of his many lives" (1982: 4).

Yet Kakar himself found "common understandings" between psychoanalytic theory and the "demonological" worldview of a Muslim folk healer operating out of a mosque located near Delhi (1982: 24). And I suspect that Obeyesekere's proposition that there is an inevitable reciprocity between the public, culturally sanctioned meaning of a symbol and its personal-psychological significance (1981) derives not solely from Freudian psychology, or Weberian social theory for that matter, but from Hindu-Buddhist epistemology as well.

For their congruence strikes me as consistent, for example, with literary conventions of classical Tamil love poetry, which, as we have seen in the Introduction, collapse distinctions between objectivity (in the form of actual exterior landscapes of Tamil country) and subjectivity (Ramanujan 1967). It also fits with the larger Hindu proposition that to "see" is "a means . . . of participating in the essence and nature of the person or object looked at" (Gonda 1969, in Eck 1981: 9). Finally, it is reminiscent of a form of knowledge that, according to Valentine Daniel, is called in Tamil *inaippāl arital* (1984: 234). Daniel explains that "inaippu means join, unite, coalesce, to be alike, connection, copulation, sameness, and so forth" (ibid). And that "*inaippāl arital*, then, means to know by establishing relationships of unity, sameness, coalescence, to know by connecting, joining and so on" (ibid). To him the goal of this kind of knowledge, which he translates as "synthetic knowledge," is "to discover the self in the other or to know the self by getting to know in the other that which is also in the self" (ibid). Both psychological anthropology and the Tamil worldview would seem to break down subject-object dualities, and any conventional distinction between personality and culture.

My problem with the application of Western psychological models onto Indian religion lies elsewhere. Specifically, psychoanalytic readings of the Hindu pantheon seem too simplistic, reductionist, and rationalistic, especially for anthropology. The prevailing assumption, for example, that the goddess known in most Indian vernaculars as simply "Mother" is a direct representation of all human mothers, and that therefore much of the myths and rituals associated with her have to do with oedipal dynamics, reflects a narrow understanding of religious meanings.[8] And the supposition that sacred symbols with sexual overtones refer to biopsychical drives and early conditioning in the elementary family is too literal. When we do investigate the specific associations of such symbols in Tamil religion, we realize that it is problematic indeed.

For throughout Tamil history new cult figures have been incorporated into local, or even national, pantheons by means of metaphors of sexual union and putative marriage ties. According to some scholars these symbolic processes are very old, as George Hart writes, "It is evident that, from the very beginning, the Tamils applied their own poetic conventions to the gods and mythological figures from North India, and that from the first they emphasized the roles of the new gods in what was for them the central and most sacred act of life, love between man and woman" (1975: 57). From the fifth century a.d. onward, the Tamil Bhakti poets encoded their devotional hymns to Viṣṇu and Śiva with metaphors of emotional and sexual love (Ramanujan 1981; Yocum 1973; Hardy 1983; Zvelebil 1973). Then in the fourteenth century female tutelary cult figures, previously enjoying the devotion and patronage of local communities, were incorporated in the state religion of the Chola kings by means of what William Harman calls, "sacred marriage" (1989). They became consorts of the great Bhakti gods, most notably of Śiva (Stein 1980: 239, 330-331; Bayly 1989: 30). And today myths, ritual performances, and temple worship still reenact "the wedding of the goddess" as well as her marital life with this great god (Hudson 1982; Fuller 1984; Harman 1989; Shulman 1980). But marriage remains a powerful trope of union between devotees and supernaturals as well. Recently scholars have documented how worshippers push the humanization of their gods to the point of viewing them as spouses or lovers (Harman 1989: 160–62). In the region of Koṅku, Manuel Moreno observed that a young, female initiate of the god Murukaṉ was "engaged in the process of becoming his ascetic wife" (1985: 118). Thus it is not surprising that the *cāmis*' initiations borrow from the same pool of metaphorical conventions. In Tamil society sexuality and marriage are connotative of unity, fusion, and incorporation and therefore become the perfect metaphors for understanding, experiencing, and internalizing those who, like the goddess, appear from the outside. Internalization of this sort is precisely the fundamental movement of these initiatic testimonies.

The problems derived from the psychological-centered perspectives also affect the interpretation of religious experiences. Like the Western psychotherapies to which they are often compared, religious experiences are presumed to free the self from repressed memories, childhood traumas, and whatever else inhibits its adjustment. Yet a closer look at the *cāmis*' testimonies suggest that their initiations by the Tamil goddess were not simply liberating. At the very least, they tell us that paradoxically release from problematic relationships and coercion may go together, may even be intrinsically interdependent.

For the *cāmis* did not have much choice about their recruitment; the goddess ruthlessly penetrated their bodies in the guise of sickness, or actively lured them with the suggestion of sexual opportunity, until they could only surrender to her. There is a clear pattern here of demands and attacks that are dangerously aggressive, particularly sexually violent. At the time of his dream Suresh suffered from an infected cut in his foot, where he had been pierced by a "trident." In South Indian ritual tradition, as Alf Hiltebeitel has recently argued, symbolism of flesh piercing and impalement with "objects of iron" are often "connotations of a marriage" (1991: 198). Since the trident is a weapon that commonly serves as the goddess's metonymic representation, we may wonder whether Suresh's cut is not an indirect representation of sexual aggression. Symbols of forceful penetration also underlie the manifestation of the goddess as smallpox. The disease is commonly understood as a form of possession, where the goddess lodges herself "inside" her victims' bodies. That this intrusion is conceived as an intimate union is evidenced by Margaret Trawick's observation that the goddess of smallpox "enters the body of a person out of 'desire' for them, love for them . . . ," and that in Tamil the infectious pustules are known as her "pearls" (*muttu*) or "kisses" (*muttam*) (1984: 26).

These initiatic representations seem also consistent with the goddess's various mythic personalities. Thus the supernatural called Kaṉṉiyamma, who "cut" Suresh's foot fits David Shulman's definition of "the lustful bride" who unsuccessfully pursued the great god Śiva (1980: 166). Likewise the same female Śakti who seduced Nagaji was also said to have yearned for union with Śiva and did succeed in marrying him, despite the fact that in this story this god was her son (see chapter 10 and Meyer 1986: 6–9).

Such continuities between mythic narratives and initiatic accounts, between the way the goddesses recruit partners in both heaven and on earth, suggests that the *cāmis*' experiences partook of a "deep" narrative structure in Tamil culture. And what this strata of belief and pattern seems to be saying is not merely that the "sacred" is fused with the "erotic" as so many scholars have noted of South Indian devotion at large (Zvelebil 1973: 253), or that the "sacred" reflects real "dynamics of desire in kinship" (Nuckolls 1996). Rather it strongly suggests that recruitments by the goddess are conceived as inherently unsafe and all engulfing. A sense of real and present danger was common in all their experiences; most of them emphasized their feelings of "fear," and Basha even mistook the goddess for a demonic spirit (*pēy*), an interesting slip because in Tamil culture *pēys* are notorious for causing mental disorders—in other words, for threatening one's sense of balanced self.

And the intensity, if not forcefulness, with which these goddesses reveal themselves was also fitting within the Tamil religious ethos. In his analysis of the South Indian story of *Ciṟuttŏṇṭar*, David Shulman notes the same "aggressive impulse" on the part of the god Śiva (1993: 36). But at least in that story, the Little Devotee was looking for god, whereas here none of these four *cāmis* recalled turning to Amma on their own for protective intervention, and none expressed any prior inclination for spiritual encounters. In fact, two of them displayed an initial reluctance to succumb to her. Nagaji recalled an inner voice telling him, "don't stay here," while Basha grew anxious that the goddess was placing him in a compromising situation, and begged her, "Come back in the morning!"

And yet, in all four narratives the *cāmis* transited from being passive or reluctant recipients of the goddess's apparition to becoming her enthusiastic followers and devotees. The same dynamic is also documented by Charles Nuckolls as he describes how the Telugu men mentioned above recalled their "mixed feelings about the goddess's first visitation," sentiments that soon "began to give way to expressions of intense love for the goddess" (1991c: 68–69). Thus Basha's resistance was short-lived, as he told me, "I remembered that I had wanted to die . . . there was no point in being afraid." Nagaji too followed the goddess, thrashing his way through thorny bushes—conceivably a literal representation of his "crossing." In the end, both men succumbed without a second thought.

For Raghavan, the urge to join the ongoing ceremonial procession of his village goddess proved irresistible. The Tamil expression he employed to describe this compulsion, *maruḷ ōṭutal* ("bewildered run"), conveyed his eagerness to surrender, to the point of usurping the emblems of the parading deity, impersonating her,[9] and suddenly uttering her "decoding" speech (*kuṟi*). Within minutes Raghavan moved from an abject state of helplessness (sickness) and marginality to that of a sanctioned incarnation and mouthpiece of the goddess.

All these testimonies end here. There is no return, or at least no permanent return, to the intimate family place or the domestic situation that was alluded to at the outset. These accounts depict a linear movement from "inside" to "outside" without a reversal in the opposite direction. The *cāmis* left home, were invaded by the goddess, reincorporated into her exterior landscape—a field, a clump of thorn bushes where Suresh and Nagaji permanently settled—and all were instructed to solve matters hidden or outside ordinary scrutiny—the death of a village temple priest's son, for example.

It is in relation to this irrevocable movement toward the space identified in Tamil as *puram*, the "outside domain" that we may understand the violent symbolism of these initiations. Whatever personal "synthesis" the *cāmis* manage to realize through their visions, whatever they "see" in the goddess, leads them to withdraw from domesticity and undergo, as Anthony F.C. Wallace generalizes for reborn visionaries, a kind of death, a "funeral" as he puts it. But unlike the prototype of the Hindu renouncer who leaves the world in the final stage of life after completion of his worldly obligations (the perpetuation of ancestors, for example), the *cāmis* receive these revelations in their prime. It is perhaps because their departure from intimate arrangements is premature, and even untimely, that they are made to suffer so. It is as if Tamil culture was saying that one cannot disconnect from kin, disengage from familial responsibilities, with impunity. And these Tamil cases resurrect Edward Tylor's old speculation whether "religion itself has its origin in the experience of visions and dreams" (quoted in Noll 1985: 444). For the same message, and similar dynamics of violence and submission, will resurface throughout many of the religious experiences in chapters to come.

2

FRUIT FROM THE GODDESS

To each of the four *cāmis* profiled in the last chapter, the arrival of the goddess caused a profound and irreversible rupture in their lives. Some fell unconscious for days, all were struck mute, lost their appetites, and were left in a daze. But this initial shock wore off, to be followed by a striking splurge of vitality: Basha soon felt "different" and "stronger"; Suresh and Raghavan quickly recovered from their "sicknesses," revitalized and reenergized and in possession of strange new abilities. All claimed direct empowerment by the goddess in the professing of *kuṟi*. What is this gift of divine speech in Tamilnadu?

Kuṟi

The paramount meaning of *kuṟi* is "sign." The Reverend Carl Diehl translates *kuṟi collutal* (literally "saying signs") as "interpreting signs" (1956: 59), a gloss that seems preferable to " 'foretelling' " the future (Moffat 1979: 230) since *kuṟi collutal*, as we will see, is more often used to disclose what has *already* happened.[1] Thus *kuṟi collutal* can be more generously defined as speech that decodes "signs" whose referents are generally obscure to ordinary humans. In Tamil practice it specializes in identifying causes of personal affliction and misfortune, in revealing, for example, why a young bride is withdrawn, why a child is sick, why a married couple frequently disputes, why a merchant has lost his business or a court case, why a home erupted into flames—in short, in making cultural and psychological sense of the host of issues that clients bring to these consultations.

But a second meaning of *kuṟi* is "aim" or "target," suggesting that it also offers direction, "aiming" the afflicted toward a specific solution or redress. For these *cāmis* seem to do more than offer "advice and reassurance," as Stephen Inglis characterized the work of the Vēḷar god-dancers of Madurai (1985: 91). More pointedly, they give "fruit" (*kaṉi*), which, according to William Sax, is also the word used in North India (*pal*) to describe what devotees obtain from pilgrimages to holy places, namely "transformations of themselves or their life situations" (1991: 13). This gloss applies to Tamil seances; the *cāmis* offer solutions that are intended to transform their consultants' existential predicaments.

Yet not all *kuṟi* tellers (*kuṟikārar*) acquire their clairvoyance by means of spiritual initiation.[2] In rural Tamil villages and towns women of the *kuṟavar* community often rely on chance devices such as dice to interpret "signs" (Peterson in press). Indeed, these random divinations may have been used for the past two millennia, since we find them in *caṅkam* literature from the first three centuries of the Christian area. A priest of the god Murukaṉ, called the *vēlan*, tossed a handful of molucca beans (*kalaṅku*) into the air, and interpreted their patterns on the ground (Kailasapathy 1968: 66). And Fred Clothey has pointed to evidence in early poetry of a "priestess" who performed the same technique with grains of rice to explain "a maiden's languor" (1978: 27; also see Dikshitar 1930: 304).

Today's *cāmis* are not (and they disdain any need to be) versed in these ancient, esoteric formulae. On the contrary, their divining functions require regular, self-induced personifications of, or direct communications with, the goddesses whom they serve. Only this intimate, embodied rapport with the supernatural world can release the "gracious speech" (*aruḷ vākku*) of their auxiliary goddesses to third parties. Twice a week, generally on Tuesdays or Fridays (the propitious days known throughout Tamilnadu for worshipping the goddess),[3] they produce a socially accessible person with whom supplicants can physically and verbally transact.[4]

Their clients are drawn from all of the non-Brahmin sectors of Tamil society, including those high-ranking castes who often dismiss such "backward" practices. Yet they (or, more exactly, their mothers, wives, sisters, and daughters) are not above seeking advice from *cāmis* in times of distress. They come by bus from villages or towns located one to three hours away, to consult under conditions of relative anonymity, for the *cāmis* usually pronounce their forecasts in open air, nonconfidential settings. Most petitioners are referred by relatives or acquaintances who have had positive personal encounters with this or that *cāmi*.

I would also argue that the problems that bring most of these visitors cannot be narrowly analyzed as indicators of larger social discontents, as much literature on divination suggests (Evans-Pritchard 1937; Turner 1968, Park 1963). To be sure, at the fifty seances or so that I documented near the town of Gingee the *cāmis* counseled on a range of issues that exposed disjunctions of contemporary Tamil society. But from the clients' perspectives their predicaments were never symptomatic of broader social trends. They constituted painfully felt, immediate crises that confronted them with dramatic, threatening consequences. By the time of their visits most had exhausted all other options—sojourns in the government hospital in case of sickness, calls to the local judicial system in case of quarrels with neighbors, etc.—but none bore "fruit." They were at a last-ditch point of despair, where taken-for-granted assumptions of their world had broken down.

The *cāmis* were well-positioned for resolving personal situations that had gone haywire. The exclusive communications that they maintained with the goddess were predicated upon a collapse of the physical and moral order—their initiatory moments of distress, helplessness, and danger. Having learned to interpret the "signs" of their own suffering, the *cāmis* could now turn around the lives of their consultants. It is in the light of the initiatic, knowledge-engendering trials that the *cāmis* have experienced that we must consider the revelations and "fruits" they can now extend to their clients.

Kuppu's Unfulfilled Vow

Our first case of a "sign saying" seance involves a *cāmi* by the name of Murukan, whose Rastafarian-like-hair and soft brown eyes made him look much younger than the forty years he claimed. Although he once told me that he was totally free of ambition and concern with fame, this slender man with delicate features had become one of the most famous *cāmis* around Gingee. Widely known for his diagnoses and cures, the fact that he was a *Paṟaiyaṉ* (Untouchable) did not prevent people of all castes (including Muslims), and from all places (even Madras), to take the uncomfortable bus ride to his remote sanctuary at the eastern border of the North Arcot district. As one of my neighbors put it, "The grace of Amma doesn't look at caste membership."

My relationship with Murukan was different from that I had with other *cāmis*. Over a period of eight months he let me record whatever he was doing and always greeted me with a wide smile. But then he paid little attention to me. On the rare occasions when he was willing to sit down, he only gave minimal responses and remained aloof throughout the exchange.

Regarding his spiritual vocation he only revealed that it began about twelve years before. In his dream the goddess Kālī announced that he would recover from a sickness and say *kuṟi*. At this Murukan grew long locks of matted hair, which in Hindu culture, as Gananath Obeyesekere has underscored, symbolizes "detachment from sexual interests" (1981: 19). But Murukan's professed asceticism remained a source of gossip: many whispered that he was not "only married to the goddess" but kept a woman on the side.

Like Protestant "charismatic prophets" studied by Lionel Caplan in Madras city, Murukan surely understood that he was popular "partly on the basis of material success" (1988: 15), for he was constantly renovating the shrine he had built right on the grounds where the goddess had originally appeared. All the structures of his burgeoning compound were built of cement and brightly painted with deities and demons. Its main sanctuary even shared the architectural sine qua non of village temples—an inner sanctum (*garbhagṛha*, "womb chamber") housing his stone image of Kālī, boxed in by a larger antechamber. Throughout my fieldwork he kept refurbishing his precinct, adding a shrine to the god Ganesh and "waiting" facilities for patients who resided on the premises until their time for treatment, all of which proved, to borrow Caplan's words again, "visible evidence of divine and human favour" (ibid).

On a bus ride to Murukan's temple one Tuesday I happened to meet a *Nāyuṭu* family on their way for a consulting session with the *cāmi*. Almost immediately after boarding the bus, the oldest woman volunteered that she was hoping Murukan would help her son, Ravi, resolve an unfulfilled vow. It seemed that her daughter-in-law, Kuppu, had vowed to the god Perumal (also known as Viṣṇu) that if she gave birth she would deliver the equivalent of the child's weight in rupee coins. Among such middle-class families of Telugu descent these vows were not unusual and are customarily fulfilled on the seventh month after birth, at the famous Vaisnaivite temple of Tirupati in Andhra Pradesh. But the problem, as my new friend lamented within earshot of her daughter-in-law who was seated beside her with an infant girl on her lap, was that Kuppu had waited over a year after the delivery to inform Ravi of this obligation.

Perhaps Kuppu feared her husband's wrath for making such an extravagant bargain on her own. But, anxious about the consequences of the unfulfilled vow, she finally broke the news. By then, of course, the baby had gained weight, making it all but impossible for the couple to fulfill their pledge. Now the situation was serious. Failure to give the gods their "due" (*nērttikaṭaṉ*) leaves one vulnerable to divine retribution, even death. When Ravi informed his mother she advised them to talk with Murukan, whom she knew from a prior consultation. So, all dressed up in their best clothes—as is proper when visiting a deity—they were searching for a way out of this spiritual bind.

At Murukan's sanctuary they joined some 200 to 250 devotees who were also waiting for the seance. Murukan himself was out of sight, a cloth curtain hiding him in the sanctum so no one could witness his embodiment of Kālī. But the telltale sounds of a *pūjā* were audible: a ringing bell, the smashing of a coconut shell, the ritual musicians (*pampaikkārar*) whom Murukan had hired singing the goddess's praises, while burning camphor infused the air.

When Murukan finally emerged, his long red dress with puffy sleeves made him look like a colonial wife on an evening out—except for the jingling anklets.[5] But then he became the Kālī of popular Hindu iconography, rolling his eyeballs and extending his tongue. While he was not entranced, everyone now addressed him as "Amma" and henceforth he spoke from her point-of-view.

Gliding to the palmleaf-roofed entrance, he ascended a "divining stage" (*kuri mēṭai*) and sat cross-legged before the enshrined Kālī, on a deer hide, a substitute for her usual tiger skin which, apparently, was beyond Murukan's means. On the cement floor his supplicants encircled him, men to one side, women on the other, waiting their turn.

Instead of addressing them in order of their arrival by passing out numbered tickets (as do some *cāmis*), Murukan called out their places of origin. When he shouted "Gingee," Kuppu and her family were brought below the "divining stage," as the surrounding crowd watched with intense interest.

When the "goddess" understood the reason of the family's coming, she said: "The vow was supposed to be fulfilled the seventh month after the child's birth. You should have gone to Tirupati right then." Both Ravi and his mother hastily explained that had Kuppu not "forgotten" to tell them they would have gone right away. But Amma was adamant: "The baby should have been weighed in the seventh month. Now she will weigh more. Even five thousand rupees in coins won't be enough." When Ravi begged, "We don't have that kind of money, tell us what to do," Amma was sarcastic, "Live on rice!" But she impatiently threw in: "No one is going to object if you are late in fulfilling your vow. Go to the temple! Though the child is more than seven months, it will be okay. You'll just have to pay." Here is Ravi's response and the ensuing dialogue:

RAVI: "That's the problem. We don't have the money. Please, tell us what to do. We can't leave the vow unfulfilled."

AMMA: "Yes, you must give the child's weight in rupees, whatever the cost."

RAVI'S MOTHER: "Please, what can we do to get the money?"

AMMA: "Rob a bank!"

RAVI'S MOTHER: "What can I do? I only found out about the vow yesterday."

AMMA: "Weigh the baby, give the money."

RAVI: "But how?"

AMMA: "Get a loan!"

RAVI: "Where?"

AMMA: "I'll give you one. Now leave."

RAVI: "When will the loan come?"

AMMA: "Within the next two years."

RAVI: "But won't her weight increase?"

AMMA: "Oh yes, it certainly will increase."

The seance was not going well. The goddess's curt and caustic responses made it clear she was unmoved. By now Ravi and his family were in great distress; Kuppu was weeping, her husband threatened to beat her. The goddess allowed herself one last scornful query, "Didn't *I* grant your vow to bear a child?"

This reminder that *she* had originally granted Kuppu's vow, and not the other supernatural option, the more demanding god Perumal, suggested that her gifts were a bargain. Moreover, as she now logically reasoned, since it was *she* who had first responded to Kuppu's prayer what was the need to enlist Perumal's help? Beside, the goddess also asked, who was this Perumal after all? She answered her own question, "Perumal will tell you that he was the one who created the world. But who created him? Śiva created him. And I am Śiva's wife. Without me Śiva cannot live. I am guarding him." Speaking as the goddess, Murukan was implying that Lord Perumal was something of an impostor. The true creator was Lord Śiva, but since Kālī herself sustained his existence, it was actually *she* who embodied the true cosmic potency of the universe.

This sortie into cosmological politics, which seemed more addressed to the attentive crowd than the distraught family, had thrown Amma off track. So Ravi's mother softly reminded the goddess of her obligation to protect human beings who were unfamiliar with the inner workings of the divine order. Appealing again to the goddess's compassion, she asked, "My daughter-in-law only wanted a child. Won't our savings be enough?"

Refocused, the goddess calmly instructed the family, "We want weight (*pāram*). Your vow needs weight." Ravi's mother pleaded, "Amma! Are you telling us that we must pay five thousand rupees?" Quickly Amma responded, "Three thousand rupees in coins will be enough."

That concluded the seance. The vow must be fulfilled; "it needed weight." Yet the reduced settlement was not considered unreasonable. Ravi's mother sighed with relief. The entire family profusely thanked the goddess and promptly left.

Gita's Proper Marriage

My second example of a *kuṟi* session featured the *cāmi* Nagaji, an extraordinary man who proved the most contradictory "recruit of the goddess" I was to encounter. His initial meeting with his goddess Śakti, when he was a miserable milkman some eleven years earlier, had dedicated him to bringing the goddess's love (*anpu*) into the hearts of other sufferers. His devotion was reflected in a warm rapport with his clients, so many of whom hung around his sanctuary that it seemed like an ashram.

But no less than Murukan, he was also a consummate showman. As I witnessed over a period of thirteen months of regular visits to his compound, he was always experimenting with different styles of dress and speech. Although I could never predict what he would say or do on any given seance, his performances were always infused with a sense of empathy. But Nagaji would not hesitate to employ what first appeared as cruelty to bring "fruit" to his consultants.

He practiced out of his home near Gingee, right where Śakti had first appeared and also where the auspicious conjunction of three sacred trees, a banyan (*āl*), a pipal (*aracu*), and a margosa (*vēmpu*), partitioning off his sanctuary from the surrounding rice paddies, was further evidence that this spot was imbued with her essence. He had chosen the margosa ("abode of Amma") to shelter her shrine—an uncarved, pointed rock with a trident stuck upright in the ground. Since the goddess Kālī also guided his exorcisms, she was represented in an adjacent shrine by a roughly shaped stone endowed with painted eyes.

It was under the banyan tree of that temple that I met Gita, a young woman with light complexion and fashionable sari. It was easy to tell she was not a villager, and from the way she kept her eyes averted from the surrounding crowd, one sensed that she wished to be anywhere else.

In fact, this visit was her parents' idea. They had brought her from Pondichery, where Gita studied at the prestigious Tagore College, because she was refusing to marry a man of their choice—a defiance which, in Tamilnadu, as Sara Dickey points out, "is one of the greatest transgressions children can commit" (1993: 99). And the problem was only compounded when Gita's mother discovered that her daughter was turning him down not because of Gita's excuse that she had no inclination for matrimony, but for a deeper reason. She was already in love with someone at the college. But this young man was from an Harijan family, the lowest rung of Hindu caste society. In the eyes of Gita's *Mutaliyār* parents the fact that he was also a Christian convert did not make him any more suitable. The situation reached a point of crisis when Gita threatened to elope. Beside herself, her mother had alerted her brother in Gingee, and he had consulted the *cāmi* Nagaji who had urged the entire family to seek the goddess's counsel. Now all of them were in his compound, sitting silently on the ground.

Around mid-morning, only a black cloth around his waist, gray hair falling freely down his shoulders, Nagaji made his appearance. All stood up as he applied holy ash on their foreheads. His regular male clients he briefly held by the hand, engaging in intimate whispers, curious whether his last recommendations had proven helpful, carefully attending to their answers.

Then Nagaji embodied his goddess by contacting items that metonymically stood for her. Climbing onto the bottom branch of the margosa tree, he leaned on the trunk and waited for her essence to suffuse him. Now the sixty clients below watched him transform into a ferocious-looking being. His chest heaving in and out with heavy breathing, his body suddenly contorted violently, his tongue protruded, and out of his throat came deep, threatening growls.

Springing down to earth, he demanded that a large brass pot, already filled with water and margosa branches (*Śakti karakam*), be placed on his head. Immediately recognizable throughout Tamilnadu as a central icon of goddess worship, this crown caused his body to shake so vigorously that he looked about to collapse.[6] Slowly regaining his strength, he crawled on his knees to a bed of margosa leaves to proclaim his *kuṟi*.

Sitting before his Śakti shrine, he invited his supplicants to settle down and grabbed the divine trident, brandishing it above his head before replanting it in the ground. His fourteen-year-old son lifted the pot off his head and set it on the margosa leaves. As Nagaji told me later, he no longer needed this external contact; Śakti was inside his body, he was ready for his first client.

When their time arrived, Gita's family sat cross-legged and handed over their numbered, two-rupee ticket. Emerging from his trance, Nagaji demanded nine limes, which he laid aside, then the *pūjā* materials: coconut, plantains, jasmine flowers, betel leaves, araca nut, incense, and camphor, which he placed on a banana leaf. Above this assemblage he swirled a camphor flame, the gesture that, to Christopher Fuller, is the quintessential symbol for signaling unity between Hindu gods and devotees (1992: 73).

With eyes closed, Nagaji invoked the goddess's protection for Gita during this family crisis. When he interrogated her directly, "How far are you in college?" Gita replied, "in second year." But when the *cāmi* instructed her to ask him (the goddess) for a husband, the advice did not sit well, and Gita stiffened, saying "I only want a job."

At this Nagaji turned to the crowd, as if they had become a jury. "This girl may come from a good family," he pronounced, "but her mind is not working too well; she only wants to earn a living!" Back to Gita, he said,

> You are asking me to give you justice but do you have it within you to live a correct life? Right now you have no peace. The time has not come yet. You should destroy your anger. Look at the position you have put your family in! You should spare them trouble and controversy. What do you want? Now, ask!

Since Gita was downcast, her mother broke in, "We have conducted her betrothal (*niccayatāmpūlam paṇṇa*).[7] But she loves another. Please, show us a way out! We want to live with respect!" Nagaji answered, "I didn't ask for the whole story, I knew you people were hiding something. Why keep things secret? Don't we have the Mother to hear our troubles?"

Nagaji was well aware that not all clients began with what Katherine Ewing calls the " 'real' trouble" (1984: 109). As she observed among Sufi diviners in Pakistan, "The actual problem may be a vague anxiety, or it may be something that the person is too embarrassed to talk about. Therefore, he or she presents a standard problem instead" (ibid). Here Gita's mother was omitting the crucial information that Gita's beloved was an Untouchable. Of course, Nagaji already knew this, and now he berated the young woman,

> Why is there a world? Why is there justice? Why is there a mother to give birth? Why do we have a margosa tree? Why do we have doors to our houses? Why do we have cloth to cover our bodies? Why do we have a mind to cover our cloth? Why do we have knowledge? You should take a husband only after knowing his origin. Give yourself only after studying that person. Otherwise you become a sinner. Didn't they teach you about civilization (*paṇpāṭu*), knowledge (*aṟivu*), love (*aṉpu*), and justice (*nīti*)? Weren't you born to a proper family? Or were you born as a prostitute (*potumakal*)? You may have studied, but you are proof that the mind of a girl cannot change. You went beyond justice. Your life became like a fire. You are like an ax which cuts the tree. Your life will be spoiled, that's your fate. This man's caste is different from yours! YOU DOG! DON'T YOU HAVE ANY SHAME! [He spat at Gita.]

Now that the crowd was cued to the "real" problem of Nagaji's clients, they seemed gripped by the unfolding plot, which echoed those intercaste love stories most of them had seen on big screens in Tamil movie houses (Dickey 1993: 108). And Nagaji knew that he had been dealt a good story, and one not without irony. Here was an illiterate, poor man, preaching to his richer and better-educated clients that hierarchical values such as *intra*caste marriage were essential to healthy social life.

As Gita sat silently, Nagaji tried more personalized persuasion,

> Don't you like the man your parents chose for you? Haven't you already gone through the betrothal? What is the matter with you? Do you want to kill your parents? Do you want to walk on their dead bodies? What do you want?

This was more effective. The thought that her behavior might harm her mother and father prompted Gita to reply, "I want my parents." Then Nagaji attacked again,

> No you don't! That man spoiled you. He gave you some love potion (*maruntu*: "medicine").[8] That was his wicked plan, his fire has burnt you. Do you know that? If you want to spoil your life at least do it with people of your kind, with good people. But you have studied. How far have you studied, the goddess does not know?
>
> GITA: "I have studied with a Tamil pandit."
>
> NAGAJI: "You have studied with a Tamil pandit! What does that mean? There are so many kinds of Tamil, the Tamil that the pandits speak, the Tamil that the shepherds (*kōn̲ars*) speak, the Tamil that is spoken at home. Each of us only knows a handful of ways to speak Tamil. Which Tamil do you know? The Tamil that leads to elope with another man? Do you think you have wings to fly? Fly! Run! You won't go far. He is a Christian, you are a *Mutaliyār*. The world will laugh at you."

Resignedly, Nagaji turned back to Gita's parents,

> You will die of shame. It is your fate. I cannot tell anything. There is no story to tell. They have already conspired to run away. They have fixed the date. She has been weeping for the last seven days, thinking of him all the time. She is not searching for a job. She is searching for him. She is in need of pleasure (*in̲pam*). You thought she was studying, she was telling you, "I am going to class," "I am going to the type-writing lesson," "I am going to the temple," but she was lying. Now it is too late. This has been going on for over a year. You came too late. What can I do now?

Nagaji looked defeated, Gita's eyes were fixed on the ground. The crowd was glued to the scene. A scream from Gita's mother finally broke the silence:

"Amma! Remove the love-potion! Help her forget him!" A voice from the crowd added, "Remove the love-medicine!" This seemed all that Nagaji was waiting for, and he announced,

> I will make her forget. Though the bastard has put some medicine on her, I can remove it. I will bring him a life of danger. I promise to make him pay. I will yank his intestines from his stomach. I will kill him. I will separate them. I will cut her marriage necklace (*tāli*). She will become a young widow." [As if re-energized, he addressed Gita]: "This is going to happen unless you wish to forget him. Do you wish to forget him? Can you?"

> GITA: [in a low, submissive voice]: "I will forget him."
>
> NAGAJI: "Do you promise?"
>
> GITA: "Yes, I promise to forget him."
>
> NAGAJI: [more softly]: "If you forget him, I will protect you. You won't be in any danger. You're not thinking of killing yourself, are you?"
>
> GITA: "I will not kill myself."
>
> NAGAJI: "You promise?"
>
> GITA: "Yes, I will not kill myself."
>
> NAGAJI: "And I promise to light a lamp in your life. From now on I will give you peace. You have studied. You have knowledge. You should live with respect and pride. Śakti should live in your mind. Don't worry, I will protect your marriage. That ceremony (*kāṭci*: literally "scene") is there for you. It will be a great occasion. Don't you try to kill yourself! If you ask me 'why?' I will tell you, 'wait and see, something good is in store for you.' I will protect you. Don't worry!"

With these parting words, Nagaji returned Gita's the nine limes. Imbued with the goddess's essence, they were now prophylactic devices for the "love-medicine" that had afflicted her. Her parents were to place them in various locations in and around their home. Nagaji called for his next client. On that day he consulted with fourteen people. I never saw Gita again, but my English-speaking assistant felt confident that she "would never elope with her sweetheart."

The Seances Analyzed: The Goddess Against Her Petitioners

Many *cāmis* explained that before actually giving the "fruit" we have witnessed, they also gave "darśan" to their devotees. Thus an observer who recorded only these question-and-answer sessions would probably neglect the whole premise of their seances. Much as they had originally "received" the goddess through that "line of sight" experience, so these *cāmis* began to impart their revelations by targeting their clients' eyes. This is why our two *cāmis*—Murukan and Nagaji—started their seances by producing their embodied goddess in front of their assembled petitioners.

Murukan embodied his behind a closed curtain where he dressed up in what he fancied to be Kālī's distinctive attire. Here he manipulated what James Frazer called the "Law of Similarity," the principle "that like produces like" (1965: 300), an impersonation that was consistent with broader Hindu representations of temple deities in anthropomorphized icons. But Murukan activated the humanization of his goddess, for when he emerged and opened his eyes, a "live" Kālī stood before all.[9]

In contrast, Nagaji incorporated his goddess by physically contacting substances (the margosa tree) or objects (the brass pot filled with water and margosa branches) that were culturally associated with her.[10] So he resorted to Frazer's "Law of Contact," the notion that "things which have once been in contact with each other continue to act on each other at a distance" (1965: 300). Less instantaneous than Murukan's mimetics, Nagaji's absorption produced the same result. His flock also treated him as the goddess incarnate, despite the fact that he repeatedly addressed Śakti as if she were a second-person entity.

But it would be misleading to suggest that these performances arouse great awe or credulity. Far from being gullible spectators, observers at these events seem fully aware that the goddess's presence in this world is mediated by fallible men, and some may criticize and question what they see. So it is the task of the *cāmis* to prove that what they offer is not just theater nor complete reality but something in between. They must create, as Edward Schieffelin also observed at Kaluli spirit seances in New Guinea, a sufficiently compelling and credible dramatization of a supernatural "presence" (1996: 64). But if the Tamil seance is to bear any real "fruit," they must also make people internalize what they see.

They accomplish this in various ways. First off, they behave imperiously with their clients, taking liberties that would be resented in ordinary settings. In harsh, commanding words, they order people to stop moving, pay attention, and keep quiet. Their slang and use of singular pronominal forms to address petitioners, regardless of caste or age, contribute to this intensified, controlling atmosphere.

The *cāmis* know full well that their reputations are measured not only by accurate forecasts but by their maintenance of authority, which is why they bully clients around. But these behaviors are also symbolic of the cosmological proposition that factored into their owns initiations: in Tamilnadu religious power is manifested within a contest that comes down to who coerces who. Moments of supernatural revelation occur within a relationship of command and obedience. We may recall how the goddess cut, infected, and seduced the *cāmis* until they had no choice but to surrender. Having originally discovered the goddess through this ordeal, they now turn from "prey into hunter," as Maurice Bloch would put it (1992), attacking others the same way and in her name. Means and goals may vary but the object remains the same: the individual (initiate or petitioner) must capitulate. Aggression is essential to revelation. But another dynamic also propels these seances forward.

Initially the goddess displays no compassion for the suffering of her petitioners. We have heard how the Kālī embodied in Murukan was almost aloof to the problem that prompted Kuppu and her family to consult her. All she kept on repeating was that their vow must be fulfilled, no matter the baby's weight, and refusing to accept dispensation for any special circumstances under which this pledge was made. Her rigid code only produced ludicrous, mocking "solutions," such as "rob a bank!" As for the goddess embodied by Nagaji, she too was not very helpful. "You came too late . . . What can I do now? . . . You will die of shame," was all she could tell Gita's parents. These pessimistic prognoses were also noted by Manuel Moreno in the Tamil town of Pa<u>l</u>a<u>n</u>i, where he heard how replies of a female initiate personifying the god Muruka<u>n</u> were "not always reassuring," as they "forecast the death of a husband or a child, the failure of crops, or the postponement of a long awaited marriage" (1985: 117).

Such systematic resistance to clients' proposals underscores a theological point: divining is not for the consultant's personal interests.[11] Before anything else the *cāmis* need to quickly assert that their goddesses do not intervene in this world to sanction what people already want. But there is even a larger message here, which is nicely captured in David Shulman's analysis of a mid-twelfth-century Tamil devotional narrative. "The moment of revelation," he writes, "is first one of loss and hiding; one discovers the god has been present only by a sudden absence" (1993: 30). This same sense of a missing presence surfaced in the *cāmis*' initiatic testimonies. The goddess had appeared to Nagaji on the road to Gingee only to "disappear" when he tried to pursue her. Similarly they reproduce that experience in their seances, no sooner materializing the goddess in their bodies than rendering her unavailable, inaccessible, indeed, disinterested in her petitioners.

At this point an ethos of shock customarily descends upon and envelops the proceedings; consultants fall prey to confusion and fear, unable to cope with the goddess's apathy or anger. Some refuse to "see" what is happening, such as the young husband's response to the goddess's malicious forecast that she would grant him a loan within two years. "Meanwhile won't the baby's weight increase?" he logically and laughably reasoned, unable to perceive how she was making fun of him.

It is true that when consultants sank to such levels of despair or denial, the *cāmis* loosened up their grip and assumed a protective role. But more often it was the clients who turned things around. They fought back, contesting the goddess's framing of their predicaments. Women often took the lead, arguing on behalf of their families. "Can't we give what we have saved at least?" we heard one reasoning with Kālī, while another begged the Śakti embodied in Nagaji to "remove" her daughter's love medicine. As they pursued the goddess, pressing her to "see" their situation from their perspectives, clients were drawn to "complete"—as Schieffelin also observed at Kaluli spirit seances (1993: 271)—the reality produced by the *cāmis*. Even reluctant participants like Gita came to internalize the factuality and logic of their revelations.

Because such seances provoke people to reach for something that initially seems beyond their grasp, they parallel the *cāmis*' initiations. All these specialists reported the compulsion to run after an evanescent goddess so as to incorporate what they had first seen in her. The susceptibility of these seances to the processual dynamics of the *cāmis*' visions may, in fact, be the reason why they had such a profound effect in redirecting a person's life, in other words, in bringing "fruit."

One may argue, however, that the specific treatments advocated by the *cāmis* Murukan and Nagaji were not of a magnitude to their own life-transforming outcomes. Far from offering such cataclysmic experiences that transcend conventional social roles, their embodied goddesses accomplished quite the opposite, reencompassing people within the social (gender, caste, parental) values and hierarchies of Tamil "public" society. This was clearly evident by the kind of recommendations they prescribed. "Don't you want a family life?" Nagaji demanded of Gita, and we have heard his/her views about Gita and the Untouchable, "Don't you have any shame!" Nor, for all his advice to rob a bank, was Murukan a societal subversive. Vows must be fulfilled, at any cost. Clearly, the recruits of the goddess did their part to uphold the protocols and prescribed orders of both this and other worlds.

But these days their embodied goddesses address fewer and fewer of the situations in this chapter. The greater percentage of their interventions consists in "decoding" sorcery powers. With this diagnosis these goddesses, once again, focus on extricating people from troubled, personal bonds.

3
IN THE GRIP OF BLINDNESS

We have seen the goddess counsel human beings through her intermediaries, but her interventions in this world are usually much more aggressive and engaged. At the fifty or so *kuṟi* seances that I documented, the goddess was caught up in revealing the causes of people's ills and overcoming them. Although one hears a wide range of explanations in Tamilnadu for affliction (see Hiebert's detailed taxonomy 1983), almost always the goddess, through her recruits, attributed it to what is called in Tamil *ēval*. This word means "command," which implies that people are in the grip of a sorcery spell.[1] What does this diagnosis mean? What does it reveal? What kinds of "fruit" does it yield?[2]

The Outer Configuration of Tamil Sorcery

The scanty documentation in South Indian ethnography on sorcery may not be surprising, for as Reverend Carl Gustave Diehl noted in 1956, in Tamilnadu the topic evokes widespread "disgust and hatred" (1956: 268).[3] Much as John Beattie observed of sorcery among the Nyoros, "the less it is spoken of the better" (1963: 28), which may explain why, in Tamilnadu, drums do what voices should not. One gloss for the denigrated practice is *cahaṭai*, which designates the largest of the drums played by Untouchables at death. Like that mortuary instrument, sorcery in Tamilnadu alerts everyone to a form of killing, a presumed action that unleashes mystical, malevolent forces that aim to disempower or eliminate another. Even if victims are not physically killed, they are intended by their opponents to be rendered socially dead.

Given these dire consequences it is no wonder then that in fourteen months of fieldwork no one admitted that he (or she) ever paid a sorcerer to harm anyone else. I never witnessed the execution of a sorcery spell, nor met a sorcerer (*mantiravāti* "one who says mantras"). Rumors had it that some *cāmis* engaged in these deadly practices, but every specialist that I confronted issued an emphatic denial. All reported that allegations were well founded when some other *cāmi* was concerned, but their involvement was only limited to its cure. Like the Madrasi priest who was asked by Reverend Carl Diehl whether "he would do it," they "smiled and said: 'No, but I can stop it' " (1956: 269).

Most of the *cāmis* I knew were available to combat spells. For despite the fact that the "sorcerer" was always *somebody else*, that spells appeared to be imaginary, and that feelings of disbelief, fear, and abhorrence surrounded the subject, they performed countersorcery rituals on an impressive scale. Nor were they shy about sharing the knowledge of sorcery upon which the efficacy of their responses depended. Their clients were also conversant about their sufferings from sorcery. For them, however, the real aggression did not stem from sorcerers or demons, and unlike the *cāmis* they were unconcerned with technical aspects of the original spell. What disturbed them were the personal implications of the diagnosis: *someone* had tried to "command" them. Through their consultations to identify the culprit(s) the *cāmis* and their clients generated a discourse about sorcery. To understand the configurations, repetitions, and transformations of this discourse is the task of the following two chapters.

Commanding Forces

To cast their "commands," sorcerers are said to shape little effigies in the form of their victims. To activate these figures with the human life-force (*uyir*), they dot their bodies, especially the eyes, with a black substance (*mai*) that is concocted from the boiled then charred skull bones of first-born sons.[4]

Observing ritual precautions of austerity and avoidance of pollution,[5] sorcerers then direct their "commands" into these effigies so as to damage their victims' ability to move, speak, and reproduce. Moreover, their spells are quite specific: there is *tampaṉam* (Sanskrit), the spell that "paralyzes"; *vāy kaṭṭu*, the spell that "ties the mouth"; *pētaṉam* (Sanskrit), the command that brings marital divorce; or *māraṇam* (Sanskrit), which can actually kill (see Diehl for other such spells, 1956: 269).[6] These spells operate on the notion common to many ritual traditions that "like produces like," that whatever is said or done to the effigies affects their human targets (Frazer 1965: 301).[7]

But the *cāmis* told me that sorcerers do not activate their malevolence through the impersonal forces that I have just described. To them the sorcerers' real expertise lies in their ability to recruit the services of specific demons, known in Tamil as *pēys*. This term usually characterizes the spirits of people who are barred from transiting into the hereafter because they have met "untimely" (*ahālamaraṇam*) deaths (Reiniche 1975: 182; Caplan 1989). Rather than being ordinary victims of this inauspicious (*tūrmaraṇam*) fate, however, most sorcery demons are what Gananath Obeyesekere calls, in reference to the Sinhalese *yakas*-demons, "named beings in the pantheon, with fairly clear-cut identities and myths of origin" (1981: 121).

But I faced a problem when I began to investigate their pedigrees. Many of these sorcery *pēys* are also lineage tutelary deities who in that respectable role protect the fertility and the health of the descent group (Moffat 1979: 229). Then I was told that the females among these demons are also avatars of the goddess Kālī, and my *cāmi* friends agreed that Kālī is implicated in casting most spells; some claimed that sorcerers prefer actually her assistance.

How can the goddess whom we heard in the last chapter lecturing people on their obligations to fulfill vows side with evil sorcerers, the goddess on whom the *cāmis* call to neutralize spells, and who is renowned throughout Tamilnadu for fighting demons on behalf of human beings? The *cāmis* explained that she is pressed into service through *vaciyam*, a term that refers to the binding power of ritual prestrations.[8] "If I do a lot of *pūjās* and sacrifices (*palis*) to the goddess," one told me, "she'll obey me. She'll have to reciprocate and I'll be in the position to ask for certain benefits." They also reported that sorcerers oblige Kālī with offerings of "blood" (*rattam*) or "life" (*uyir*), in the form of animal (*kāvu*) and human sacrifice (*narapali*), and especially that all-powerful *mai*—the residue from the first-born son. To obtain this substance the goddess will perform the sorcerer's bidding, enforcing any spell upon his request.

The way the goddess, or her demonic manifestations, "takes command" of targeted victims is reminiscent of her recruiting techniques: she appears before them and commands their line of sight. Whereas she appears to the *cāmis* as a beautiful woman, she now becomes a terrifying, disheveled, blood-dripping creature. Now she casts no seductive glances, but stares with the destructive force of the "evil eye." Not surprisingly, human recipients play a part in these oracular transmissions. For a split second, I was told, victims glimpse the malevolence that is streaming toward them. This instantaneous awareness infuses them with fear (*payam*), the identical, intense emotion that characterizes some of the *cāmis*' initial responses to the goddess's original manifestation. But whereas the *cāmis* quickly overcome this "fear," victims "surrender" to it, a dangerous lapse, for in Tamilnadu, as Margaret Trawick noted, "To submit to *payam* is to lose control, to come under another's power, to let part or all of one's life flow away" (1990b: 190; also see Caplan 1989: 55).

In the context of sorcery attacks, the "fear" strips from the self its natural "command." Victims of the goddess's "evil eye" are thus left in the opposite predicament to that of her recruits: instead of gaining heightened sight and control over the hidden "signs" of life, they lose focus and sink into a helpless fog and disempowerment.

Perhaps we find the goddess's implication in this sorcery so puzzling because our dualist Western cosmologies forbid any possible confusion, or even collusion, between God and evil (Russell 1977). But numerous scholars have observed how the Hindu worldview tolerates if not welcomes such ambiguities. The noted historian of religion, Wendy O'Flaherty Doniger, characterizes the Hindu pantheon, "The opposition between the gods and demons is purely structural; they are alike in all ways except that, by definition, they are opposed" (1976: 64). In such a cosmology the notion of deities as channels of sorcery is no contradiction in terms. Hans-Georg Turstig finds this notion in the Sanskritic sorcery tradition (*abhicāra)*:

> Often a difference is made between "white magic" as opposed to "black magic", the one being supported by God, the other by the devil. Such a distinction is totally inapplicable to Indian magic, where "white magic" and "black magic" are not seen as functional opposites, but rather as complementary functions related to ambivalent aspects of one single power. (1985: 71)

The Tamil folk theory of sorcery does not go that far. *Cāmis* emphasized the risks of exercising *vaciyam* or "control" over the goddess: sorcerers can go "mad" or suffer violent deaths from unchecked greed. These *cāmis* fight them, they said, out of devotion and love (*patti* or *pattu*) for Kālī. As for sorcery's victims, so long as they keep faith with the goddess spells will not work; Amma never harms her true devotees.

Sorcery in Tamilnadu incriminates not just a sorcerer and his demons but a third participant as well—the alleged person(s) who deliberately order and pay for the spell. One *cāmi* used a legal analogy: "The person who orders the sorcery is like a plaintiff (*vāti*); he holds a grudge (*kuṟai*). The person who suffers the sorcery is like a defendant (*pirativāti*); he has caused the grievance of his injurer."[9] When I asked why these "plaintiffs" and "defendants" do not seek judicial redress, he replied, "The Panchayat [the local adjudicative counsel] cannot solve their conflicts."[10] For these domestic conflicts between blood kin, in-laws, lovers, and co-wives usually revolve around the contradictions between kinship norms and individualistic conduct rather than legal codes. Alleged victims failed to follow customary rules of reciprocity or the moral order of kin relations, or they behaved selfishly by reneging on financial obligations or marital transactions or stealing a husband. Let me illustrate with the experience of a businessman who resided in the North Arcot town of Chengelput.

I first met Kumar at the Mēl Malaiyaṉūr temple where he often worshipped. He had become a devotee of the goddess Aṅkāḷaparamēcuvari ever since she undid the "command" that a sorcerer had placed on him a few years before. At the time his life was going well. After seven years of unsuccessful attempts at last his wife was pregnant. Their rock quarrying business was so successful that one of Kumar's *paṅkāḷis* (a male patrilineal cousin who stood vis-à-vis Kumar like a brother) asked to merge their respective businesses. But Kumar was leery about the prospect of this partnership. As he told me: "My cousin was not successful. I was worried about losing money so I refused." That made his cousin seek "revenge," according to Kumar. "His sorcerer sent a demon to catch me. For five years this demon made my life miserable. It came on [possessed] me as often as ten times a day. Each time

I would be frantic and utterly confused from five minutes to one hour. I had so much energy that seven men could not hold me down. I didn't know what I was doing."

From Kumar's perspective "jealousy" and "revenge" had motivated his cousin. But my inquiries with others in the village revealed that his injurer was not unrealistic in expecting a partnership, for their kinship tie prescribed them to share worldly benefits (paṅkāḷi means "partner," "shareholder," "coheir" and comes from the noun, *paṅku*: a "share"). In their view Kumar disregarded a primary obligation incumbent upon all lineage members to mutually assist one another.

Tamil Sorcery in Anthropology

Let me place what we have heard about Tamil sorcery in theoretical perspective. To the extent that Tamil spells are commissioned by a social agent, my information underscores the old, anthropological argument that sorcery is a social fact (Evans-Pritchard 1937; Turner 1968). To the degree that there is a consensus on the clear relationship between sorcery and personal enmity, it also supports the notion that sorcery is indicative of failed social bonds (Douglas 1970). As for the proposition that alleged perpetrators and victims are entangled in some hostile relationship that cannot be redressed through customary legal channels, my documentation on the Tamil language of "command" confirms that sorcery allegations express recurrent tensions and conflicts that society fails to resolve (Marwick 1982; Beattie 1963; but see Crick 1976: 109–27 for a criticism of these sociological approaches). Finally in so far as these sorcery "commands" are commissioned out of "jealousy" and "frustration" caused by breaches of "traditional" expectations, this discourse also corroborates ethnographic observations that sorcery accusations thrive in times of rapid social change (Redfield 1941). And there is sound reason to suspect that not all Tamil communities fare well in, or welcome, modernity. As Kalpana Ram has observed, in the fishing villages of Kanyakumari, "New forms of capital accumulation, new deployments of human labour power . . . are experienced as introducing disequilibrium, exciting deep-lying resentments" and "relations of envy, always active, have come into greater prominence in this time of great social upheaval" (1991: 54).

Powerful as it is, however, the argument that sorcery is "an index of the malfunctioning of the system, of its objective disorder, or [is] symptomatic of the chaos of transition" as Bruce Kapferer characterizes it (1997: 15) only takes us so far. It overlooks the fact that in Tamilnadu sorcery is first and foremost a *psychological* expression. Let us not forget that I met no sorcerers, no perpetrators, saw no empirical evidence of spells, and witnessed no accusations ventilated in public. To be sure, I did find a systematic and coherent symptomology of sorcery "commands," but in reality such physical manifestations could easily be reinterpreted; for as Luc de Heusch reminds us, pathologies rarely fit into received classifications (1981: 171). As for the *cāmis'* diagnoses of sorcery, they too could be dismissed in favor of more satisfying explanations—karma, inauspicious planetary influences, "natural" sickness, and so on.

The ontology of Tamil sorcery is grounded in the subjective experiences of the sufferers; its cosmology and sociology depend on their psychology. They are the only ones who can answer the paramount question "Who did it?" For in the public divinations those personal enemies are never identified by the *cāmis*. Because the key of this entire discourse lies in the victims who alone can unlock the mystery of their own afflictions, we must understand and analyze Tamil sorcery from their perspective.

To do this we must conceive of sorcery as a cultural process that begins with a person's sickness, climaxes at the revelatory dialogues with the *cāmis*, and reaches its denouement with the spell's "removal." But it was only when I followed cases from beginning to end in real time, rather than from when they were over and done with, that I realized how this cultural process had its logical and dramaturgical trajectory that went far beyond the functional arguments just described. It was only then that I discerned how through this process people formulated the realities of their personal experiences with sorcery so as to effect them.

To grasp the transformative powers of this process, we will take a detailed look at one case of sorcery, from divination of origin through ritual treatment (known as *kal̲ippu*) to resolution (in the next chapter). However, I must emphasize that its protagonist, a village woman I call Laksmi, was not a typical target of sorcery spells. Since money and property were commonly at stake in sorcery suspicions, men—particularly well-off, urban men—were the main "defendants" of this discourse.[11] But as exceptions can confirm the rule, it was this tall, thin, and powerless woman with sad eyes and ragged sari who first revealed to me something of the emotional conflicts and personal torment that found catharsis in the conviction that one was under another's "command."

The Plight of Laksmi

Laksmi was a low-income, Untouchable (*Par̲aiyan̲*) woman in her late twenties who lived in the western part of South Arcot. Nine years before I met her she began to experience convulsions, jerking and shivering on the dirt floor of her single-room house. A neighbor rushed to alert her mother, but Laksmi was soon unconscious. Momentarily she returned to her senses but then collapsed into a deep sleep, grinding her teeth, suffering from nightmares. In the morning, when Laksmi refused food her mother sent for a local priest who whipped her with freshly cut margosa leaves, a plant imbued with the goddess's powers to ward off affliction. The next day, feeling a little better, Laksmi resumed work in the peanut fields.

But over the next few years Laksmi continued to suffer from chronic convulsions and pains in her arms and legs. She grew thin and weak and three of her four children died. Alarmed, her father took her to a nearby village where a temple priest made an amulet (*tāyittu*)—a thin piece of copper foil that he engraved with protective symbols and rolled up in a small cylindrical case for Laksmi to tie around her arm. But she continued to suffer, so in spite of his fears of the medical bureaucracy, her father took her to the Tindivanan Government Hospital about seven kilometers from his village. After waiting for two days, Laksmi was diagnosed with epilepsy (*valippu*), but prescription drugs were unable to control her convulsions.

For Laksmi's parents the doctor's failure confirmed their suspicion that she was afflicted with another kind of illness. In Tamilnadu it is common knowledge that biomedical treatment has no therapeutic efficacy against afflictions caused by supernatural or moral agencies. The only cure is a ritual procedure. First one must identify the cause. Is it a demon, an inauspicious astrological configuration, sorcery spell, the evil eye of an envious neighbor, sinful actions committed in past lives?[12] To find out, Laksmi's parents decided to consult someone to "say *kuri*," and settled upon Nagaji, the practitioner who in the last chapter persuaded the young, high-caste woman to stop seeing her Untouchable friend.

As they waited for the *cāmi* in the shade of his banyan tree, Laksmi's mother talked about her daughter's suffering and their helplessness. Neither Laksmi nor her father said a word, but other eavesdropping patients joined in, reassuring the family of Nagaji's gifts and recollecting his famously difficult cases.

Around mid-morning, his forehead and bare chest smeared with strips of holy ash, saffron wrap tucked around his waist, Nagaji made his appearance. Everyone prostrated themselves, touching his feet. He greeted everyone and, in no apparent hurry, idly conversed with some young men. When Nagaji at last signaled his readiness, about fifty visitors stepped back a few steps to leave him facing them. Dropping into his cross-legged posture on the ground, he gestured everyone to settle around him and, using tickets again, called his first client.

Laksmi was seventh in line. At her turn she sat with her parents, watching him wave the camphor flame around some offerings. Eyes closed, Nagaji gracefully folded his body, shut his eyes, and invoked his goddess's guidance:

> Give me your grace, protect me. Light the lamp in my life. Come to my mind, and protect me. Hardship has come to the lady. It has become sorrow, it has become a disease. We have to dispel it. NOW! It is good, but will you be happy if her body is happy? Protect us. We are burned, we have suffered, we have put our hands and legs inside out. In order to prevent us from hopping instead of walking we have become different castes. We must destroy the fluctuation, the disturbance of our minds. You must protect me,

Amma! I have no one else! Please become my guardian and peace will come to me.

After this stream-of-consciousness preamble, swinging between hyperlucidity and what my assistant called in English "nonsense," Nagaji opened his eyes. He addressed Laksmi:

Desire for a body? Desire for a mother? Desire for protection? What is your desire? Ask! Ask, my daughter! Whatever there is in life, we must grab it, we must control it. We must light a lamp. We must be good people. In this world we must not look at darkness, but at pleasure (*iṉpam*). But for some people, pleasure becomes trouble. It becomes a story of pleasures which are over for good. Amma! protect us from this story! There is Amma, there is Śakti, what are you asking for?

It was clear that the goddess was ready to hear Laksmi's problems, but her mother spoke up: "Our daughter is sick, she won't eat, does not sleep well."

NAGAJI: "She won't eat or sleep? Did it just happen or did it start five years ago?"

LAKSMI'S MOTHER: "It began some years ago."

NAGAJI: "Five years ago, I already told him. Didn't he hear me then? No, he did not hear me. He did not obey me. People have tricked your girl."

LAKSMI'S MOTHER: "We didn't do it!"

NAGAJI: "From then on your family has had difficulties. Your pleasure was broken. Sorcery [*ēval*] is walking around your house, *Kāṭṭēri* [a demon] is there. This is why there is no justice. Your girl cannot go on, cannot eat, cannot see the figure [*uruvam*]. She suffers from pain in the arms and legs, from many dreams. Weakness, tiredness, destruction have overcome her body. Incurable suffering may have come."[13]

Here the *cāmi* revealed that Laksmi suffered from a "command." His diagnosis also implicated the customary three participants in such an entrapment. First was the sorcerer. Nagaji hinted that he knew his identity but only allowed himself an obscure reference to a previous communication five years before, when he warned this very individual to leave people alone. Clearly the sorcerer had not desisted, and Laksmi's case now unfolded, in part, as a power struggle between these men.

So the "command" required a demon, and Nagaji had specifically blamed *Kāṭṭēri*, who was widely known to be the ghost of a woman who had died in pregnancy (or childbirth) and now vented her frustrated instincts by attacking other childbearing women, snatching their unborn babies and small children.[14]

Lastly, the spell incriminated the person(s) who paid for Laksmi's suffering. "People have tricked your girl" was all Nagaji would tell her parents about these enemies.

Yet Nagaji made it clear that Laksmi was unaware of this sorcery. The way he phrased it was revealing, "She cannot see the figure," implying that Laksmi's blindness was indicative of her victimization by *Kāṭṭēri*, a diagnosis only reinforced by the young woman's "pain in the arms and legs" and "many dreams."

Nagaji next offered a solution, assuring Laksmi's parents that Amma would intervene through the ritual called *kaḻippu*, which would neutralize *Kāṭṭēri*'s spell; as he put it, "Amma will take care of this. With love (*aṉpu*) we can conquer it. If we do the removal rites, we'll definitively obtain victory." Heartened, Laksmi's mother asked, "How can we do that?" "We cannot do it now," Nagaji replied. "Let the full moon come. If we do that then there will be joy (*mahiḻcci*)." Today's visit was only a diagnosis, without therapeutic value. For treatment Laksmi had to return on the full moon (*paurṇam*i).

In the meantime, he offered temporary protection, returning the five limes that Laksmi handed him over at the outset imbued with the goddess's power. The first should be buried under the threshold of her home, the second hung over the main entrance, so the family could safeguard their domestic life. A third lime was for "the path of the god of death, Yama"—the entrance to the funeral grounds. In South Arcot this area is usually marked by a stone (*kal*) representing Ariccantira, mythological guardian of this inauspicious zone. For the time being, this prevented Laksmi from figuratively entering funeral grounds—from dying. The fourth lime she had to ingest, absorbing the goddess's strength. And the fifth lime was for *pūjā* to the goddess, a reminder that Laksmi must pray to Śakti throughout this perilous period.

To conclude his seance Nagaji waved his fist full of margosa leaves, Śakti's vegetal representation, in smaller and faster circles before Laksmi's face. With the coming power of her defending goddess hanging in the air, Laksmi rose to her feet and departed with her family.

Two weeks later, when I visited her at home, Laksmi was a somewhat different person. The shy, speechless woman now told me in no uncertain terms that Nagaji was on the right track. In the privacy of her small hut, I also learned that she had good reason to suspect that someone did not wish her well.

At age sixteen, she married a "drunk" who squandered her dowry and beat her. After three unhappy years, she returned to her parents. She was about twenty when she began seeing another man whom she addressed as "my husband." Over the years she bore four children, three of whom died in infancy. But five days after she delivered their fourth child, a girl, the man returned to his first wife, for he was already married. Then Laksmi experienced the convulsions that prompted her parents to suggest the original consultation with Nagaji.

To Laksmi the "husband's" abrupt desertion was clear evidence that her jealous rival, the first wife, had resorted to sorcery to win him back. But Laksmi never brought up Nagaji's recommended exorcism to "remove" the spell. Was the diagnosis enough of a vindication on its own? Did she hope the sorcery would weaken and her lover would come back without further effort or expense? Why did she seem so passive about her victimization?

A month later Laksmi visited Nagaji for a second consultation, this time in private. On that occasion he clarified that *both* the rival wife and the father of Laksmi's children were plotting against her. To my surprise this news seemed to energize her. During our initial conversations Laksmi yearned for the man's return, now she lashed out, "I don't care whether he dies. I would not cut my marriage necklace [*tāli*; the rite that turns a Tamil woman into a widow] since he never tied it anyway." Only now did I discover that Laksmi had never married this man, but still wore the marriage badge from her first, legal husband. Although her lover could have wed Laksmi—polygamy being illegal but not uncommon in Tamilnadu—he had failed to do so.

The *cāmi* had deliberately stirred up Laksmi. His words carried weight because they confirmed what she was beginning to suspect, that her lover had left of his own free will and was not coming back. And she had no legal recourse; they were not married. Nor could Laksmi have made case to get him back since by Tamil standards she had deprived his real wife of her marital rights. As the *cāmi* enigmatically predicted two months before, "For some people pleasure becomes trouble. It becomes a story of pleasures which are over for good." Only when she fully accepted this finite rejection was she ready to undergo Nagaji's treatment.

The Inner Configuration of Tamil Sorcery

Through seven cases like this, I gathered that sorcery suspicions were commonly formulated on imputed resentments or jealousies. Usually the suspects were already known personal enemies so revelations that they were at the root of suffering were met with a degree of "resignation," as Michael Lambek also observed on the island of Mayotte, near Madagascar (1993: 262–63). In those cases there were often insufficient grounds for mounting a counterattack. But the sorts of intolerable victimization that did justify action incriminated loved ones whom it was too emotionally painful or frightening to initially suspect. Only when one confronted the agonizing realization that these intimates had tried to assume "command" over the relationship, generally by abruptly and unilaterally terminating it, was one impelled to seek a remedy. The experience of being manipulated and rejected by relatives and lovers provided the necessary level of emotional pain for defending oneself.

It was not simply a sociology of insoluble conflicts, nor a history of unprecedented changes, that seemed to fuel this Tamil sorcery discourse. Rather, it was a private logic, a psychology of painful revelations: one was made to "see" what one vaguely knew but could not accept or internalize. This state of blindness conforms with what we have now learned about the key condition of sorcery victimization; these "commands" grip people, like Laksmi, so that they feel "fear," the emotion that, according to *cāmi* Nagaji, "tricks" them. This emotion, in turn, prevents them from "seeing" the negative forces heading their way, from discerning, for example, that they no longer exist for the father of their children, and worse from acknowledging that that person took deliberate measures to eliminate them from the world. Their inability to face such personal repudiation becomes the cause of their suffering, with such symptoms as paralysis, mutism, frantic trance, convulsions, nightmares, violent head or stomach aches, and infertility.[15] This Tamil logic is very clear: what we do not or cannot "see," what remains hidden from us, ends up stalking us and "commanding" us.

To arrest this degenerative process and regain the capacity for independent action, victims must be empowered to "see" what is blocking them through the *cāmis*' "decoding" seances. But as Nagaji warned Laksmi, *kuṟi* is only a diagnosis, a first step. To complete this remediation and obtain full "fruit" a cure is needed. For in Tamilnadu there is little to be gained from making public allegations of sorcery. As Michael Lambek also found in Mayotte, "Making an accusation can unleash forces whose consequences the accuser cannot predict" (1993: 263). It is impossible to gather tangible evidence of the spell, there are no legal procedures for punishing any culprits. The best thing to do is to remove the "command" through the private, secret *kaḻippu* ritual.

In Laksmi's case, an additional two months elapsed before her father could raise the 125 rupees (approximately five dollars) to pay for Nagaji's countersorcery.[16] In the following chapter we will witness the completion of the process through which this troubled woman reggained power over her life.

4

LAST RITES FOR COMMANDING RELATIONSHIPS

On a full-moon night in the Tamil month of *Māci* (February), Nagaji scheduled Laksmi's "removal" rite.[1] The breeze during my motorscooter ride to his sanctuary east of Gingee was cool and dry. The path was utterly deserted; in the late hours when Nagaji conducted these rituals every one was fast asleep. Nor were these rituals casual spectacles; people without business there avoided them. Only some dogs barked at my silent passage through a succession of villages leading me to the *cāmi*'s grove.

Laksmi and her father were standing motionless with several other visitors around a camp fire. That night two women (including Laksmi) and seven men had arrived together with clusters of immediate relatives. No one talked, but they stared wide-eyed at me, completely bewildered why I would record such an inauspicious even dangerous ritual. But Nagaji, who understood and even exploited my research for his own ends, explained that I was learning how he dealt with enemy sorcerers and their demons. His job was to stop spells, mine was to be an attentive but neutral spectator. His patients nodded in approval.

As Nagaji waited for the midnight hour the air of expectation only intensified. That was when the original spells were cast, he once told me. Since Nagaji considered each ritual a counterattack on an opposing sorcerer, he had to strike back at the same time and in like manner. When I pointed out that he had personally not witnessed the evil sorcerer's ritual, Nagaji explained that the tutelary goddess guided his actions.[2] But for this healing, his supernatural assistant was *not* the goddess Śakti who regularly spoke during his biweekly divining seances, but the goddess Kālī—well known throughout Tamilnadu for her bloody battles against demons. Yet when acting as exorcist he did not identify with Kālī but retained his own male, human consciousness and personality.

Neither ritual terminology nor practice corroborated Nagaji's suggestion of the cosmological dimension to his confrontations with sorcerers and demons. Normally the procedure to counteract an evil "command" is simply glossed as *kalippu*, which means "removal," "casting out," or "rejection" (Fabricius 1972: 35). The word also describes rites regularly performed in households to ward off "evil eyes." In that domestic context circular hand motions draw the troublesome malevolence into absorbing, purifying substances, which either leave no residue, such as camphor lumps lit just outside the home, or which can be discarded, like cooked rice (Maloney 1976; Pocock 1973). The same logic underlies the countersorcery rite, for sorcery victims have been likewise incapacitated through visual means, only by the gazes of sorcery demons rather than envious neighbors.

But those visual assaults do require a more elaborate intervention, since human "eye-focused" assaults are often considered involuntary, a sort of subconscious "witching" power, if you will. The demons, on the other hand, are consciously intent on doing harm. And while the effects of human-cast "evil eyes" are relatively benign, and may be neutralized without help from specialists, demonic gazes can kill. Their "removal" entails a complex rite that, commensurately, as we will see, borrows its process and symbols from Tamil mortuary ceremonialism.

The *Kal̲ippu* Ritual

To initiate the *kal̲ippu* ritual, at exactly midnight, Nagaji drew three horizontal, chalk powder lines across the open patio of his sanctuary, each about fifteen feet apart. Positioning three of his patients an equal distance apart on each line, he indicated for them to face east in cross-legged, sitting positions. Next he duplicated the small effigies (*pāvai*) that the sorcerer was believed to have shaped, one for each patient.[3] As the original "commands" were personalized attacks, they required customized counterprocedures. Nagaji fashioned his seven-inch anthropomorphic effigies out of the identical ingredients—rice or wheat dough, dung, clay, or ashes from funeral grounds.[4] Each was encoded with the same iconographic characteristics applied by the sorcerer. But all shared the dominant features associated with demons: protruding tongues rouged with red vermillion powder, bulging eyes, and oversized sexual organs.

Moving from one patient to another, Nagaji worked calmly neglecting no detail, taking an average of fifteen minutes for each effigy. Under the moonlight, his patients witnessed the gradual birth of their "doll." But the mood was neither tense nor ominous. In fact, Nagaji seemed remarkably relaxed as his hands molded and adorned the effigies, monitoring in a teasing way the progress of his two young assistants, announcing in some detail his plan to sponsor a festival in the Tamil month of *Āṭi* (July/August). At one point he asked me if the dolls were frightening. By then I had attended a number of such sessions and was no longer impressionable, but I knew what he wanted to hear and nodded vigorously. He laughed, "Don't be afraid, Amma is on our side!"

It was fitting that these opening procedures engaged his patients' eyes. At his divining consultation for Laksmi, the *cāmi* emphasized that he knew she was under the sorcerer's "command" because she "could not see the figure." Through these little incarnations of the invisible forces that controlled them, now patients could begin to objectify them. Symbols of this separation were also encoded into the crafting of the effigies. Nagaji laid his finished dolls on their backs in a winnowing fan, known in Tamil as *muṟam*, or in a pot with their limbs drooped over the rim. Used daily to sort grain from chaff, the fans were markers of differentiation between "pure" and "impure." Elsewhere in India, anthropologists have noted how winnowing fans used in rituals denote what Christopher Fuller calls "the separation out of polluting and inauspicious elements that can then be cast away" (1992: 193; Fuller also cites Hanchett 1988: 141–43; Raheja 1988: 123–24). During Tamil funeral processions for caste Hindus, I observed village washermen carry such fans in order to signify, as one such specialist told me, that the living wanted to distance themselves from polluting corpses.[5] In the context of countersorcery rites, the laws symbolized the dissociation between afflicted and healthy selves.

Nagaji finished his effigies by dotting them with charcoal paste to "open the eyes" (*kaṇ tiṟappu*) and bestow "life" (*uyir*) on them, more hints of the link between sight, vitality, and consciousness. After this activating process—known in Tamil as *ceyviṉai ceytal*—[6]he offered the dolls cigars, palm liquor, and puffed rice, the delicacies preferred by demons.

Then Nagaji proceeded to destroy these icons of affliction. As each patient was called forth he drew a *cakkaram*, or protective enclosure, around each of them on the ground with yellow turmeric powder. Inside these circular, rectangular, or square shapes he traced Sanskrit and Tamil syllables (*uyirmey*), always under the guidance of the goddess, for he was illiterate. Explaining these signs, he once told me,

> The combination of a vowel [*uyir* also the word for "life"] and a consonant [*mey* also means "truth"], for example, h + a = ha, or p + u = pu, is the fusion of life and truth. Like the letters that the god Brahma, the creator, writes on people's foreheads at birth [*talaiviti*: literally "head fate"] they create order [*amaippu*: literally "structure"] in the world. They are like a mother and protect us.[7]

Along with these esoteric, prophylactic symbols, Nagaji added others with different connotations. Inside each enclosure he placed small, round fruits from two shrubs. The first, *ūmattaṅkāy*, is known to have emetic properties (V.A. Vidya, personal communication). The second, *kumaṭikkāy*, is poisonous when eaten raw (ibid).[8] The *cāmi* sliced both in half, smearing their insides with turmeric and vermillion powders to symbolize the manifestation of the benevolent goddess.[9] This proximity of opposites represented, in ways no words could achieve, her inevitable victory over noxious forces.

Since he was treating his clients in order of their arrival, and Laksmi was eighth in line, it was not until four-thirty in the morning that Nagaji positioned her into her turmeric circle, seating her to face east, her effigy resting on a winnowing tray before her. Now her enthralling forces could not escape. Now Laksmi was reencompassed within a moral and divine "structure."[10]

Across from her sat Nagaji, facing West, directly opposite a crudely carved stone image of Kālī. First he placed a burning camphor lump on the doll's belly. Lighting a cigar, he drew a few strong puffs and addressed the effigy,

> Don't try cheating me. I'll control you. I'll suck your blood and wrap your intestines around me. Stop your tricks. They won't work. I'll burn and stab you. Today you and I will fight [*poru*], and *I* will win. You have brought suffering to the girl. Today will end it.

Of course this challenge was uttered from Kālī's point-of-view, who is commonly depicted with intestines and skulls of enemy demons draped around her neck. Although it appeared that the rite was borrowing from Hindu cosmology, the following proceedings bore little evidence of any epic "fight" between demons and goddesses, or even of duels between sorcerers and *cāmis*. What followed was a funeral for the effigy.

The *cāmi* first poured uncooked rice (*arici*) into a cloth that he and Laksmi's father stretched above the effigy; this was so that Laksmi could "feed" the doll. Under normal circumstances, this action is performed by living kin on behalf of their dead. Prior to formal processions to the cremation grounds, a towel stretched above the corpse is filled with "*vāykkarici*" (literally "mouth rice"). Each gripping a fistful of this substance, consanguineal and affinal kin circumambulate the corpse and "feed" it. "At times of separation," one female consultant said of this procedure, "one always gives uncooked rice."[11]

In Nagaji's ritual the cloth was dropped, enshrouding the doll, whereupon he quickly tied a rupee coin into one corner. Then he abruptly ripped off the knot. This too seemed derivative of funeral symbolism, where the village barber tears the knot (*muṭittuṇṭu*) that contains a rupee coin (*kāl paṇam*) just before cremations or burials.[12] As one of them explained: "At birth the god Brahma gives man a knot, the umbilical cord. On the last day of life that knot must be removed. In doing so the dead person's relationships are torn apart."

But the next phase was even more suggestive. Pouring water into a new clay pot bought by Laksmi's family, Nagaji had her carry it on her right shoulder clockwise around the effigy three times. Before the first circuit, however, he punched a small hole in the pot so that water dripped out. By the third round, the pot was empty. Then he told Laksmi to smash it on the ground.

At Hindu funeral rites there is also this "breaking of the trickling pot" (*kalikuṭam uṭaittal*) (Good 1991: 135). The chief mourner, usually the son, concludes three circumambulations of his mother's or father's corpse by breaking the pot. Once again, a village barber, whose ceremonial duty was to perforate the vessel, helped me out: "At birth we come out of a pot, our mother's womb. The breaking of this pot symbolizes the end of life" (for a similar exegesis see Srinivas 1952: 151). In real funeral contexts, this action preceded internment, or cremation, and climaxed the ceremony. Here, too, Nagaji set the cloth covering the effigy on fire, and Laksmi stared intensely at the flames. But then the *cāmi* invited her to work her own way to recovery. Handing her metal nails, Nagaji instructed Laksmi to insert them into the doll's arms and legs.

At this, the *kaḻippu* ritual was essentially over, the doll was "dead," the spell was neutralized. Nagaji lit a small lamp near the crucified effigy, again reminiscent of funeral practices. Once a human death has occurred, an oil lamp burns for sixteen days until all ceremonial responsibilities have been fulfilled to assure the soul its successful journey to the afterworld.

But a larger finale still lay ahead. In Sinhalese sorcery rituals, according to Gananath Obeyesekere, this "is generally achieved by cutting some object" (1976: 205). Now Nagaji had Laksmi crush limes in the northeastern corner of her enclosure. Then he lit a camphor lump atop a pumpkin and waved the flame around her face. Suddenly smashing the pumpkin on the ground, he had her chop up the broken pieces with a large knife.

In Tamil popular rituals limes and pumpkins are common deflectors of the inauspicious. Crushing pumpkins concludes such "beginning" rites as consecrations for new houses; stomping on limes is associated with the blessing of newly purchased vehicles, such as bicycles and rickshaws. In Laksmi's ceremony, it seemed to protect her as she recovered the capacity for volition and mobility, since the *cāmi* now ordered her to hop three times over the winnowing tray.

Finally, he sent Laksmi to the presiding goddesses of his sanctuary. Circumambulating the shrines of Śakti and Kālī with palms pressed together above her head, she bowed each time she passed their images. On her final circuit she stretched out fully on the ground, arms extended toward the goddesses.

Close to dawn Nagaji carried the used or "dead" effigies to the nearby river bank. Because he insisted that only men could join this expedition, I never saw what happened. Later he said that near the water he enclosed them in another, rice flour circle. "This *cakkaram*," he told me, "was a form of arrest. It meant to say, 'do not come back!' " Then he lit some dry brush and cremated them all together.

Interpretations of the Funeral Symbolism

On at least thirty-six separate occasions I watched five different exorcists perform this ritual. All followed the same sequence of actions and manipulated the same symbols. Healers first objectified the invisible forces of sorcery affliction. Then they employed the winnowing tray to dissociate patients from these negative powers. Next they borrowed from such funerary actions as "the feeding of the corpse," "the tying of the knot," "the breaking of the trickling pot," and the cremation. It was not merely the exercise of violence against sorcery effigies nor their abandonment in the "jungle" that extirpated their malevolence, as appears to have been Sinhalese practice (Yalman 1964: 126; Kapferer 1983, 1988, 1997). It was the fact that *kalippu* rituals were so richly encoded with mortuary symbolism, which was consistent with W. T. Elmore's description of one "method of exorcism" he observed in 1913 from the adjacent state of Andhra Pradesh, in which an "image of dough" was placed in a pot that was then interred in the funeral grounds, in line with "*usual burying ceremonies*" (1984: 50, emphasis mine).

But contemporary, Tamil "removals," at least, do not actually incorporate all of the "usual burying ceremonies." They seem to skip rites that are integral to a "real" funeral in the South Arcot district, and an examination of what is left out confirms that this ritual works to exorcise outlandish and unwanted forces.

First, the countersorcery rite differs from a usual funeral by the conspicuous absence of formalized mourning. For whenever a death occurs the household's women huddle in arm-linked clusters near the corpse to sway, moan, weep, beat their chests, and intone their lamentations—a genre of song called *oppāri*, meaning "comparison." By means of metaphors and hyperboles their mournful words contrast a happy past before death with the desolate present, always honoring the deceased as the prototype of the ideal kin, always deploring his or her absence.

Second, the *kalippu* ritual also suppresses other representations of the social order that are constitutive of a "real" funeral. There are no male lineage members to observe strict pollution taboos, no grandchildren to ceremonially circumambulate around the corpse while holding a torch (*neypantam*), no in-laws to make ceremonial prestations, and no sons to perform "the breaking of the trickling pot." It is as if the individual whose "funeral" is underway had been a complete stranger, with no social identity, no kinship role, indeed no kin at all.

What is additionally striking, almost shocking, about this "funeral" is that, save for the final lighting of the lamp, it pays no attention to the fate of the soul. This is in sharp contrast with the prototypical Hindu funeral, which, after the disposal of the polluting corpse, always adds a second, crucial ceremony, known in Tamil as *karumāti*, which dispatches the departed (*preta*) to the hereafter as an honored "ancestor" (*pir*) (Parry 1994; Knipe 1977; Malamoud 1982; Hopkins 1992). All preoccupation with reincorporating the deceased into the extended kinship web of ancestors, which for some scholars constitutes the hallmark of Hinduism, is entirely missing (Knipe 1990). This facsimile of a funeral, which begins with no emotional "comparison," no public display from the living kinship community, simply ends with abolishing all that the person once was.

But who exactly does this funeral seek to completely eliminate from this world? To answer this question we must take a second look at the effigies themselves, for it is the dolls that actually undergo the death rites. And as we will now see, it is in the variable meanings invested in these symbols of affliction that the real efficacy of this "funeral" resides.

While Nagaji had encoded them with some distinctive features, all looked greedy, (tongues out), shameless (oversized sexual organs), and scary (bulging eyes). Save for their size, their iconography was also typical of the giant-size, horizontal effigies that are sculpted out of mud for ceremonial purposes in South Arcot (see Meyer 1986: 167; Hiltebeitel 1991: 321–24). They represent demons who threaten the order of social and cosmic worlds. They must die, and their anthropomorphic representations are given "life" for the sole purpose of being destroyed. Emphasizing this destiny is the fact that their heads, like that of corpses at funeral rites, generally face south, the realm of Yama, god of death.

The miniature effigies fashioned by sorcery—exorcists, which worked as healing dolls, were clearly modeled after malevolent powers.[13] In Laksmi's case, Nagaji fashioned her effigy to hold a decapitated baby in its right hand—a representation of the demon *Kāṭṭēri*, who was known to vent her frustrated maternal instincts by snatching unborn babies and infants. He also made the demon, *Varāki*, identified by her distended belly and streaming hair, who made her victims' bodies swell, and the demon *Kuṭṭi Caittāṉ* ("small Satan") holding his characteristic fork, a Christian demon, who, Nagaji claimed, killed "whomever the sorcerer ordered him to do."[14]

This iconography is consistent with popular knowledge of these demons and common understanding of countersorcery rituals. Since in Tamil cosmology demons are beings who have perished before enjoying marriage or childbirth, they have no direct descendants who can perform their funerals and postfuneral rites that normally convey the dead to the afterlife (Knipe 1990: 124). One sure way to hasten these untimely dead from this world, where they trouble the living through sorcerers' spells, would be mortuary rites. Since the ritual aims to "remove" sorcery, it would appear that Elmore was correct when he understood in 1913 that "the demon has been left buried" (1984: 49–50). His interpretation also explains why the living remain unmoved by the demons' "deaths."

According to both Nagaji and Laksmi, however, the effigy stood for someone other than a demon. Furthermore, their divergent interpretations suggested that ritual symbols could be invested with contradictory meanings and apparently still do what they were presumed to do.

One week after the *kaḻippu* ritual just described, I returned to Nagaji's compound when he was off duty and napping inside his hut. We drank coffee and discussed the coming hot season. But then Nagaji looked me in the face and said, "Ask me!" So I did, and he explained:

> That woman was seriously sick. She almost died. The *kaḻippu* was her last chance to return to life. The goddess restored her life. . . . She [Laksmi] is

> coming back to us. . . . She is like a new born. Because she died we had to perform her funeral and give the things required for a death ritual. . . . *The doll was a representation of the lady*. . . . This ritual was not dangerous for her. On the contrary, it brought relief and a new life. . . . The message to the lady was "forget about your past! it is dead now, you are entering a new life where things will be better."

The *cāmi* made it crystal clear that his ritual action was not simply or primarily concerned with expunging any demon. More importantly he had stood in as primogenitor by giving life to Laksmi through the doll. Then, in the role of funeral specialist, he officiated over the effigy's death. Third, as we have just heard from his own lips, he functioned as midwife for Laksmi's rebirth, giving her the tools (such as the nails) to incapacitate the forces that previously "commanded" her. He guided her piercing, crushing, smashing, and slicing her own way to recovery and personal freedom. Through this symbolic process he had facilitated her reincarnation, destroying her old life and reconceiving her into profoundly altered conditions of existence. Rather than performing a healing rite, he seemed to have carried out a rite of passage, a "twice-born" experience that "moves" a person into a second existence entirely dissimilar from the first (Van Gennep 1909). And Nagaji's own interpretation followed customary understandings of mortuary rites. The French Indologist, Charles Malamoud, for instance, argues that the old, Brahmanical funeral rite was "the *samskara* par excellence" (1982: 445). The term, which he glosses as "perfectionement," designates Brahmanical rites of passage that initiated individuals into more purified ontological states (ibid). Other writers confirm that, in modern ethnographic contexts, it is the "timely" death that constitutes the truest form of this "perfecting" (Parry 1994; Kaushik 1976).[15]

For her part, Laksmi interpreted the effigy's symbolic funeral quite differently. At first she claimed only a minimal, perfunctory memory of what had transpired. "To avoid *karma* (here meaning 'bad result')," she said, "the *cāmi* dealt with the spell in the appropriate way." Except for chopping the pumpkin, she only recalled Nagaji saying something like, "Today is your last day of suffering, from now on you won't have any convulsions." This was a relief, because, at that moment, "I was trembling. I was experiencing the symptoms that normally come before my convulsions."

Yet when I probed what she made of her participation in what paradoxically had been characterized by Nagaji as a life-giving funeral, Laksmi snapped at me. "You ask why I did that death ceremony? I already told you, to break with my 'husband.' I wanted nothing more to do with him." She needed no decoding of symbols to tell her that its purpose was the ritualized "death" of her living relationship with this "husband," who had never married her and had returned to his legal wife once Laksmi bore their fourth child. To eradicate the cause of those excruciating self-negations, she enacted the only familiar ritual that would provide a sense of meaningful closure. This "funeral" gave her permission and power to initiate retroactively an end to a relationship that her lover had already denied her.

But to effect this separation she had participated in a rite that in social reality no Tamil woman in the South Arcot district would ever be allowed to perform, or even to witness. At real funerals, under no circumstance can a woman ever break the "trickling pot" or even watch a cremation.[16] Female mourners are even prohibited from entering the funeral grounds and must remain within the family threshold where their mourning clusters express sorrow over the loss of relatives or beloved ones.[17] For her part, however, Laksmi had sat alone in the middle of a circle where she neither cried nor wailed nor evoked better times. Instead, she had assumed the ritual posture of a male mourner, cooly officiating over her "husband's" definitive "removal" from her life.

Countersorcery as Open-ended Therapy

Laksmi was not the only participant to contradict Nagaji's interpretation. Over time, I elicited radically different exegeses from healers and patients. I also discovered that the *kal̲ippu* ritual contained transformative resonances that exceeded its apparent purpose. It could even become an attractive "cure" for those who were *not* victims of sorcery. As the young son of a village school teacher told me the morning after having a *kal̲ippu* done for him (his second in five years):

> I did the *kal̲ippu* not because a sorcerer placed a spell on me. He did not. Not because there was a demon on me. There was none. I did the *kal̲ippu* because I was getting crazy. I read too much, I think too much. I needed to forget, to let go [*pōhaviṭa*] of my thoughts, that's all.

For this young man the "removal" rite was neither a way to end an unfinished relationship nor to rebirth but simply a way to obtain release from the "command" of a self-absorbing mind.

These quite different interpretations of the *kal̲ippu* ritual cast doubt on Bruce Kapferer's argument that the "self" of a patient is simply or automatically reconstituted in accordance to the sequential, objective structure of a healing ritual like a Sinhalese exorcism (1979a, 1979b, 1983: 179–226). For in these Tamil "removals," the successive manipulation of symbolic forms—making of effigies, positioning patients inside the circle, "borrowing" from funerary practices—does not appear to produce similar inner transformations. In fact, the Tamil countersorcery ritual seems better characterized by Jean-Marie Gibbal's description of the Ghimbala healing cult in Niger, "To each his or her own truth, almost" (1994: 108). It also rather seems to fit Gananath Obeyesekere's definition of a "standard ritual," which may be used by patients to express different psychological conflicts because it "has sufficient flexibility to cope with them" (1977: 289). Yet Tamil countersorcery does not seem to catalyze the kinds of primordial motivations that Obeyesekere found in Sinhalese exorcisms. Instead, as we have seen, it clearly addresses emotions that spring from ongoing personal crises and interpersonal dramas.

Central to the participants' understanding of how and why this therapy works in such idiosyncratic ways is Sudhir Kakar's contention that while an Indian shaman may "symbolize" symptoms he does not "translate" them (1982: 82). Let me review his comparative study of Western psychoanalysis and Indian exorcisms, based upon his observations at the Balaji temple in the North Indian state of Rajasthan (1982).

A Western-trained psychoanalyst, Kakar reminds us that a customary psychoanalytic cure is based on the assumption that mental or physical disorders can be the symbolic expression of a personal or emotional problem that has eluded a patient's consciousness. This is why, Kakar adds, the psychoanalyst must "foster a self-reflective attitude in the patient toward his bodily signs or symptoms," a process that involves concentrating on what he calls "the *text* of the mental illness—on its understanding, translation and genesis" (1982: 81–82; his emphasis). Kakar himself is quick to point out that this is not what the Indian shaman does. The healing rituals he saw performed at the Balaji temple "seem to be more concerned with the *context* of the illness . . . [with] connecting (or reconnecting) the individual with sources of psychological strength available in his or her life situation" (ibid). To Kakar, this shift in emphasis explained why "the special idiom" underlying the symptoms of sickness treated at Balaji "is left at the symbolic level without any attempt at translation" (1982: 82).

In my experience, however, Tamil sorcery healers were not concerned with reintegrating patients in their social fold, as seems the case at Balaji (and elsewhere in India, for example, see Carstairs and Kapur 1976). They concentrated on giving to patients some kind of "text" of their afflicted selves. Another look at what the healer Nagaji tried to impart through his effigy-making activities makes this clear.

For Nagaji the little doll could only represent Laksmi because that was what it had stood for in the original sorcerer's hands. Yet he produced a different effigy, for he had not simply modeled it after Laksmi's physique but drew upon received demonic iconography to portray her. Nagaji's work was thus reminiscent of the Cuna shaman whose recitation of a birth incantation, according to Claude Lévi-Strauss, eases difficult labors because it gives parturient women a "mythic language" to predicate and overcome the physiological duress of delivery (1963; also see Laderman 1987). Nagaji's cure was premised on the patient's receiving if not exactly the same sort of "language" Lévi-Strauss is talking about, at least an expressive "image" derived from Tamil mythology. But unlike the Cuna shaman, whose incantation invoked a social myth that did not correspond to the patient's personal state, Nagaji had fashioned his "representation of the lady" herself.

This is why I cannot follow Sudhir Kakar when he writes that the Indian healer offers personal resolutions that, while "personal," are nonetheless less individualistic than those provided by the Western psychoanalyst (1982: 82, 115–16). Far from focusing his therapy on the social "context" of Laksmi's sickness, on roles she had assumed or her relationship with her child's father, Nagaji presented her with a symbolic expression of the very problems that eluded her awareness. In other words, he had produced a personalized "text" of her afflicted self. True, he had not helped her reconstruct her individual past through verbal associations, nor had he given a narrative shape to her conflicts. But through his effigy-making he had objectified her interior state so that her greed, jealousy, fear, and sorrow became transparently embodied *in* and *to herself*. By "opening the eyes" of the doll, Nagaji intended for Laksmi to "see" the negative feelings that had disempowered and blocked her from finding a way out. Much like the psychoanalyst praised by Kakar, Nagaji had tried "to foster a self-reflective attitude in the patient" (1982: 81).

And Nagaji must have been aware that ritual symbols are enacted and hence derive their communicative powers, as Edward Schieffelin suggests, "also from the practices and contingencies involved in how they are put across" (1996: 61). For it was not merely the inert dolls but the whole performative confidence in which he molded them—his authoritative posture, upbeat demeanor, calm pace—that communicated his therapeutic goals. At the same time his small talk, teasing his young apprentices, casual announcement that he might soon hold a festival, all conveyed his message that the "commanding forces" were banal, unworthy of obsessive fears, and that everyday life could resume.

But much as Kakar also observed at Balaji, Nagaji did not "translate" his therapy. He never told Laksmi, "Look lady! you need to focus on this image because it embodies the kind of emotional motivations and longings you have been denying for too long!" His *kaḻippu* ritual entailed no instructions, no intersubjective dialogue, almost no words at all.

This was why I found myself with different exegeses from healers and patients. Without a didactic gloss, or clear-cut prescriptions about how this ritual functioned, patients read its open "text" from their own perspectives and vested interests, as Edward Schieffelin might say, "completing" the symbols with meanings relevant to their own experiences (1985: 721). In the absence of an all-encompassing hermeneutics, they seemed freer to associate and project whatever "commanded" them onto the ritual effigies.

Because participants were at liberty to infuse and personalize this ritual with specific, felt significances created out of their current existential predicaments, my research would seem to corroborate Kapferer's recent argument that in Sri Lanka "sorcery *is* power" (1997: 261; his emphasis). Indeed, his contention that sorcery is the "power that human beings exercise" (1997: 263), and that it symbolizes "the potencies of human beings to change the circumstances of their lives" (1997: 20–21), may ultimately explain the open-ended procedures of Tamil countersorcery. For this "undecoded" ritual becomes a pragmatic practice through which people reconstitute their private worlds and restore their place in them.

But I must still disagree with Kapferer on the nature of sorcery power. Although he notes that myths, ideas, practices, and rituals related to *Suniyam* are predicated on "metaphors of the political—of violence, authority, command, control, containment, division, and transgression" (1997: 34; also 1988), he sees the power released by Sinhalese sorcery as neither simply moral or immoral. "Nor is it," he cautions, "necessarily ordering or disordering, creative of the social or destructive of it" (1997: 263). In the Tamil case, as I will now show, the transformative potential of this power is always destructive, and its regenerative capacity is and must always be predicated on death and its role in Tamil culture.

The Destructive Powers of Sorcery

The working cosmology that is reproduced and exploited by Tamil sorcerers and their language of "command" draws on and exerts forces that are fundamentally destructive and antisocial. Their effigy-making activities clearly abrogate the life-giving power of the Hindu Creator, Brahmā. The activating substance of their spells comes from the disinterment and dismemberment of the corpse of a first-born child, a body that is a supreme symbol of generational continuity. Their mantras aim to disempower and exile someone from his or her social milieu. Their recruits are always the untimely dead, such as the demon *Kāṭṭēri*, who threaten the fertility of women like Laksmi. Because Tamil sorcery is from beginning to end concerned with the abortion of biological and social reproduction it is compared to *cahaṭai*, the funeral drum that, as one ritualist told me, "announces the loss of a human bond."

These details may not always be known to the average Tamil person, but they are consistent with general understandings of sorcery. From my consultants' perspectives there was nothing "moral" about sorcery. True, they could view it as a kind of self-help adjudication employed by those with no other avenue for redress. And some conceded that perpetrators had genuine reason to be frustrated by their victims' actions. But they were also quick to point out that the moral position of these "plaintiffs" was undercut by their self-serving motives, that their claims to whatever had been denied them were fueled by an inflated sense of self-importance, and that perpetrators' idea of equity was to "take command" over those who failed to behave according to their expectations. In short, everyone agreed that sorcery was not about rightful justice but about its dark side, about exercise of the wrong kind of power.

But in Tamilnadu, paradoxically, the very people who tap into this "commanding" power are not those who commission spells, but those who suffer from them. For we must never forget that Tamil sorcery is a speculative or experiential discourse with no objective reality; it is only authenticated by subjective impressions. It is therefore always a given perspective on what happens, on what, in this time and place, specific people say, what they do, what is done to them, on interpretations of the whole business of real life events and personal dramas.

This perspective, we now know, begins to crystallize when people "see" that someone whom they did not consider to be an enemy, in fact, whom they did not wish to have for antagonist, has rejected them. When at last they "see" (or as we might say "project" into) their rejecters in the demonic-looking effigies that are then crucified and cremated, they experience a kind of catharsis. The therapeutic powers derived from such a perspective go without saying. People take "command" of their relationships and execute their executioners. Laksmi realized that her "husband" had tried to erase her from his life and memory, so she sought an identical revenge, expelling him from her life for good.[18]

This fits with Hildred Geertz's observation that in Bali, "to fight sorcery you must sorcerize" (1995: 16). But one can even go further and argue that in Tamilnadu, at least, countersorcery is the only sorcery that is actually commissioned. For the perspective that I have just described is the only one that I was able to elicit, as I never met any sorcerer or any one who had paid for a spell. And the funeral that I have just detailed is the only empirical evidence of "removal" that I could document, for I never witnessed a spell's execution. Those who participated in countersorcery were casting the sole "command" of this discourse: they had activated the drums of death. Something of this shift in emphasis is captured in the widespread belief that the alleged perpetrators, those who are thought to commission the sorcerer's spell, are the primary "plaintiffs" of this discourse.

These repositional meanings take us into the heart of a sorcery cosmology that itself is volatile, but in a bipolar way. The powers recruited by the sorcerer to enforce his spells are the same as those who assist the *cāmis*' destruction of sorcery. Although in the abstract the distinct personalities of these supernaturals never coexist at the same time—they are *either* demons *or* gods—in reality one can never know for sure what they are, for they can easily be persuaded to switch sides. In such a worldview supernatural entities may be on your side one moment and against you the next, which may also explain why a young woman could be subdued by her lover one moment and may vanquish him the next.

Even the birthlike transformations envisioned by the healer Nagaji were not without destructive import. The *cāmi*'s intervention did not stop with the making of the effigies or with their simple unmaking, but more emphatically with their funeral. To understand the full significance of this mortuary treatment, let me explore the larger perspective of Hindu funerals.

Many scholars have noted how Hindu mortuary rituals and their Brahmanical antecedents sought to obliterate not just the physical remains of the dead but their personal characteristics and biographies as well. Charles Malamoud, for example, describes the old Brahmanical crematory ritual as a "rite of suppression of the deceased's worldly person" (1982: 443, trans. mine), while Jonathan Parry has written how such representations still prevail in contemporary Benares: "No place is made in the mortuary rites for a celebration of [the dead's] individual achievements; no eulogies are delivered in praise of his particular virtues, and no recognition is given to the passing of a unique life" (1994: 210). The Tamil funeral also attempts to efface the individuality of the deceased. What is ceremonially lamented is an idealized and somewhat stereotypical relative, what is officially commemorated is a member of a kin group, and what is ritually preserved is an ancestor.

We begin to understand that the rebirth that Nagaji extended to his patients was premised on the repudiation of past experiences, previous relationships, and former identities. This suggests that it was not merely patients but healers like him who filled the countersorcery ritual with meanings drawn and relevant to their own individual experiences. For this *cāmi* had personally undergone a rebirth following a deathlike separation from his former self. In retrospect, one can see how his entire therapeutic philosophy was predicated upon his own initiation as a recruit of the goddess.[19] That was when he had envisioned himself as "commanded" by personal intimacies and emotional entanglements that, like destructive enemies or spells, needed to be "removed." Consequently, those who assimilated his therapeutic "text," like the dead who undergo real funerals, emerged "newly born" from his *kaḻippu* rituals, without biographies or senses of continuity with the past, or even personal memories. The resumption of life that Nagaji's "funeral" facilitated, the new relationships and new pleasures that it anticipated in an ongoing, revitalized existence were dependent upon "removal" of all that a person once was.

And this appeared to also be Laksmi's experience. Before I left India, I paid a final visit to her village. As her father led me to the peanut fields, I recognized her tall silhouette among the group of women picking the pods. She approached with a broad smile, and we sat under a scrawny tree. For the first time since that day when I met her ten months before, she did most of the questioning, asking about my daughter and nodding attentively. She never alluded to the circumstances of our original meeting when she had been so miserable. Nor did she seem to recall what had led her to consult *cāmi* Nagaji in the first place.

In the end, we learn again that sorcery *is* power. Its complete cycle—from initial diagnosis to successful defeat of spells—opens new forms of consciousness. The Tamil countersorcery ritual therefore verifies Kaplerer's formulation that sorcery highlights that truly extraordinary capacity of human beings . . . to construct and transform their life situations" (1997: xi–xii). The open-ended procedures of the *kaḻippu* ritual make it possible for ordinary Tamil villagers, like Laksmi, to make their own analyses and reconstitute themselves and their realities on their own terms. But for all its "creativity," indeed, "regenerativity," Tamil countersorcery is not so good to "constitute lifeworlds" with, as Kapferer implies for Sri Lanka. The practice above all aims to eliminate, or (in Tamil) "remove." Its regenerative potential, its "power" to reposition the Tamil person, is always bound up with death of injurious others, the injured self, and of whatever forces hold people in their thrall.

5

OF WOMEN AND DEMONS

In this chapter and the next we explore a form of exorcism that, in sharp contrast to the countersorcery ritual, does seek to reintegrate participants with their former identities and milieus. What is peculiar to this ritual process is how it inhibits the kind of idiosyncratic exegeses we have just heard about. Far from enabling endless, private interpretations, it is prescriptive, even "totalizing," as Bruce Kapferer also characterizes Sinhalese exorcisms (1983), that is, it enforces a reality in which only one kind of consciousness and subjectivity is possible (1983: 5).

The objective of this ritual is to "drive away" (*ōṭṭutal*) demons known as *pēys*. Now these malignant beings have a different ontological personality from that of the sorcery demons we have just met. Those supernaturals had proper names, clear-cut identities, and myths of origin that correlated with the careers and narratives of members of the great Hindu pantheon. But the category of *pēy* that concerns us here represents the spirits of unknown, ordinary human beings who suffered unnatural or untimely deaths. Their inauspicious fates prevented any normative transit into the hereafter and stranded them in this world where they possess, or "catch" (*piṭi*), the living, most conspicuously young married women (also see Caplan 1989).[1]

Throughout India anthropologists have noted the propensity for new brides to be afflicted by the untimely dead.[2] Usually this sort of "ghost-possession" (Freed and Freed 1993) is explained as a safe means for young wives to vent frustrations over their powerless role in their new families (Opler 1958; Freed and Freed 1964; Harper 1963; Kakar 1986; but see Skultans 1987).[3] As Christopher Fuller writes, "Women's possession episodes are . . . culturally tolerated opportunities to complain about female inferiority and subordination within Indian society" (1992: 233). From her research on the Mukkuvars, a Catholic fishing people in the southernmost Tamil district of Kanyakumari, Kalpana Ram also contends that demonic possession enables women to reinterpret "dominant" symbolic constructs of the female body and sexuality, and to "challenge the daily discipline of living within the confines of respectable femininity" (1991: 93).

But my research will cast doubt on this widespread anthropological wisdom. That analysis may have the virtue of translating puzzling practices into terms that seem accessible and even ethically pleasing. But it was never corroborated by my Tamil consultants and stands at variance with the exorcisms that I recorded on twenty-four separate occasions in South Arcot. To the contrary, my analysis unveils how this ritual coerces women and their spirits into articulating a sense of self that is entirely alien to them.

Nor does my documentation of Tamil exorcisms support three other interpretations of female demonic possession that have stemmed from nearby Sri Lanka. The first, proposed by Bruce Kapferer, argues that "women . . . are subject to demonic attack as a function of their cultural typification, which places them in a special and significant relation to the demonic" (1983: 128).[4] At first blush his reasoning seems consonant with what I heard from Tamil consultants. Women and men agreed that women are more susceptible to being possessed by demons because of an inherent weakness attributed to their impurity, which also explains why women are likely to be "caught" while menstruating (also see Bharati 1993: 345; Caplan 1989: 55; Mosse 1986: 474). It was also said that women are mentally and emotionally deficient, more susceptible to the "fear" that, as we have already seen, can strip the Tamil self of protection against malevolent powers such as *pēys*.

But this argument fails to explain why, at least in Tamilnadu, it is not women as a whole but predominantly new brides who are at risk. Of my cases of demonic possession, twenty involved young women who had married within the past six years (also see Mosse 1986: 473). Such statistics might be understood by invoking the Tamil belief that "the odour of sexual activity . . . [is] said to be particularly strong and attractive to demons in the period immediately after marriage" (Ram 1991: 90). But this would not explain why, of my sample, sixteen had run away from their husbands. Here, too, the Tamils have their own perspective: the spirits known as *pēys* cause grave psychic disorders and incite women to reject their spouses. But to formulate any analysis based solely on such beliefs can blind us to the social practices and ritual processes that enact this discourse. And when we do link those patterns and actions to the real lives of the women in question we discover a deeper motivational layer.

The relationship between culture and the individual in South Asia is addressed in Gananath Obeyesekere's now familiar premise: in any society demons belong to a class of cultural symbols that may be invested with subjective significance in order to articulate "deep" psychological conflicts (1981). From this perspective, demonic possession is a culturally constituted idiom available to women for expressing and managing their personal problems (1970, 1977).

The argument that culture is created and manipulated by individuals is one with which I agree, for all of the religious activities presented in this book hinge upon subjective or reflexive engagement. But my investigation into possession by untimely dead suggests that the production of Tamil culture is not always such a spontaneous or free-form endeavor. As we will see, Tamil women are taught, even pressured, to frame their personal predicaments within the cosmological framework of demonic possession.

My analysis leans closer to that of R. L. Stirrat, yet another ethnographer of demonic possession in Sri Lanka. At Kudagama, a Sinhalese Catholic shrine specializing in exorcisms, demonic possession is "primarily concerned with attempts to impose power over others, particularly young women" (1992: 112). Stirrat bases his conclusion on the observation that individuals defined as "possessed" often exhibit more than symptoms of physiological illness; they display a "whole series of problems," which include "odd behaviour" and "irresponsible sexual attraction" (1992: 112–13; 1977: 138). To Stirrat, a demonic possession diagnosis and subsequent exorcism allow close relatives to regain control over such individuals.

While this is what I observed in the South Arcot district of Tamilnadu, the field of power relations at stake in my research on *pēy* possession seems narrower. For at the heart of the Tamil process that defines a woman as "caught" appears to be control over marital sexuality. Here is a discourse that focuses on women who are disenchanted with conjugal life, accusing them of surrendering to fantasies of extramarital intimacy, and of therefore jeopardizing the reproduction of their husbands' families. The exorcisms we are about to examine force women to repudiate publicly this reprehensible behavior and rededicate themselves to cultural expectations of the "good wife" (*cumaṅkali*).

On *Pēys* and Their Environment

German missionary Bartholomaeus Ziegenbalg was correct when he wrote in 1713 that "those men who die by their own hands" are particularly prone to become "evil spirits, called *Peygel*" (1984: 152). Of the demons I tape-recorded in the midst of exorcist rituals, one had been murdered and six spoke of bus or train collisions. But fifteen, the majority, told of hanging or drowning themselves. Furthermore, virtually *all* of the suicides had suffered from what my field assistant, in English, called "love failure." These *pēys* had taken their own lives due to an unrequited passion or because relatives opposed their marriage plans.

After death their limbo-like time on earth *remains* dominated by an unrelenting yearning to fulfill their frustrated desires for sexual intimacy. This is their driving obsession and why they stalk and "catch" the living. *Pēys* do not seem to be compelled to possess people, as missionary Robert Caldwell (1984) believed, because of their hatred of human beings, nor, as Lionel Caplan more recently put it, out of a diffuse "anger" (1989: 55). All my consultants—specialists, lay people, and *the spirits themselves*—were unanimous that *pēys* are motivated by "love" (*aṉpu*) and "lust" (*ācai* or *kātal*).[5] This understanding also resonates with one of Wendy Doniger's key points about Hindu mythology in general. "The origin of evil," she writes, "is inextricably associated with the appearance of sexual desire" (1976: 212).

While twenty-two out of the twenty-four *pēys* I encountered were male, my consultants' explanations for inactivity on the part of the female untimely dead was always the same: "They are too shy to catch people."[6] Furthermore, women are prudes, I was told, and after death behave with the same modesty that guided their conduct when alive. Since *pēys* are predominantly young males craving for intimacy, young women are their favored prey.

Symbols of sexual passion are also evoked in my consultants' descriptions of the landscapes in which *pēys* usually carry out their attacks. When I heard that *pēys* hover around the place of their death and asked for topographical specifics, I always learned that these spirits had perished in an inauspicious zone which people call *taricu nilam*, or the "wasteland" (also *kāṭu*, or "forest"). Rarely was this landscape given more specific features, for such "fallow" and "dry" land lay beyond the periphery of every settled community (also see Caplan 1989: 55; Mosse 1986: 471). Likewise, the Reverend Caldwell noted in 1849 that the Nadars of the Tinnevelly district believed *pēys* occupied "inhabited wastes" and "shady retreats" (1984: 163; also see Dumont 1986: 451). Their association with wilderness perhaps clarifies why the term *pēy*, as Gustave Oppert noted in 1893, can also be glossed as "wild or obnoxious plants" (1893: 559, in Caplan 1989: 53). Sometimes this forbidding territory is also depicted with imagery symbolic of the demon's untimely death: the pool of stagnant water where he originally drowned, or the tamarind tree from whose spreading branches he hung himself. The hardy tamarind has natural and cultural properties that make it especially compatible with such an unseasonable landscape, for it thrives during severe droughts, and is classified in Tamil folk taxonomy as "sour" and "inauspicious."

This was the desolate landscape in which virtually all my consultants imagined *pēys* launching their attacks. And their timing was always at highnoon, when there is maximum heat and maximum light. That is also when their victims are usually traveling "alone" outside their community; or as I often heard, "The girl gets *caught* on her way to the fields" (also see Dumont 1986: 451).[7]

These representations derive from Tamil aesthetic conventions of considerable antiquity, specifically from the last of the five categories of landscape described in Tamil love poetry (*akam*) compiled between the first and third centuries a.d. (Ramanujan 1967; Hart 1979; Shanmugam Pillai and Ludden 1976). Named *pālai* after an ironwood tree characteristic of this arid country, this fifth landscape was glossed as "wasteland" (Ramanujan 1967: 105). To evoke its barrenness, the classical Tamil poets used phrases such as "dried springs" and "stagnant water" (ibid). Even the key metaphor for this landscape, the *pālai*, a leafy tree with the same characteristics as the tamarind, was aptly chosen, for, as A. K. Ramanujan points out, it was "unaffected by drought" (1967: 105). The poets also located this "wasteland" in a specific temporal setting: its climate corresponded to the peak of seasonal and daily heat—midsummer and at high noon (Shanmugam Pillai and Ludden 1976: 18).

These formulaic references to landscape served to intensify emotional descriptions and to characterize a particular phase, or *uri*, in the development of love between a man and a woman (Ramanujan 1967: 105; Hart 1979: 5; Shanmugam Pillai and Ludden 1976; Sopher 1986: 6–7). In the classificatory system of *akam* poetry, this "wasteland" landscape pictorialized their "separation" and, according to Ramanujan, it connoted "the hardships of the lover away from his girl, but also the elopement of the couple, their hardships on the way and their separation from their parents" (1967: 106).

Transposed to the equivalent landscape of *pēy* aggression described by my consultants, commensurate meanings prevailed. When depicting the typical scenario of a *pēy* attack, exorcists and lay people alike embroider it with seductive connotations and emphasize how gorgeous the woman looks. The initial contact of demons with their prey is strongly visual and erotic: in broad daylight the *pēy* can clearly see the girl's beautiful skin daubed with turmeric paste and vermillion powder, her hair dressed with flowers.[8]

Once seduced by her allure, in a lonely place, the demon "touches" her. Startled, the woman grows "fearful," the emotional state which, as we know, renders one vulnerable to external forces. And so the demon is able to "catch" his girl, and according to my consultants, he does so by "sitting" on her head, the locus of sanity, driving her half-crazy before "entering" her body through a lock of hair.

Much like the lovers in *akam* poetry, the demon-*pēy* then elopes with "his girl," forcing her to separate mentally and physically from her community and husband. For it is well understood that *pēys* "not only sexually enjoy their victims" but also prevent normal conjugal sexual relations, inciting wives to "kick" and "bite" their husbands to keep them at bay. And since a woman's liaison with a *pēy* is also said to make her barren, the husband is deprived not only of legitimate control over his wife's sexuality, but of her fertility as well. If the couple is ever to resume a "normal" life, it is absolutely necessary to conduct the ritual that "makes the spirit run away" (*pēy ōṭṭutal*).

How Shanti Was "Caught"

In day-to-day life the production of a cultural symbol such as *pēy* is never as monolithic or straightforward as the foregoing synthesis suggests. Personal histories of Tamil women involved in demonic possession reminds us that the utilization of such a symbol generally depends on highly specific family details and marital tensions. To illustrate how crucial these social and psychological dynamics are to the making of a given *pēy* I will describe the case of Shanti, a frail, high-caste (*Mutaliyār*) woman in her early twenties who grew up in a village near the town of Salem.

When she was four years old Shanti's father left home to start a new family with his second wife. The sole offspring from his first marriage, she was raised by her mother and paternal grandmother. At seventeen, while attending the wedding of a relative, her soft, attractive looks caught the attention of a widower fifteen years her elder. He proposed marriage and her family accepted. As Shanti told me, "He did not ask much in terms of a dowry. My mother was poor. As for my father, he was relieved to give me away, for he was saving for the marriage of his two younger daughters."

After her wedding Shanti moved to Madras where her older husband worked as a government clerk. Her life became miserable: "He would come home drunk, irritable, quarreling over any small thing. I cried every night. Tears would flow and there was no stopping them." Eight months later Shanti ran away. Back in her village she resumed her old job in a puffed-rice factory. But when her mother died six months later, Shanti's father returned her to her husband, where life was little better than before. But she did make a few friends and began "to go to the cinema." Around this time she experienced mood swings: "One day I would be drowsy and could not bring myself to get up. Yet the next morning I would be giddy and restless." She rejected her husband's sexual overtures and soon they were no longer speaking. She became withdrawn, lost her appetite, and "lost all interest in life." Alarmed by her physical deterioration and sullen disposition, her mother's younger sister took Shanti to a suburb of the city for a consultation with the healer named Raghavan.

This was the man who was recruited by Kālī in his teens during a life-threatening siege of smallpox. His trance-diagnosis quickly attributed Shanti's trouble to a *pēy* and prescribed a ritual to "make this demon run away." *Cāmi* Rhagavan recommended that this exorcism be performed on the next new moon day on the grounds of the Aṅkāḷaparamēcuvari temple, located in the town of Mēl Malaiyaṉūr. When Shanti arrived in Mēl Malaiyaṉūr that day, accompanied by her mother's younger sister, I met her at the temple.

The sequence of events that led to this ritual was typical, and followed the pattern noted by R. L. Stirrat in Sri Lanka (1992, 1977). "First," he writes, "there is some sort of abnormal behaviour" (1992: 104). In Tamilnadu, women also acted in ways that struck their kin as odd or inappropriate: they were withdrawn, apathetic, anemic, aggressive, incoherent, and barren (also see Dumont 1986: 450). Like Shanti, they often refused to have sexual intercourse with their husbands, even fleeing from their sight. These behaviors precipitated what Stirrat calls "suspicions of possession" by close relatives—usually parents but also siblings, spouses, and in-laws (1992: 105). In my experience women sometimes confirmed these *pēy* suspicions by spontaneously entering into trance, "dancing" like demons, and even speaking from their perspective on occasion. But since few *pēys* were rarely bold enough to entrance their victims, their influence was usually expressed through the attitudinal symptoms mentioned above (also see Stirrat 1992: 101).

The next step was for the family to find a *cāmi*-like practitioner (male or female) to verify that they were indeed under a demon's sway. Women rarely resisted this explanation, and from that point on they were forced to comprehend their distress within the discourse of demonic possession.

Now their relatives filled in the blanks of the diagnosis. They ceaselessly conjectured as to how, when, and where the *pēy*'s attack occurred, drawing upon well-established collective representations. As David Mosse observed among Christian communities of the Ramnad district, the basic plot of these retrospective accounts typically included the identification of "some preexisting condition of vulnerability to demonic attack" and the "frightening incident" that came as a consequence (1986: 473). For instance, people told me how a possession must have happened on a day when the woman was sent alone to fetch firewood outside the village; or the attack was traced back to the week of her last heavy menstruation; or it was said to have occurred when she returned from a nearby town with a "shaken" or "startled" expression on her face. Hearing these hypotheses, neighbors contributed their own details.

As Stirrat observed in Sri Lanka (1992), activities leading up to the exorcism ritual also impress upon these women the reality of their possession. Many were prescribed a minimum stay of ten days at the shrine where they would undergo the ritual (also see Mosse 1986: 479). They were made to fast, to circumambulate the temple 108 times a day in order to "purify their bodies and hearts," and some were whipped with freshly cut margosa leaves to drive off the *pēy*. All the while their relatives anxiously consulted exorcists who offered advice, additional details on demons, and on what they could expect from the forthcoming ritual. From the moment a woman was diagnosed with possession, she was also "caught" in this encompassing world of symbols, stories, and meanings. Out of this discourse her demon was constructed in three dimensions, and the exorcism rite only furthered this convincing objectification.

A Healing Temple and Its Musicians

Shanti may have been shocked that the temple of Mēl Malaiyaṉūr was built adjacent to the town's cremation grounds. The location of a funeral ground within a town precinct is odd enough, for such zones are customarily situated well outside the community, usually along a river bank. To find the abode of a goddess alongside this inauspicious place is more unusual, for normally Hindu deities will not tolerate contact with the polluting forces that are released by death.

A second striking feature of this temple is found in the antechamber of the main shrine. Here the nonanthropomorphic representation of the goddess Aṅkāḷaparamēcuvari stands in the form of an old, earthen termite mound (*puṟṟu*) that rises unevenly over a rectangular base; the mound is about five feet high, fifteen feet long, and five feet wide.[9] Shrouded in an old, tattered canvas smeared with ochre-colored turmeric powder, it is said to shelter a nest of cobras. According to Eveline Meyer, this form of the goddess as both termite hill and snake,

> is Aṅkālammaṉ before she is recognized as a goddess, it is the power which manifests itself in an extraordinary way. This power is as yet without attributes, it may be male or female or both, it may be benevolent or malevolent or both. It is the moving force behind some event, before that force has revealed its name or identity. (1986: 58)

To primordial powers latent at this site, where the deity herself was first conceived, devotees present offerings of milk and eggs at orifices of the termite mound, and pinch its yellow earth to daub on their foreheads. Upon entering the inner sanctum, the "womb" (*garbhagṛha*) of the temple, they face the goddess who is seated in her usual posture—left leg folded under her hip, her right leg slightly bent at the knee.

"At this spot," writes David Shulman of Tamil inner sancta in general, "the pilgrim is conceived afresh, to be reborn without taint, with all the powers latent in the new born child" (1980: 19). His observation fits the Malaiyaṉūr temple. Progressing from the outer gate near the funeral grounds toward the anthill and into the inner "womb" chamber, devotees recapitulate the road from death to life, emerging reborn from their contact with the goddess.

The chartering myth of this temple claims that Lord Śiva himself once undertook this very journey. And on the Malaiyaṉūr funeral grounds, Aṅkāḷaparamēcuvari, a frightful manifestation of Śiva's wife, Pārvatī, cured his madness (also see Meyer 1986). Like the Mahanubhav temple studied by Vieda Skultans in the state of Maharashtra, this divine precedent for recovery of sanity has turned the Malaiyaṉūr temple into a "healing centre . . . for spiritual afflictions, in particular, those which give rise to mental illness" (1987: 663). Since this is the identical disorder that besets the women "caught" by *pēys*, and as victims of sorcery spells have similarly lost "command" over themselves, this popular shrine is primed for the performance both of exorcisms and "removals." This explains why Raghavan always advised his consultants to undergo treatment here, and he was not alone. On new moon days, the lunar juncture said to have favored Lord Śiva's cure, his fellow practitioners, many as far away as Madras, "heal" their patients on Malaiyaṉūr's funeral grounds.

But not only healers and new patients converge on this temple. Many ex-patients, like Kumar in chapter 3, return to thank Aṅkāḷaparamēcuvari for releasing them from debilitating spells or mental disturbance. Other devotees come to fulfill vows, to take *darśan*, to pray, or to "dance" in the temple courtyard to the accompaniment of musicians' drums. Its air thick with vibrating percussion from drumheads and metal bells and bangles, high-pitched screams, and odors of smoking incense, the temple becomes an arena impossible to grasp in its varied intensity. To enter it is like plunging into another, more urgent dimension of human yearning, one in which frantic agitation, passionate enthusiasm, and ecstatic self-absorption are permitted and encouraged.

Shanti was not treated by Raghavan, who only practiced as a diviner. In exchange for a percentage of their treatment fees, Raghavan turned his patients over to his long-time associates, a troupe of all-male ritual musicians known as *pampaikkārar*, who were well positioned to share in the temple's thriving business. Three of their troupe belonged to the temple's priestly lineages, from their necks hung its distinctive insignia, a miniature silver casket enshrining a *liṅkam*.

These musicians can contact with all supernaturals of the Tamil pantheon—deities, demons, spirits of the untimely and timely dead. But unlike the *cāmis*, *pampaikkārar* do not enter states of trance or impersonate supernaturals, and they claim no intimate relationship with the goddess, or any deity for that matter. Instead, they sing and beat drums, brass rattles, and bells in order to stir one (or more) member of the party sponsoring their services into trance.[10] During exorcisms, for example, they accompany the demon as he "dances" through the possessed woman's body. In this state she conflates cosmic realms and provides the musicians with a direct verbal channel to the demon itself.

But as Gananath Obeyesekere has documented for Sri Lanka, spirits of the untimely dead are "a known *category*, but they are not known beings" (1981: 115, emphasis in original). So the job of these musicians is to establish who exactly is now lodged within a woman's body. They must extract a number of facts about this unwelcome visitor's personality: his or her name, gender, ancestral village, caste membership, age, marital status, number of children, and the ominous circumstances that left him or her wandering in unfulfillment and yearning (also see Mosse 1986: 479). Only when they have reconstructed the *pēy*'s personality, can they proceed to evict him or her.

The structure of their exorcist operations thus differs from that of a *cāmi*-like practitioner, who, as Lionel Caplan rightly points out, first "becomes a medium for the goddess, who then drives out the *peey* either by appeasing it with a sacrifice or threatening it with her superior power, or both" (1989: 66, citing Moffat 1979: 241–42). It is beyond the power of these musicians to stage such grand confrontations. To oust the demon, they are limited to the possessed woman's kinetic and verbal participation.

It would be misleading, however, to view the musicians' mode of exorcism as devoid of cosmological resonance. For all their claims to exclusively technical expertise, the *pampaikkārar* also operate in a world in which Amma remains the ultimate opponent of demons. All of them knew that it was she who had originally built their principal instrument, the *pampai* drum, by stretching a vanquished female demon's skin over a wooden cylinder, and that of a male demon over a thinner tube of brass. Then she tied the "male" drum on top of the "female" one, giving her double drum to human beings whenever they needed to cast out demons (also see Meyer 1986: 3; for a similar origin myth of a South Indian musical instrument see Assayag 1992: 286).[11] According to the Malaiyaṉūr musicians, the beat of this *pampai—their* gift from the goddess Aṅkāḷaparamēcuvari—made the demon dance, speak, and ultimately leave this world.[12]

Yet the license to command the coming and going of supernaturals also demanded rhetorical virtuosity, humor, performative creativity, and psychological insight, all of which this troupe had in abundance. These charismatic, talented musicians were also my favorite consultants. With the *cāmis* I was asking clarification on matters "hidden" to me, and fell into the category of a supplicant who was expected to defer to them. Since our interactions followed the model of a regular *kuṟi* seance—I asked questions, they answered—we seldom struck a looser, intersubjective style of conversation. For when they "decode the signs" these recruits lecture people in the name of the goddess and never level with them.

No such distance existed with the Malaiyaṉūr musicians. Since I could not enter trance, they never considered me one of their patrons. And since they too did not "dance," they seemed to view me as an equal, often visiting my home and asking many questions about life in the United States—which was not surprising, for their line of work consisted of a sort of skilled debriefing. Our conversations were highlights of my fieldwork and gave me temporary hope that cultural differences could be transcended. Moreover, such troupes brought together a cross-section of caste affiliations and seemed relatively uninterested in social inequities and hierarchical values of traditional Hindu society. Their almost universalistic sociology was also reinforced by some skepticism toward the very epistemology within which they worked. In contrast to the *cāmis*, who embraced the sacred reality of what they had "seen," not all *pampaikkārar* kept faith in matters of spirits. One once told me that he was sure that the dead could not "dance" with the living.

Paradoxically, in actual ritual practice these musicians were more absolutist than the *cāmis*. At least the recruits, who depended on no one but the goddess and themselves to "decode" signs, permitted clients to make their own interpretive choices and construct, to some degree, their truth. In fact, they did not so much "permit" as push people to "complete" and "translate" curing scenarios all by themselves. By contrast, these musicians forbade their patrons such hermeneutic leeway. Perhaps because they received their expertise through inheritance and apprenticeship, rather than by means of transformative visions, they enforced a ritual reality that participants could not "see" and therefore could neither debate nor contest. At the same time, their services were in high demand and very expensive: while *cāmi* Nagaji took only 25 rupees for Laksmi's countersorcery ritual, the Malaiyaṉūr musicians demanded 500 rupees to cast out Shanti's *pēy*.

Making the Demon Dance and Speak

Whenever they are contracted to transact with deities, human spirits, or demons the Malaiyaṉūr musicians issue what they call a "notification" or "warning" (*eccarikkai*).[13] In the case of exorcisms, this occurs around midmorning in the entrance to the Aṅkāḷaparamēcuvari temple. So on the morning of Shanti's ritual the musicians "alerted" her demon to come "outside" later that day," on the temple's funeral ground.

Immediately Shanti's *pēy* responded to their drum beats by "dancing" his willingness through her body. And speaking through her mouth, he promised to show up on condition that he receive a "life" (*uyir*) in exchange—a sacrifice. After this draining experience, Shanti slumped to the ground in a faint. Meanwhile the musicians made her aunt purchase offerings that *pēys* are known to relish: puffed rice, cigars, arrack, toddy, bread, cooked rice, dry fish, and the chicken that would be sacrificed.

At two o'clock in the afternoon, amidst the hammering heat, the cluster of musicians, Shanti, and her aunt converged near a stone slab representing Mayāṉavīraṉ, son of the goddess Aṅkāḷaparamēcuvari and guardian of Malaiyaṉūr's cremation grounds. The grim, silent expanse held no sign that while here one stage of human existence ended another began. The sparsity of trees, the dirt piles of graves, and the gaunt, jackal-like dogs rolling in human ashes, everything pointed to death's finality.

Scratching a circle into the dusty ground, the musicians positioned Shanti in the center, facing east. As with countersorcery rituals, the enclosure aimed to "tie down" (*kaṭṭivaikka*) her demon; a musician emphasized, "inside this circle the *pēy* cannot escape." With Shanti's aunt and onlookers watching intently, the five *pampaikkārar*s divided into two groups (three on one side, two on the other) and surrounded the enclosure.

The splashy crack of a smashed coconut signaled the instrumentalists to begin their rapid drum rolls, regularly punctuated by metallic clicks on bell and rattles. A handsome young man with a melodious voice summoned the major Hindu gods and the local pantheon to guide him through the ritual. In exorcisms, this lead singer told me, the obligatory, formulaic invocation called *kāppu*, or "protection," is critical because the demon may have "tied the mouth of its victim, rendering her mute." "When we have the gods on our side," he added, "they'll break the tie."[14]

But once this divine protection had been secured, the singer threw all his vocal energy and talent into inducing Shanti into her trance. Switching to free-verse, his prescribed sequence of entreaties mounted with rhetorical intensity. First, he addressed the *pēy* directly with a mocking tone of deference: "Whether you are king, minister, or governor [*turaicāmi*][15] open your golden mouth, please speak up. Where did you catch her? Dance, and tell us your name, we removed the gag over your mouth [*vāykkaṭṭai*]. Please, speak!"

His appeal was encouraged by the chorus: "He's a good and civilized person, he won't let us down, he'll tell the truth."

Getting no response, the singer resorted to threatening the *pēy*, "You'll be scolded if you don't open your mouth." Then he pleaded for the goddess's assistance. "Amma! Put some knowledge (*aṟivu*) and sense (*putti*) into this evil spirit. Bring him here. He is so arrogant. Beat him in the chest."

Meanwhile the musicians kept their eyes on Shanti, alert to any fixed gaze, body quiver, or stiffening motion to indicate that she was on the verge of "dancing." Her gaze locked on the camphor flame. Although her preoccupation had not yet taken kinetic form, the singer hastened to initiate a dialogue. Signaling a sudden halt to the music, he threw out the overriding question,

"WHO ARE YOU?"

No answer was forthcoming, so he turned to imploring,

"Why can't you speak? We haven't done anything to you!"

When this failed, he was reduced to begging,

"Who has come on this girl? Tell! I won't scold you. I won't beat you."

Suddenly he switched back to his threatening approach,

"So far we have asked our questions respectfully. If you don't want to be mistreated, you better speak up!"

When she remained silent, the singer squeezed lime juice around Shanti's face and upper body. "It contains Amma's essence [*kuṇam*]," he explained later, "it scares the *pēy* and makes it speak." But still the spirit neither spoke nor danced. Over the next fifteen minutes, the singer's frustration increased, and in his lyrics he directly addressed the spirit world:

"From *Yama lōkam* [the world of the dead] we have to pull him, give us two ropes! The one who wanted a chicken, it's time for you to come. How did you die? Did you hang yourself? Were you murdered? Unable to bear some grief or pain, did you commit suicide? If you want this girl, please dance and talk to me. If you speak, we will give you the girl."

"Say one or two words! Speak up! Dance and speak! Don't just stand there! He hung himself. So many girls passed him, but he did not like them. He only liked this one. What is your name? What is your home town? If you dance and answer my questions, I'll give you whatever you want. I won't beat you, I won't scold you. Please tell your name! Give me your hair!"

His chorus sang back, "He told us that he would give his hair. He is not a bastard, he will keep his word."

But Shanti failed to move a muscle.

At this point, the musicians' invocations attracted an unexpected visitor. Upon hearing the drums, a heavy-set woman in her late forties, circling the temple precincts on a devotional round, entered into a "dancing" trance in front of the musicians. Since the singer was of the temple's priestly lineage and officiated at most temple functions he recognized the signs: the matted hair and bright yellow sari identified her as a recruit of the goddess.

It was not unusual for the musicians' drumming, which could be heard many kilometers away, to compel devotees of Aṅkāḷaparamēcuvari to "dance" their way into an exorcist session. Customarily the musicians acted annoyed by these intruders and tried to abort their trances by swiping holy ash across their foreheads and resting their anklet-shaped rattle on their heads. But since this exorcism was not going well, the singer welcomed the diversion, engaging the woman in an entertaining if somewhat mocking, metaphysical discussion. "Amma!" he yelled, "In this world there are so many spirits, so many demons and so much sorcery! Isn't it true?"

The goddess embodied by this woman did not seem to notice the musician's sarcasm and irreverence, as he insolently called attention to the multitude of evil forces still "in this world," hinting that she was not doing her job of protecting human beings. Ever preoccupied with "seeing" through people, she simply replied, "there is a male on her [Shanti]." And ever ready to assert her divine authority over demonic forces, she requested a bunch of margosa leaves to beat the *pēy* out of Shanti's body.

But the singer refused her margosa leaves and seemed unimpressed by her responses. He even admonished her, "Why didn't you bring the *pēy* to *us*?" making it clear that the goddess was his assistant rather than the other way around.

Amma agreed through the woman to help: "Call him now!" But the singer held off, complaining, "We have tried for so long." Vexed, the goddess now protested that she would have helped out earlier if the musicians had only called on her.

This did not sit well with the musician; he called the shots here.

"You must answer *our* questions," he said, "or you can go and sit by the mound [in the temple]. Are you going to protect this woman [Shanti]? Can we call the *pēy* now?"

The goddess agreed, but not before reiterating that if the musicians had brought Shanti to the town where her recruit resided, she could have driven the demon away.

The singer scoffed, "Isn't there any Śakti [female divine power] in Malaiyaṉūr?"

Put in her place, since that was where she *was*, the goddess backed off. "Call the *pēy* in two hours," she meekly replied, "I'll drive him away."

At this point the singer abruptly halted the proceedings, postponing the exorcism until later.

He resumed the ritual two hours later at the same location, and soon Shanti began to sway and roll her head from side to side. As the musicians intensified their drumming, her gyrations accelerated, her braid loosened so that her hair swung wildly. Once she was fully entranced, the singer signaled the music to cease and began to interrogate her *pēy* in an everyday tone of voice.

"Do you want this girl?"

For a moment the question hung in the air. Then the young woman nodded and grabbed a lock of her hair, volunteering it to the musician. Since *pēys* are said to be "on" their victims' heads, specifically "on" a lock of their hair, the demon's offering expressed its readiness to surrender. But the singer turned down the overture because any successful exorcism dictated that *pēys* first submit to a structured interrogation for revealing their identities. So the musician picked up his earlier inquiry.

"WHO ARE YOU?"

"I don't know," answered the *pēy*, speaking through Shanti's mouth.

The singer was relentless.

"WHO ARE YOU? Male or female?"

At "male," the *pēy* nodded timidly. But the musician wanted a verbal response.

"Male or female?" he said insistently.

"Male."

"What is your name?"

When the spirit was silent, the musician tried humor,

"You could say *something*—'Donkey,' for instance!"

Laughter rippled among the gathering onlookers. Setting aside the crucial question of identity for the moment, the singer ventured the second most common query, familiar to foreigners in Tamilnadu, regarding identity.

"What is your natal home?"

"I am from Tiruppur."

"Where is that?"

"Near Salem."

"And your caste?"

"Why do you care?"

"How old are you?"

"Twenty-two."

Trying to catch the spirit unawares, the singer sprang the central question on it again.

"What is your name?"

"I don't know. Please leave me alone!"

"WHAT IS YOUR NAME?"

"I don't know, I'm from Tiruppur."

The musician tried a different tack,

"How did you die?"

"I hung myself."

"On what kind of tree?"

"A tamarind."

"Why did you hang yourself?"

"They did not want me to marry."

"So you died. But you must have had a name. What was it?"

"Yes, they gave me a name. But I don't know it."

"Come on, these people will beat you. Tell me your name and I'll arrange a proper funeral marriage [*karumāti kalyāṇam*]."

"Will you arrange my marriage?"

"Yes, I promise."

"My name is Shankar."

Often the musicians have to play for many hours before achieving this sort of contact with the *pēy*. No matter the stream of compliments, sermons, or threats, spirits are usually in no hurry to speak or dance. Meanwhile, the afflicted woman stands awkwardly in a kind of limbo, hands clasped and eyes downcast. These behaviors are striking in light of the fact that usually they "dance" so readily during the ritual's "warning" phase. Perhaps this is because that requires little psychological effort; the spirit's demand for "life" is formulaic, for "life" is what an untimely dead invariably wants. By contrast, the *pēy* is next required to reveal its true and unique identity, a confession that entails a complex investment on the part of the "possessed" woman.

To this critical question of the name, our demon first pleaded ignorance, which was not surprising. All *pēy*s whose testimonies I recorded swore up and down that they did not know who they were. But eventually biographical details and personal names do emerge. After examining a number of my transcripts, it dawned on me that the *pēys* were constructing their identities by patching together vital statistics *from their victims' lives*. In Shanti's case they shared similar ages (twenty-three/twenty-two), and similar places of origin (two villages near the town of Salem) and similar names (Shanti/Shankar).[16] Upon my comparative analysis of two dozen *pēy* testimonies, I was also struck by how often the existential predicament that led most *pēys* to commit suicide were likewise reminiscent of their victims' own lives. Shanti's family, much like that of her spirit, had failed to arrange her marriage. Her father had not wanted to pay her dowry and she had been hastily wed to the first suitor who made no financial demands. Other women, much like their possessing *pēy*s, had been prevented from wedding sweethearts or were mistreated by spouses.

Since *pēy*s are encouraged to voice their personal problems, the dialogue with the exorcists did enable women to talk indirectly about their distress. But I think it would be misleading to see in this process an unconscious expression of feminine protest or therapy in any Western sense of freeing the self from past experiences. It is true that this ritual seems to conform to the Western therapeutic proposition that recounting traumatic memories to an attentive, well-meaning audience can help people recover aspects of their identity. It is precisely when the *pēys* recapture the most troubling stage of their lives (the cause of their suicide) and are offered a way out of their misery that the women complete their own identification with them. Only then do the spirits name themselves and women, like Shanti, can be said to "find themselves" in their demons. But these women are not at liberty to exorcise their past through any free association. The formulaic interrogation requires them to articulate a sense of self consistent with what is culturally known about the *pēy*. Since *pēy*s are predominantly male malcontents with loose libidos, women are only able to speak of themselves through symbols of a frustrated masculine sexuality. We can understand why this process could not occur without its drawn-out trial: women are slow and reluctant to "dance" because they resist taking on the personality of a sexually obsessed male.

But from the moment they are "caught" in the discourse of demonic possession there is no going back. As Stirrat notes in Sri Lanka, "[O]nce defined as possessed . . . the subject has little alternative but to go through the rituals of the shrine" (1992: 106). A woman brought to Mēl Malaiyan̲ūr to be exorcised is, similarly, "exposed to extreme forms of pressure" (Stirrat 1992: 105; also see 1977: 140–41). Surrounded by the five musicians who closely monitored all her movements, Shanti, we have seen, was incessantly, aggressively urged to dance and speak. To hasten her entrancement, she was told to stare at a burning camphor flame and lime juice was frequently squirted around her face and body. As David Mosse observed at a Christian healing shrine in Ramnad, when these procedures were of no avail there was "an escalation of verbal abuse and physical violence directed at the *pēy*" (1986: 479). Then one of the goddess's recruits broke into the exorcism and threatened to beat the *pēy* out of Shanti's body. Although she was restrained, I have watched others in the temple grabbing "possessed" women by the hair and pulling them to the ground so they could have the demons whipped out of them with braided leather straps. Although these women sobbed and wailed, they made no attempt to avoid the blows or fight back, perhaps because they knew that any show of resistance by their *pēy* would only prolong the beating.

This reading of the phase of this exorcism known as "making the demon dance and speak" is in opposition to the old functional interpretation of "ghost possession." At the least it forces us to rethink the relationships that the untimely dead have with women. As we follow Shanti's experience in the next chapter, we will see how the ritualized eviction of these spirits confirms the impression that a patriarchal ideology can be more encompassing and resistant than some anthropologists might allow.

6

THE DECAPITATION OF YOUNG BRIDES

The musicians had achieved their first objective: the *pēy* who was possessing Shanti was personified. So far her exorcism had followed the processual logic of the *kal̲ippu* countersorcery ritual, which also began with the typification of afflicting forces. The difference was that here the musicians had not embodied the demon in an effigy; instead, they had drawn him out of Shanti's body with their music. Nor was this incorporation accomplished by means of any visual, "eye-opening" procedure. Rather, they had employed verbal, dialogical conventions to assimilate the demon's personality with key aspects of Laksmi's identity and biography. Speech had replaced sight as the organ of recovery.

With the demon's and Shanti's identities sufficiently merged, the musicians could now proceed to separate them. For this dissociation no winnowing trays or any funeral symbols were necessary, only words. Let us return to that scene in the late afternoon light at the Malaiyan̲ūr temple. Tottering from side to side in the middle of her circle, Shanti looked dazed and oblivious to the ritual's progression. But the lead singer glared at her and demanded of her demon:

"Where did you first catch this woman?"

"In Salem. She came with her husband and relatives. I caught her on the way to the movies. She often went to the movies with her friends."

"Why didn't you catch the other girls?"

"They were Muslims."

"You don't like Muslim girls? I know many *pēys* who have caught Muslim girls! When did you first catch her?"

"Two years ago."

"What trouble have you brought her?"

"She no longer speaks to her husband. I brought dissension [*pirivu*] into her family. She laughs at everyone, she is shameless, she is like a cow, she has no feeling."

"Is there anybody else?" [Not infrequently it is revealed that more than one *pēy* are "on" a victim.]

"Who else, when I am around?"

"No Kāṭṭēri?" [the same demon who had troubled Laksmi earlier.]

"No! My whole body is aching."

By reconstructing precisely where and when Shankar "caught" Shanti, the singer created a resonant, familiar narrative for all witnesses to the ritual, which also confirmed the purgative steps to follow. And by itemizing the troubles the *pēy* had caused her, the musician also substantiated a cultural verdict that their encounter was pathogenic. Shankar had confessed to being the culprit who had visited these ills upon Shanti. He was to blame for Shanti's marital conflicts; he had rendered her "arrogant," "shameless," "insensitive," and "like a cow." The *pēy* and its associated mental disorders became synonymous.

Now the singer felt free to ask the demon to leave Shanti alone for good, and Shankar agreed. But since these spirits are notoriously untrustworthy, he asked the earth goddess, the sky goddess, the sun and the moon to bear witness. Then Shankar swore over a camphor flame "to leave this girl now" and "to never bother her and her husband again," and mashed out the flame with the palm of his/her right hand.[1]

Here the musicians completed their banishment of the *pēy*. First the singer asked the demon to indicate the precise lock of Shanti's hair "on" which he resided. "Search for the hair my dear king!" he sang. "My dear handsome king search for the hair!" After the musicians knotted the lock, the singer begged the departing spirit, "Once you leave, who will come on this hair? Search and tell us!" Shankar said the goddess Aṅkāḷaparamēcuvari would take his place—the auspicious replacing the inauspicious.

In exchange, the *pēy* would now receive his promised "life." But as the singer held out the chicken, he warned, "We'll give you the life, but you'll have to drink the blood." When Shankar balked, "I do not want to suck the life. Just give me puffed rice (a common vegetarian offering for demons)," the singer became insistent, "If you don't take this life, who is going to believe that you're leaving? I want to slap you. You asked for this. Drink! Bite!"

Shankar refused to sink his teeth into the bird's neck, but consented to drink its blood. Tearing off the chicken's head, a musician shoved its bloody neck into Shankar's mouth. Immediately the *pēy* spit it out, an act which signaled his imminent expulsion. Again the singer warned that if he ever turned his head to gaze at Shanti again, he would make him "eat her shit." Handing him a cup, the musician added, "You're about to go far away. Drink this water before you leave!"

"Help!" Shankar screamed in response, "Help!" (*apāyam!*). The mood of the gathering abruptly changed. Everything speeded up, as the exorcism's cover term in Tamil, "making the *pēy* run away," became dramatically explicit. Placing a large, round rock in Shanti's hands, the musicians began chasing her/him. Staggering under its weight, she zigzagged toward a nearby tamarind and dropped the stone. Two musicians caught her and dragged her up to the tree. Slicing off the knot of hair, they nailed it to the trunk (cf. Mosse 1986:

483). Shanti fell unconscious. Returning to her senses a few minutes later, she was pronounced free from her *pēy* at last.

Analysis of the Sequence Known as "Making the Demon Run Away"

This final sequence of the exorcism appears to be a symbolic process of long-standing. In 1709, in what may be our earliest Western source on this ritual, the French missionary Jean-Jacques Tessier witnessed an identical enactment in Pondichery less than one hundred kilometers away from Malaiyaṉūr:

> To cast out the demon, the priest (*pūcāri*) whips the possessed. The demon surrenders via the mouth of the possessed. But, at once, this one seizes a big stone, and the *pūcāri* still whipping drives him outside until the possessed exhausted, falls down on the ground and drops the stone. Then the *pūcāri* ties him to a tree by the hair which he cuts to offer in sacrifice to the demons, thereby delivering the possessed who barely moves on account of the received blows. (in Dharampal 1982: 131–32, translation mine)

Tessier made no effort to explain what he saw, concluding only with his denunciation, "all this is useless. . . . Only the disciples of Jesus Christ can dispel malevolent spirits by merely making the sign of the cross" (in Dharampal 1982: 132; trans. mine).

To appreciate the sequence we should start with the notion of giving "life" to the *pēy*, since it is the exorcism's central premise. At the preliminary communication with the demon—the "warning"—the *pēy* agreed to meet the musicians on the funeral grounds on condition that he be granted the "life" missing from his disembodied existence. In this climactic episode, however, our *pēy* Shankar was horrified by the idea of consuming his sacrifice, a reaction I was to witness on several occasions.

His behavior may be understood in the light of a broader religious trend. Since "The Madras Animals and Birds Sacrifices Prohibition Act" was passed in the 1950s, many temple officials have discouraged or eliminated life-taking rites, so today, as one exorcist confided to me, "even *pēys* are becoming vegetarian" (*cuttam*, literally "pure"). But the demons may have deeper reasons for refusing this "life," or blood sacrifice that is given in compensation for their submission.

No sooner are *pēys* offered the chicken sacrifice than they customarily cry for "help!" (*apāyam*), the word that formulaically concludes the verbal operations of *all* exorcisms. They are feeling "in danger and fear for their lives," the very same emotion that left their victims open to the original attack in the first place. The demons, then, appear to be "caught" by an identical terror to that which they induced in their victims, and their fright has the same consequences; at that instant they are rendered voiceless, passive, and remote.

Losing their personal identities, the demons are also transformed into inert matter—into the heavy, round rock that the musicians placed in Shanti's hands. Now I must emphasize that this was not my comparison; a musician described the stone to me as "the weight of the *pēy*'s desire." But it is important to note that this "weight" (*pāram*) has changed location. The *pēy* is now in the young woman's hands, in the rock, and under her control. While it made vague sense for the exorcism to climax with her dropping the rock, my questions regarding this mystifying episode were met initially with uncertain answers. Shanti herself, then in the state of trance, had no recollection of it; the *pampaikkārar*, usually so loquacious, could not "explain" their own actions.

Let me suggest that the dropping of the stone symbolically enacts the *pēy*'s decapitation. Later we will see how I reached such interpretation through the comparative method, as this exorcism is shown in binary opposition to the two Tamil rituals, the investiture of the family deity and the sacrifice for a lineage god, which I will discuss in chapters 9 through 12. For now let me only contend that such structural, or "positional" meanings (Turner 1968: 17), are not my only key to this final exorcist sequence. For symbolism of decapitation also surfaces in a local myth.

The story in question is none other than the chartering myth of the Aṅkāḷaparamēcuvari temple in Mēl Malaiyaṉūr. I am not suggesting that this South Arcot folk variant of the well-known Sanskrit story of the god Śiva's Brahmanicide is a prototypical representation for Tamil folk exorcism (for Sanskrit versions, see Doniger 1973: 127). According to Eveline Meyer, it may not even be the true founding myth of Malaiyaṉūr, as it was "introduced at a relatively late stage in the history of the [Aṅkāḷaparamēcuvari] cult" (1986: 184). But as I pestered one musician about this obscure, closing sequence in the exorcism, he must have drawn a correspondence between myth and ritual, for he volunteered the following story that put it and my interpretation into a larger context (also see Meyer's detailed versions 1986: 36–38, and 176–83).

Śiva's Extra Head

Paramacivaṉ (the god Śiva) had five heads. The angels, the sun, and the moon used to regularly ask the god to grant them favors. Even the god Brahmā came and asked for one. He wanted a fifth head too. Śiva granted his request.

No sooner was Brahmā endowed with his fifth head than he began to fulfill wishes as well. Śiva felt bad about this. At the same time Ishwari (Śiva's wife) complained that she could no longer distinguish him from Brahmā. Śiva replied: "What could I do, he came and asked for five heads and I granted him the favor."

As Brahmā was becoming arrogant, and in the eyes of Ishwari too much like her husband, Śiva cut off one of Brahmā's heads. But another grew in its place. When he cut off that one, another replaced it, and again and so on.

The god Viṣṇu appeared, announcing that he had given a special boon to Brahmā that enabled his head, if chopped off, to grow back. To cancel the boon Śiva would have to keep the head in his hand. Śiva followed Viṣṇu's advice and once more cut off Brahmā's head, but this time he held it in his hand. Brahmā fell down but when he got up he cursed Śiva for having broken his promise. "You will become a naked beggar and hang around like a madman. You will never be at rest again."

Unable to get rid of Brahmā's head, which stuck to his hand, Śiva suffered the curse. He wandered like a homeless, crazy beggar. When he reached the cremation ground of Malaiyaṉūr the goddess Ishwari followed the advice of her brother, Viṣṇu, and took the form of a scary-looking being (*akōra rūpam*). She became Aṅkāḷaparamēcuvari and threw two lumps of blood rice at Brahmā, and one to the head that was stuck to Śiva's hand. Then Brahmā's head fell off and rolled on the ground where Aṅkāḷaparamēcuvari stepped on it. Delivered of the head, Śiva came back to his senses. He and Ishwari resumed their happy life as husband and wife.

This story opens with the uniqueness of Śiva's personality as epitomized by his five heads.[2] When Śiva endowed the god Brahmā with a fifth head, the identification between the two was so complete that Ishwari, Śiva's wife, could no longer distinguish which one was her husband. In several versions of this particular narrative collected by Eveline Meyer, Brahmā took advantage of this and quickly made a pass at the goddess (1986: 177).

So Śiva resolved to cut off Brahmā's fifth head. According to Wendy Doniger O'Flaherty (1980: 47), the decapitation motif is "always" a symbolic "castration," and in Tamil folk myths, at least, it often appears as retaliation for lust as well (see the Māriamma myth, in the next chapter). But as Gananath Obeyesekere (1981) has shown, castration is rarely a final solution to Hindu sexual conflicts. In this myth Brahmā's head grew back, and whenever Śiva tried to chop it off again, it grew back.

But a literal reading may lie closer to its effective meaning. Śiva failed to permanently sever the head because he was unable to let go of that extra-personality he had just created. This was perhaps why he still had one too many heads after managing to decapitate Brahmā. Now he had six of them, with his state of imbalance conveyed by the bizarre location of that extra head—in his right hand. And Śiva remained stuck to this head, effectively "possessed" *by* an additional identity.

At this point the mythic representation of Śiva's possession becomes identical to that of our demon's victim. The god was likewise condemned to dwell alone, on the fringes of society, in a wasteland where liminality became his permanent condition as he wandered around stark naked. Like a woman "caught" by a *pēy*, he was also stripped of reason, and the story eventually has him going mad.

Correspondences between myth and ethnography even extend into the exorcism, which in this narrative also took place on the Mēl Malaiyaṉūr cremation grounds, the location par excellence for separation and rebirth. There the goddess intervened, throwing a lump of rice soaked in blood upon Brahmā's head. Unable to tolerate contact with this polluted offering, it tumbled from Śiva's hand; the goddess, in effect, beheaded Brahmā. This is not the only time that a South Indian goddess triumphs over those who, like the god Brahmā, try to deceive her.[3]

In the South Arcot ritual I am describing here, the exorcism similarly opens with a blood offering: the chicken's crude decapitation. It presages the demon's own beheading, which is why he immediately cries for help. The woman now holds the *pēy*'s "weight" in her hand, a rock which is smooth, round, and about the size of a human head. The woman runs frantically and drops the stone—the demon's symbolic head—near the tamarind tree. With this act, she, like the goddess, decapitates her own impostor-husband, freed of her demon(s) at last.

Why the Symbolism of Decapitation

The decapitation symbolically enacted through the final operations of this exorcism is necessary if Tamil women like Shanti are to resume a "normal" life. But to fully understand what I am about to argue about the expressive dynamics at its heart, we must delve into Tamil representations of demonic possession.

First, we must reexamine the key symbol of this discourse, the *pēy* himself. These spirits are construed as human beings prematurely robbed of their lives. Sometimes they met their fate by accident, but more often, unwilling to accept emotional frustration, they took the ultimate step of self-destruction. Hence *pēys* lack what Tamils call *rajam kuṇam* ("courageous disposition"), a quality of fortitude considered indispensable to social life.

Second, the victims of *pēy* attacks appear to possess the same escapist tendencies as their demonized doubles. Women who are "caught" are commonly said in Tamilnadu to be afflicted with a "weak or timorous disposition" (*pūtam kuṇam*, literally "demonic nature"). Confronted with the same marital problems that frustrate the demons, they too do not "adjust" nor find a way out of their emotional entrapment. Instead, much like the *pēy* who possesses them, they succumb to disappointment and withdraw from social life, as testified by the fact that many women run away from home and that some, like Shanti, told me that before the entanglement with their demon they had already begun to "lose interest in life."

Third, my consultants always represented these women being attacked when walking alone, away from the normative landscape and its focal sanctuary, the family compound. We have noticed how their escapades led to these forbidden spaces, featuring stagnant pools and tamarind trees, an unincorporated and undomesticated terrain devoid of the secure appointments of proper social life.

To be sure, the demon Shankar contradicted these representations, and he was not alone. At most exorcist rituals I documented, *pēys* claimed that their attacks had actually occurred *not* in any of the traditional wasteland landscapes described earlier but in the heart of bustling urban centers. Nine of these spirits, for example, confirmed Lionel Caplan's observation that in cities such as Madras the *pēys* concentrated "near trees and wells, cemeteries . . . and railway tracks" (1989: 55). But twelve others, like our Shankar, announced that they had "caught" their victims on the way to cinemas, by bus stops, or even *on* buses.[4] When I inquired about this shift of *pēys* to modern sites, an exorcist replied that times had changed. "In the cities," he explained, "there are more crimes, more suicides, and therefore more *pēys*."

Yet these new venues for demonic attack still remain associated with anonymity and threat. Away from the security of home, family, and clear-cut gender domains, they are places where male and female strangers brush up against each other in dangerous proximity and where illicit passions can be kindled (or represented on cinema screens). Our *pēy*'s response to the exorcist's question as to why he had chosen Shanti over her girlfriends was suggestive of these dangers. The other young women were Muslim, he said, inferring that they were unsuitable sexual partners. But he also implied that Shanti, a high-caste Hindu, was in foreign company, hence removed from her own kind, alone and defenseless.

Female alienation was conceived as a perilous domain of experience in which women were freed from the ordinary constraints on female sexual behavior. Unaccompanied by male guardians, they ventured beyond the village or town settlement where they risked unrestrained intimacies outside the realm of legitimate sexuality ruled by their fathers, husbands, and even sons.

But the Tamil evocation of female alienation does not leave it at that. Once estranged from their constitutive relationships, women became drawn to and seduced by this desolate and dangerous alternative reality. Although their absorption into this alien world is depicted primarily as the consequence of the *pēy*'s aggression, women are also seen as setting themselves up for being "caught." On the day of their attack they are always reported to be dressed in their best attire, as if prepared to lure any available demon. Even the *pēys* stressed their visibility and sexual availability, and said that despite the crowded city surroundings their victims always stood out, as if suddenly seen with great clarity, with everything else out of focus. "She was special," the obsessed demons would say. "I saw no one but her."

What makes the woman's alleged flight into either rural or urban wildernesses undesirable is the sure fact that she inevitably gets ensnared within this landscape. As she crosses into these zones of delusional, erotic fantasy, they trap her into thinking that the *pēy*—this home-wrecker, tortured malcontent, and social pariah of the first order—loves her and wants her.[5] And the additional reason why the *pēy* must be expelled at all costs is not merely that he is such an inconceivable partner but that he is also not real.

This is an interpretation that my consultants would probably reject, because for many of them demons are real inhabitants of the world beyond human settlement and control. But I found hints that these disembodied spirits are conceived to have more of a subjective than objective existence. A demon has no personal name, nor any biography outside of that lifted or "stolen" from his victim. In this sense he is what Obeyesekere calls a "personal creation" (1981: 115), a being that only exists in the woman's mind. As the mythic prototype for this exorcism suggests, women are openly accused of having created these extra-personalities for themselves. Because they are assumed to blur the boundaries between reality and fiction, these women are derided as *aṟiyāta makkaḷ*, "ignorant ones," the identical epithet assigned to their *pēys*.

The original demonic assault also constitutes an event that is not totally "real," for as we have seen, not infrequently women are "caught" by *pēys* on their way to movie theaters. It is as if they are victimized not by the *pēy* but by their mimetic involvement in melodramatic films, whose appeal to South Indians, Sara Dickey recently argues, lies in their staging of "utopian" and "fantastical resolutions" of social and personal dilemmas (1993: 110–11). Moreover, the timing of the attack at high noon coincides with the hottest period of the day, the time when, according to Bhakthavatsala Bharathi, the Tamil landscape, "seems to have *kaanal*," a word which he translates as "mirage" (1993: 345).

A main purpose of the exorcist dialogue is to delineate and publicize the fact that these women have trespassed the boundaries of cultural reason and have succumbed to marital disappointments and erotic impulses that put them in peril of losing their minds. This is why the musicians must first identify them with the prime symbol of frustration. In Tamil culture, the *pēy* represents a quality of sexual yearning that almost always is associated with men rather than with women. This is also why the musicians must reconstitute the time and place in which the woman entered into the wild, aberrant landscape and took on this borderline personality. They must make the demons confess that they have caused *pāvam* ("evil") or *mayakkam*, a word that Margaret Trawick translates as "dizziness, confusion, intoxication, delusion" (1990a: 113), and are lecherous outsiders who have made their victims risk losing their sanity and their society.

To get rid of these undesirables, the musicians do not offer marriage therapy in a Western sense of "working things out" between wives and husbands. In league with the family, their work is closer to what Luc de Heusch calls, in reference to the treatment of mental sickness among the Tsonga of Africa, "a psychoanalysis of expulsion" (1981: 177). They must forcibly remove the *pēy* from the woman's head and make her accept that her husband *and not* the demon is her rightful sexual partner. The musician's attempt to "make the *pēy* run away" and its decapitation symbolize this. Better yet, they have the woman perform this operation on herself. Only by publicly executing her demon lover will the social order welcome her back.

Why the Lock of Hair Is Nailed to the Tamarind

But demons never die, and the ritual does not end there. When Shanti dropped the rock the musicians immediately nailed her hair to the tamarind tree. As one told me, "This prevents the *pēy* from escaping and returning to the same person or catching someone else." This was why these specialists dashed after Shanti and looked so tense. Their success hinged upon this final effort to secure their clients' reincorporation into a domesticated sociability.

In the Hindu culture of Sri Lanka, as Gananath Obeyesekere has amply demonstrated, hair is invested with unconscious potency and profound sexual implications (1981). To Sinhalese female ascetics, he argues, matted hair represents "the god's *lingam*, the idealized penis, his *sakti*, the source of life and vitality" (1981: 34). It is tempting to infer that in exorcisms the lock of hair stands for the lustful genitalia of the demon. No such equation was explicitly made by my consultants, but the ritual dialogue hinted at it. The *pēy* was said to "enter" his victim through a hair lock. The exorcist repeatedly asked the demon, "Give us *your* hair!" The lock was treated as the metonymic identity of the spirit, for no sooner had *pēy*s revealed their names than the exorcist demanded to know, "Is this your hair?" as if drawing an association between it and lustfulness. And when the musician tied the lock into a knot, the demon protested with dramatic anguish, "It hurts! it hurts!"

Yet in Hindu culture hair is also associated with contrastive representations; specifically, with the public discipline of sexuality. Women's hairstyles change according to marital status. Hair is a major symbol of self-abnegation, as devotees, male and female, offer their tonsures to tutelary deities. The capacity of this symbol to unify such disparate, even polar-opposite meanings as rampant lust, sexual control, and ascetic devotion perhaps explains its capacity, in this ritual context, to "convert the obligatory into the desirable," as Victor Turner has argued is characteristic of "dominant" symbols in general (1967: 30). In exorcisms the lock of hair seems to begin as the symbol of the *pēy*'s wayward libido and point of erotic contact with his victim. By the ritual's end, however, it has become the token of the demon's voluntary sexual renunciation of his victim and marks their point of separation.[6]

My sense is that the nailing of the hairlock in the tree trunk actually reconnects the demon's decapitated head to another body, to the body of the tamarind tree. This is consistent with broader South Indian representations of decapitation. Most Tamil myths that feature beheading usually conclude with the head's reattachment, but only rarely to the original body.[7] Since in Tamil religious symbolism the piercing of flesh by metal objects is often invested with sexual and particularly marital connotations, I suspect that at this point the demon is actually being remarried to the tree (Hiltebeitel 1991: 197–98). This interpretation is not as farfetched as it first sounds, for in South Indian rituals trees are commonly married to one another, to human beings or even to supernaturals (Biardeau 1989). In the Coimbatore district Brenda Beck documented how during a village festival the goddess Māriamma was "married to a tree trunk" (1981: 91), which was said to represent "the goddess's husband" (1981: 122). While my consultants never explicitly called the tamarind tree "the demon's wife," its botanical and cultural properties would seem to qualify it as a "natural" bride or sexual partner for a malevolent creature such as a *pēy*. As Maneka Gandhi has written, its bark is "rough, almost black, covered with long cracks," (1989: 27) and the tamarind is classified as both "hot" and "female" (Beck 1969: 569).

Unlike the countersorcery rite that culminated with a funeral, this exorcism progressed toward a life-giving transaction. Once his "divorce" from his victim was secured, the *pēy* did obtain what was missing from his disembodied existence: winning both a "life" and a "bride."[8] As for straying women like Shanti, they were reintegrated back to collective life and acceptable identity. Reunited with their husbands and decreed by the musicians to be "happy" at last.

How the Goddess Replaces the Demon

But did the ritual work? While the musicians claimed that the great majority of their female clients happily reunited with their husbands, they acknowledged that sometimes this *pēy* or another might return, in which case they had to start all over again. All agreed that the demon's expulsion was definitive when they fused the "cured" woman with the goddess, effectively turning patient into initiate, as has been documented by ethnographers in other parts of the world.

This is anticipated during the ritual dialogue, when the demon announces that the goddess Aṅkāḷaparamēcuvari will succeed him. But how could a demon possibly be entrusted with heralding the "coming" of the goddess? I asked. "There is wisdom (*putti*) to the *pēy*," a musician replied. "He has some foresight (*uṇarvu*) into what is going to happen. He knows the coming of Amma."

Normally the musicians conduct this initiation on the morning after the exorcism, but for Shanti it occurred around 10:30 P.M. the same night, on the Malaiyaṉūr funeral grounds. By then all the devotees had retreated inside the temple. This was the hour for inauspicious activities, as healers prepared to counter sorcery spells under the dim light of a new moon and flickering oil lamps. Only the implicated dared to enter here.

Amidst scattered clusters of spell-removers and their patients the musicians found a vacant spot. After a small offering, they invoked the goddess

Aṅkāḷaparamēcuvari while Shanti faced east, eyes shut and palms pressed together. In preparation she had bathed and put on a new sari the bright yellow of a goddess devotee. Her face, arms, and shoulders were smeared with turmeric paste, a large dot of vermillion powder beamed from her forehead, jasmine flowers brightened her hair. Yet she struck me as diffident and clumsy, dropping the margosa leaves handed to her.

No sooner began the songs to Aṅkāḷaparamēcuvari, however, than her face contorted into a fierce grimace and her body became stiff as a board. Stretching her arms high above her head, she jerked forward, bent over, and struck the ground with her hands. Then she skipped backward, spasmodically repeating this pattern back and forth to the rapid staccato of the drums. Suddenly halting the music, the singer addressed her spiritual visitor.

"WHO ARE YOU?"

Speaking through Shanti, the dancing spirit gasped,

"Aṅkāḷaparamēcuvari."

The musicians greeted the goddess with an intensified round of drumming and bellowed with one voice, "Kōvintā," the name of Viṣṇu that was formulaically cried whenever divine spirits manifested themselves.

"We are so happy you came!" the singer told the goddess, "This girl [Shanti] has suffered greatly. Are you going to let some *pēy* catch her again?" Emphatically the goddess replied "no," promising to stay by the woman "at all times." Hearing these words the musicians cheered. Laying a *cilampu* (the anklet-shaped rattle associated with the goddess) on the top of her head, they drew her out of her trance and sat her, still a bit foggy, on the ground.

To cement the goddess's vow of protection two final rites were performed. From a burning wick held above her head, the singer dripped flame on a betel leaf, which he had placed where he had clipped her hair.[9] And he then touched this "blade of fire" (*pū alaku*)[10] on Shanti's shoulders, knees, the palms of her hands, and tail of her sari while the musicians sang: "Aṅkāḷaparamēcuvari doesn't easily make a promise. So when she does, we are sure she will carry it out."

For the second rite the singer ran a small trident (here called *alaku*) through Shanti's tongue (*nā*), a perforation (*nā alaku*) that drew no blood (it never does). On each prong the musician impaled a lime. Though the procedure forced Shanti to adopt an awkward posture, her glazed eyes locked on some point straight ahead and she registered no pain. Only after she circumambulated the inner precincts of the temple three times clockwise was the trident removed. Now the exorcism was completely over. Replaced by the goddess, the demon was banished for good.

A Pedagogy for Errant Women

There can be no doubt that "making the *pēy* run away" is one response to a pervasive source of female distress. It is also probable that the exorcism offers women some opportunity to voice feelings of loneliness, abandonment, and marital disappointment. But other than providing a way of venting their alienation and transcending isolation, it is hard to say what is fully or finally liberating for them about Tamil exorcisms. The healers seemed to be operating from a much broader cultural premise. The source of a woman's alienation was locked in her head, in her antisocial and life-threatening fantasies of extramarital sexuality. Their "therapy," such as it was, called for these longings to be eradicated, "cut off," and the women returned to reason: the safety and structure of the patriarchal family fold and the woman's proper role in it.

The exorcism was coercive in ways that transcended its rehabilitating and resocializing functions. It enforced a reality that was not debatable and could neither be challenged nor contested. This was evidenced by the fact that I was never able to collect exegeses from participants. Normally accessible and talkative women like Shanti generally blanked at my queries, pleading that they "could not recall" what was said and done by their *pēys*. The musicians could not (or would not) decode the significance of such key episodes as the dropping of the rock or the nailing of the hair lock. Their only commentary was the myth of Śiva's Brahmanicide, the narrative that is received by, and external to, narrators and listeners.

In so far as it inhibits performers' reflexivity, this ritual is strikingly different from the countersorcery treatment that communicated precise and varied understandings to patients and healers. Since the *cāmis* did not promulgate a "correct" or "right" reading of their manipulations, participants made their own analyses, filling the "removing" symbols with meanings drawn from and relevant to their life situations. Such free-form engagement fashioned in direct relation to personal experience permitted everyone to choose their own transformations.

But no such idiosyncratic investment seemed permissible at the *pēy* exorcism. To be sure the key symbol of this ritual had a kind of plasticity as well, for the demon was infused not just with "life," as was the case for countersorcery effigies, but with the afflicted woman's own personal life. But the important difference was that this intermarriage of culture and personality was neither spontaneous nor voluntary nor even conscious.

Through a relentless, compulsory interrogation, women like Shanti are pressured to complete what is culturally known of their given *pēy* with details from their own biographies. With its fixed conventions for cross-examining the demon, the exorcism's formalized dialogue "dramatically restricts what can be said," as Maurice Bloch argues of ritual speech in general (1989: 27). Women can only speak within the code of this inquisition and only in the names and through the voices of demons. They are not even aware of what they say, as they are then, and must be, in entrapping states of consciousness. Unlike the countersorcery ritual overseen by individual *cāmis*, which allows for participant reflection and reflexivity, this exorcism run by teams of musicians robs women of any chance to understand and question its inner logic and proceedings. It falls within that category of rituals that constitute, to borrow Bloch's famous phrase, "an extreme form of traditional authority" (1989).

The Tamil exorcism is more prescriptive, or in Kapferer's words more "totalizing," than the countersorcery ritual because it addresses a more troubling order of personal and social turbulence. The typical sorcery victim was a man who failed to "see" that his reckless conduct frustrated someone (generally another man) who was more "commanding" than he, and who therefore was trying to eliminate him. The solution consisted of empowering him to counterattack or walk away unharmed.

The typical *pēy* victim, on the other hand, was a woman who perhaps too clearly realized or "saw" how she was victimized by a negligent father or an abusive husband, or as in Shanti's case by both. To a patriarchal society such insight was more threatening. Her "cure" consisted of silencing her—an operation that was accomplished by transforming her into a lecherous demon who must be beheaded and expelled.[11]

The reader may object that my analysis fails to allow for the creative or resistant potentials of ritual that have been stressed by many anthropologists (for example, Gibbal 1994; Comaroff 1985). Since I do not wish to deprive these "caught" women of any more agency than this ritual already has, let me set the record straight. Not all Tamil women subjected to this procedure are passive or voiceless victims. Many tried to boycott the proceedings by declining to "dance." Two women in my experience managed to resist their desired altered state of consciousness. I will never forget how a third one faked trance and deceived the musician-exorcists by inventing multiple personalities that contradicted cultural understandings of *pēys* (for example, one of her spirits had died peacefully in "her" bed at the age of seventy-four). She was so clever that after two days the singer declared a stalemate, halting the transactions. But the fact that such "resistance" was couched in terms that defied the ritual conventions only deepens my sense that some women at least realized that this exorcism worked by objectifying them as aberrantly sexual, demonic, and crazed beings. If the ritual was to successfully achieve these objectifications, its entire discourse had to bar this sort of awareness, and generally succeeded.

The musicians had sealed the symbiotic relationship between the goddess and women like Shanti by techniques pervaded with symbolism that was reminiscent of the *cāmis*' spontaneous initiatory experiences. Some of those "recruits of the goddess" were also "cut" with a trident while plowing their fields, while others had their flesh punctured by "heat" or smallpox pustules. Those who ritually contracted the goddess's "grace" in the manner described in this chapter might also serve the goddess for life. This meant that if women like Shanti did not obtain love and intimacy from their husbands, they had found an alternative; they could withdraw from domesticity altogether and embrace, with newly won impunity, an ascetic life-style. But before we are tempted to conclude that this initiation was meant to provide any escape from social control, let us reexamine its symbolic logic.

First the goddess (represented by the flame) was forced to "enter" the woman at the precise spot—the missing hair lock—where the demon targeted its maddening assault. Then her power (represented by the trident) was driven through the woman's tongue, the main organ of speech. "Previously," a musician explained, "the *pēy* rendered the girl confused, unable to communicate who she was or what she felt. This perforation gives her the faculty to speak the truth (*uṇmai*), which was lacking in her previous life."

According to Saskia Kersenboom the same message was imparted when in the past young Tamil girls (*tēvatāsis*) were dedicated to temple male gods. Glossed as *muttirai*, which literally means "branding," the procedure culminated with branding the arms of these *tēvatāsis* with the sign of a trident. As Kersenboom explains, "The proposition expressed in the burning mark is the proposition of 'truth' as absolute identity of 'spirit', 'thought', 'speech', 'soul', 'action,' and 'being' " (1995: 189).

Now we can appreciate how the theory that demonic possession and rituals of exorcism somehow empower Hindu women does little justice to the fuller female predicament in the Tamil world. Far from working toward their emancipation, the ritual I have described is an assertive pedagogy and not a dialogue. Women are silenced through the interrogation, the symbolic decapitation, and the "tortures rituelles," as the French anthropologist Jackie Assayag would characterize the final procedures (1992: 331), which invade their person and imprint on their beheaded bodies society's "mark" or "truth" so that they will never forget it. Now these young women know not to venture beyond the boundary of the supervised, life-giving sexuality of the home, for it can lead only to madness, an utter absorption of wasteland symbolism by the self.[12]

Furthermore, these fresh initiates are expected to pass this "truth" on to others. Some may actually set themselves up as interpreters of "signs." So far as I could learn, Shanti never pursued this career. But she did take her new role of devotee quite seriously, returning every new moon to the Malaiyaṉūr temple where she continued to "dance" the goddess. As I would watch her dance, the kinetic and verbal expressions of her trances conveyed a new found sense of self, of a goddess prepared to vanquish any demons possessing other women brought to Mēl Malaiyaṉūr who might endanger their families and society.

7

LEARNING TO LIVE WITH A SPLIT SELF

In the South Arcot district of Tamilnadu human beings who meet untimely deaths through suicide, murder, or sudden accidents cannot exactly die. Their ghosts linger on earth where they entrap the living and inflict various pathologies that are usually "cured" by means of the demon-chasing ritual we have just seen. But possessions by these untimely dead do not always call for such programmatic, definitive resolutions. To understand these exceptions we must pay renewed attention to the matter of social context, or more specifically, kinship.

Most of my consultants gave consistent, almost generic responses to the question of what happened to people who died in bus accidents or other traumatic circumstances. Invariably they stressed the spirits' demonic side and the clear imperative to "make them run away." But when I asked about the fate of *their* relatives who died in such an untimely fashion, their answers strayed from these hard and fast explanations. None would accept responsibility for declaring that their kin had become *pēy*. "Bad death" seemed to demonize Tamil human beings only in the abstract, and it always afflicted someone else's relatives, never one's own.

When it came to the tragic fate of their loved ones, my consultants came up with inventive, revisionist interpretations. It was said that the accident that prematurely cut short the life of a son or father was written by the creator, Lord Brahmā, on the forehead of the person upon his or her birth. Ensuing from this divine mandate, such a death hardly disrupted the cosmic plan; it could pass as a "natural" end to life.

Untimely deaths that could not be attributed to a divine plan were interpreted in the light of social rather than personal conflicts. Here the explanatory scenario was one of victimization rather than normalization. Kinfolk who took their own lives were not characterized as psychologically maladjusted or deviant as were the *pēys*. They killed themselves because they could no longer bear difficult challenges, often of an economic order, such as bankruptcy or poverty.[1]

They may have been retrospectively reconstructed as having lived full lives, but these spirits did not always achieve satisfactory deaths. Over time I learned that their funeral rites failed to prevent some of them from returning to this world where they were prone to possess their living relatives.[2] And when this happened in the South Arcot district, at least, it appeared almost inconceivable to construe their influence as pathological. For by definition these affiliated spirits were incapable of causing the psychic or biological (infertility) disorders that were attributed to unrelated, unknown spirits.[3] So where one's own dead relatives are concerned, the untimely dead are never said to "catch" (*piṭi*: the verb which describes a *pēy* possession), but rather to "come on" their living descendants, out of emotions that this chapter will explore.

Over time their insistence on keeping in touch may be met with some ambivalence—as might too frequent visits from any bothersome relations. But the consequences are never so undesirable that they are "made to run away." The culturally preferable way to deal with overzealous "good" spirits is to plead for a more viable line of communication. Again one hires the ritual musicians (*pampaikkārar*), this time to extract (or at least try to) some "promise" (*cattiya vākku*) that the spirits will only "dance" at specific times and places.

Any ritual treatment for such possessions then is quite opposite to that of an exorcism: these visitors should be placated rather than expelled. For all their emphasis on perpetuating the status quo and stabilizing rather than terminating a relationship, however, such "accommodations" still have the potential to end the same as any exorcism: eventually the spirits, whether malignant invaders or meddlesome kin, are replaced by the goddess, for all the roads in this Tamil cosmology ultimately lead to her.

But these linkages with the goddess produce different "fruit" from an exorcism. For one thing, they are not programmatic. They do not result from a one-step, one-way operation, as is the case with the ritual that "makes the demon run away," but eventually grow out of a long, lonely, and painful passage into possession; "long" because separation from one's untimely dead cannot be rushed, "lonely" because these possessed persons are all on their own to deal with their spirits, and "painful" because counterposing funeral scenarios can be psychologically and socially damaging. For another, the metamorphoses these impromptu linkages with the goddess entail are not "prescriptive." Far from enforcing a cultural rationale or a pedagogy, they permit people to make their own creative and meaningful connections with cultural representations.

At least this appeared to be the case for one young widow, whose story also reminds us that even when people are free to author their own growth within the indeterminate spaces of their lives, the work of personal transformation is not easy in Tamilnadu. Nor does the privilege to choose one's own reconstitution preclude symbolism of violence against the self. The process of parting with loved ones at one's own pace and through one's own doing is articulated through strong imagery of bodily splits. When such a process is over, when one's untimely dead have truly "departed," one is torn apart for ever.

The Story of Leila

This case study is qualitatively different from any others in the book because it concerns a woman who was my cook and whom I came to love. Our friendship continues today. This is also about a time when the issues I was documenting in adjacent communities were brought into my home, when I saw my friend go through the torment-and-release associated with possession by the untimely dead.

Leila was a widow in her mid-twenties who was struggling to raise three young children, two of whom needed special care. One daughter was afflicted with polio and required therapy to strengthen an atrophied left leg. Whereas many polio-afflicted children, especially girls, often suffered rejection by their families, Saroja's mother adored her. Through Leila's patient assistance day after day, the girl learned to walk with a special brace and crutches. No sooner had Saroja been accepted in a nearby home for handicapped children than Leila's younger son, Krisna, came down with tuberculosis. Her meager wages as a part-time cook at a local hospital could hardly cover the special medicines and diet Krisna required.

So one night I was introduced to her in the tiny room in a house that Leila rented with three other *Kavuṇṭar* families along a back street in Gingee. In the light of an oil lamp I noticed her compact, sturdy body, her alert face with the slight cast in her left eye. Immediately she agreed to help with my domestic chores, and for the next thirteen months she prepared our evening meals after her chores at the hospital.

From the very first Leila was eager for me to know about her undying love for her husband, Ramesh, who was killed in a bus accident four years before. Her recollections of their initial infatuation became a sort of overture to our early friendship and subsequent conversations. Repeating its details she always reminded me that their marriage had been arranged through no other conventions than the glances they had furtively exchanged.

Leila was clearly aware of the narrative's poignancy and melodrama and rendered it with a passion that never failed to move me. Yet it was devoid of self-pity. She always refused any commiseration, proudly pointing out that her feelings for Ramesh overcame the inauspicious stigma of widowhood assigned by her society. Her gallantry must be understood against the background of the Hindu ideal: the married woman, or *cumaṅkali*, who produces children (preferably male), grows old with her husband, and dies before him. Astonishingly, Leila told me that once she had even been invited to decorate a bride (*nalaṅku vaittal*), a ceremonial task usually performed by young married women and forbidden to widows whose envious glances or "evil eyes" could undermine the celebration. "People know they have nothing to fear from me," she laughed, "How could I be jealous? My husband is still with me."

When she repeated these words, it was as if she was inviting me to ask for clarification. But I simply understood that it was Ramesh's memory that remained in her heart and said nothing. Then, while visiting her home in Gingee one night, I learned that in fact her dead husband did keep in touch with her. And so began a series of conversations that unfolded throughout my many months in India. Here is how her account began.

> It started on the seventh day after his death (*ēḻāntukkam*: "seventh day of mourning"). On that day I went back to my natal home (*tāy vīṭu*) in Madras. This is the custom on the seventh day. A widow goes home where she is presented with delicious food such as *atiracam* and *vaṭai* [traditional delicacies] and lots of flowers. This is the last time she is allowed to see the holy lamp (*kuttuviḷakku*) in the domestic sanctuary where she was born.
>
> On that day, after the ceremony (*pūjā*), I went to the Tiruvērkāṭu Māriamma temple (a well-known temple in a northern suburb of Madras). There I cried and lamented, "How am I going to support myself and my three children? Amma please help me!" Right there in the temple I cried myself to sleep. Then I felt a tap on my cheek. I woke up frightened but saw nothing. I was feverish for three days.

Leila was aware that later I would play back her testimony with my assistant to obtain a word-for-word translation. She had witnessed this process on a daily basis and understood that these sessions produced written transcriptions and familiarized me with Tamil culture. She had also become appreciative of my need for this cultural knowledge, and not infrequently scolded my consultants for assuming my acquaintance with their "customs" (*aitiham*), urging them to enhance their answers with concrete examples and explanations. So now this intelligent, vivacious woman volunteered contextual information about the circumstances that precipitated her initial "wake-up call" from the other side.

As she rightly suspected, I was unaware that the seventh day of mourning marked a widow's ceremonialized return to her natal home. But when I finally saw these proceedings for myself, I realized that Leila had omitted one all-important sequence. The widow's journey actually starts in the dead husband's home, where female relatives decorate her just like a bride. She is given a hot bath, her hair is dressed with coconut oil and flowers, her body smeared with turmeric paste. The bridal symbolism is even exaggerated; not one but many strings of flowers are coiled in her hair, and up to two dozen glass bracelets are squeezed over each wrist. And whereas a married woman daily daubs her forehead with a small dot of vermillion powder, on this ceremonial day the widow is branded with a two-inch red disc.

Then as Leila explained, the widow enters her parental domicile for the last time with the status of a married woman and is granted a final opportunity to look at its ritual flame. As one elderly widow explained, "Never again will her glance be charged with the auspicious power (*atihāram*) of the married woman. It won't have any meaning anymore." After being feasted and accorded more bridal insignia, more flowers and bangles, she is escorted back to enter her dead husband's house as she did on her wedding day. The abrupt relocation emphasizes that she is not welcome to stay in her parents' house.

For a widow, this seventh day of mourning is traumatic in three ways. It reactivates the memory of her wedding. It announces to the world that she is about to lose the auspicious ritual powers of the married woman for good. It stresses the harsh fact that her survival (if her sons cannot yet support her) now depends on her in-laws. How people now behave to her also makes it clear that her fate is undesirable. Other women are quick to commiserate, and their ritual laments seem less to mourn the dead husband than the plight of his survivor.

Instead of returning directly to her in-laws in Gingee, however, Leila stopped at the well-known Tiruvērkāṭu Māriammaṉ temple in a northern suburb of Madras to appeal for the goddess's protection. For she had not only lost a deeply beloved husband but all financial security as well. How was she to support herself and her three children? Emotionally drained, physically exhausted, she collapsed into a deep sleep. The "tap" on her "cheek" suddenly woke her up. Unable to identify the origin of this intimacy, Leila grew frightened, the telltale emotion that is aroused in Tamilnadu from the predicament of "aloneness" and renders one vulnerable to various sicknesses. Over the next three days Leila felt increasingly feverish, a bodily symptom that my consultants customarily linked with the influence of the goddess. However, it was not Māriamma who appeared to her, as Leila described.

> On the third night, my husband came in a dream that I still remember. His legs and arms were tied in a rope. People were dragging him away. He managed to bite loose the rope that bound his hands and rushed to embrace me. He called my name and said, "I won't leave you, you will protect me." With the tail end of my sari I wrapped both of us. The people beat us with whips. They separated us and dragged him away. I ran after them, crying: "I want my husband back!" They yelled at me, "leave him with us, Go, you dog!" This was the end of my dream.

To Leila the dream was unambiguous. The ropes that tied her husband's arms and legs represented his bondage by death. Ramesh was still being "dragged" away to the afterworld and was still struggling to escape. In her view he was not so much trying to recover his life as to reunite with her. In the dream he momentarily triumphed and managed to "embrace" her. She responded by wrapping them both in her sari. But then they were separated, and when she implored for his release, she was treated much as a demon-*pēy* who refuses to let go of his living victim. For the moment it appeared that death was stronger than their love for each other.

The next episode in Leila's story took place on the sixteenth day after her husband's death, the *karumāti* day, which among most non-Brahmin castes marks the last official day of mourning.[4] If the deceased was a married man, the day opens with the widow-making rite (*tāli aṟutal*), which, once again, first transforms the bereft woman into a bride. As Leila said, "On that day they also dressed me in a new sari and gave me glass bangles, smeared my body with turmeric paste and daubed my forehead with vermillion powder." Then, one by one, these insignia were publicly removed: the turmeric paste and vermillion powder rubbed off, her flowers thrown away, the glass bangles smashed, even her toe rings and anklets taken off. Last, her marriage necklace (*tāli*) was submitted to a dramatic "cutting" (*aṟutal*);[5] She had been made a widow.

I was not surprised that Leila omitted this painful moment, for invariably it brings people, especially female onlookers, to wailing and tears. This is when the woman's feminine identity is utterly stripped away. The most dramatic disjunction to be found within Tamil society, it amounts to nothing less than a death of a self. The widow's sung lamentations speak of this terrible predicament with abject clarity. Her words address her dead husband, but they are really directed at all of her living relatives, as if inviting them to deplore a cultural verdict that has pronounced her sexually useless, ritually powerless, and economically bereft.

Nor did Leila mention the second rite of the day, when the deceased's liminal state of *preta* (disembodied and potentially malevolent spirit) transforms into that of *pirt* ("father" or "ancestor"). This omission was for a less emotional reason: this ceremony, which sends the dead off into the afterworld, is usually held by the village reservoir (or water source) and generally attended only by men, especially the son(s) whose ritual role(s) along with that of the Brahmin priest is central to the proceedings.

What Leila did remember was that once the ordeal was all over and her husband was "officially" dead, Ramesh abruptly reappeared to her.

> After the purification of the house by the Brahmin priest [the final rite of the day], I waved a camphor flame for my husband. How I despaired. I thought, "How am I going to live in this world? Take me with you."
>
> I lifted my arm and began to shake. Like my husband in my dream—legs tied by the rope, hopping around—I started to hop as if my feet were bound together. In small steps I worked my way near to my brother-in-law and asked him to light a camphor. He asked, "WHO ARE YOU?"
>
> My husband replied [through the mouth of the now entranced Leila]: "I am Ramesh. I don't want to leave my wife and my children."
>
> He [the husband] talked directly to me too, "Why are you crying? Can't you see that I am here with you?"
>
> He also spoke to his brother, "I came on her on the seventh day. On that day I embraced her. Don't neglect me! I AM NOT A *PĒY*! I am her husband, I am Ramesh. I promise to protect her." Then the camphor was extinguished

> and I began to shake again. And my father-in-law demanded to know, "WHO ARE YOU?"
>
> Now my husband's dead grandmother spoke through me and told her name. The people around us asked her, "What do you want?" She said: "I came to get my grandson."
>
> Again I was shaking and they asked: "WHO ARE YOU?"
>
> Now my husband's dead younger sister gave her name [through my voice] and she said: "I came to get the newly dead person."

Her possession had communicated Ramesh's presence to others, who now stood witness to their abiding love. His [her] feet still tied by the ropes of death, Ramesh [Leila] had hopped over to his younger brother, heir to the position of familial head and the individual upon whom Leila and her children now depended for support. Ramesh's request that a camphor lump be lighted signaled his desire to speak, for this flame, as we have previously seen, transcends the barrier that normally inhibits communication between supernaturals and human beings (Fuller 1992: 72–73). Ramesh wanted all to know that he was not a demon-*pēy*. In fact, by identifying himself and promising to protect Leila, he stood as a demon's very antithesis.

Leila's performance ended with the successive apparitions of two female spirits, Ramesh's paternal grandmother and little sister, who arrived to claim the newly dead. Since he was desired among his ancestors, the request confirmed Ramesh's insistence that he was no *pēy*. His dignified departure for the afterworld also sanctioned his new role as Leila's benefactor. Following Ramesh's remarkable intervention into the ways of the living, Leila was able to obtain from her in-laws the permission to establish an independent household. As Ramesh had vowed to her, he continued to look after his family from beyond the grave.

> On new moon nights I would light a camphor for him in the domestic sanctuary (*naṭuvīṭu*: literally "middle house") and he would appear all dressed up in nice clothes with his mustache oiled. Then I was happy, happy as when he was alive and we were together.
>
> He protected us. The day I learned that my younger son had TB I was weeping at home with my child on my lap. My husband came on me again at that time, telling me not to worry. He said, "Go and seek medical treatment in the direction of the east."

After a while these apparitions became predictable and ceremonialized; they occurred each month when Leila performed the prescribed new moon observances for the dead in her domestic sanctuary, which was found on the wall of her room facing the east. Waving the camphor flame before his photograph, she "invited" Ramesh, as E. T. Jacob-Pandian explains this most common of all Hindu invocations, "to be present in the house during the night" (1975: 71). Since Leila herself saw her husband through the flame this was clearly more than a trance. The face-to-face, almost erotic nature of their communication was evidenced by the fact that she always remarked upon his well-groomed looks, fine clothes, and shining mustache. These apparitions came to carry a seductive as well as protective and therapeutic charge. Following Ramesh's recommendation, she did place her son in the Pollur hospital, located to the east of Gingee, where the boy began treatment.

But after a while her husband's claims grew excessive. Leila described the uncomfortable acceleration in their relationship.

> He began to come on me outside our home. As soon as I would hear the *pampai* drum I would go out in the street to dance. I would dance so hard that my sari slipped off my shoulder. I was ashamed. I went to the Kārumāriamma temple here in Gingee and talked to my husband. I said, "Not only you made me into a widow but you shame me in public. Please don't make me dance in the streets!"
>
> Then, I went to Mēl Malaiyaṉūr to consult a female medium. She told me, "Your husband wants you to be in a state of fluctuation between happiness and grief. One day you may be happy, the other you may not."
>
> My husband no longer made me dance in the street, but he did want me to remember him. If I was too happy perhaps I would forget him.

For the next four months Leila received no more visits. But then began a new cycle of trances. Before continuing her story, I must add some facts concerning my own association with Leila. Working in our household brought both benefits and problems. Certainly as she earned extra income and small gifts her material life improved. The employment also conferred a not insignificant social boost. As she was an outgoing personality, she increasingly mediated on my behalf with neighbors, village officials, ritual specialists, ceremonial participants, and anyone who felt like dropping by. But this new atmosphere of almost antihierarchical conviviality inevitably led Leila to chat and socialize with men. Within a few months rumors spread that she was having an affair with one of our married regulars. Fearful for her reputation, I alerted her to the gossip, but she only laughed it off "jealousy" (*poṟamai*).

But the gossip traveled back to her own compound in Gingee. Leila was said to have skipped work in our home to meet her lover. When a co-worker in the town hospital called her a "whore," the women fought and Leila was suspended for a week. Her brother checked with me to find out whether she was showing up. I defended her and conspicuously paid her home visits to make it clear that we remained close. During this time of harassment by neighbors and relatives Leila experienced a new set of trances, as she told me with some excitement one day in March, "Yesterday [a new moon night], Sita [her girlfriend] and I went to Mēl Malaiyaṉūr to pray to Amma [the goddess Aṅkāḷaparamēcuvari]. When I heard the drum [*pampai*] I began to dance."

Her friend giggled, "She was like a snake," and proceeded to imitate her—standing straight up, extending her hands above her head, palms pressed together, and weaving her body from side to side. Without resentment, Leila grinned and continued,

> I danced in front of the musicians. When one asked, "Who are you?" the goddess Māriamma spoke her name. When the musicians also asked, "When will the rain come?" the goddess answered, "In two weeks it will rain." Then a musician placed a burning camphor in my hand. I swallowed it and fainted.

Over the next few days, whenever she remembered how Māriamma "made her dance" Leila never failed to mention that she held the burning camphor in her palm then swallowed it without hesitation. This was significant, for in Tamil culture, as E. T. Jacob-Pandian noted, "the shaman's permanent relationship with the deity is confirmed with the seal of burning camphour placed on the tongue or the palm" (1975: 74). For the next eight months, or until I left India, it was only the goddess who now "came on" Leila, as if her fixation on her husband and their fruitless relationship and the physical ties it evoked had been eclipsed by a new, more approvable focus for her inner longings.

How Leila Intercepted a Myth and a Ritual

A Western psychologist might have diagnosed Leila's suffering as the pathological condition that Sigmund Freud called "melancholia" (1957). To Freud, this was characteristic of those who could not "normally" respond to bereavement, with the sheer fact of a beloved's death, to the extent that their "ego identifies with the lost object and loses interest in staying alive" (1957: 239). Nor would this diagnosis be at odds with my consultants' religious beliefs that the deceased continue to have feelings that they may communicate through the dreams and trances of the living. What is said or done during those communicative states is not simply a question of the spirit's emotional state, as Piers Vitebsky, for example, has discovered among the Soras of North India (1993: 241). As we have already seen, in Tamilnadu it is understood that entrancement by the untimely dead requires intimate, emotional engagement on the part of the possessed. If not Freud's "melancholia" exactly, my consultants would agree that her profound loss and sorrow had prevented Leila from separating from her beloved husband, and hence from accepting or internalizing the entire momentum and objectives of the various funerary rites in which she had participated.

Her disregard for the funeral process began on the seventh day after her husband's death, a ceremonial day that divests a Tamil widow of the capacity to "see" or make connections with auspicious forces. Shortly after this rite was performed, however, Leila did make that sort of forbidden contact at the Māriamma temple. True, she could not "see," but she could feel her husband's touch on her cheek; despite his supposed death, she was still a wife. And three days later she experienced her powerful vision of him. The seventh day, in other words, did not quite succeed in blinding or severing her from her former existence.

Moreover, the sixteenth day after Ramesh's death also failed to accomplish its cultural purpose. Now this is not the first time that we learn that participants may not experience identical significances or efficacies from a Tamil "funeral." We may recall the different ways in which patients and healers interpreted the mortuary symbolism encoded in the countersorcery rite of chapter 4. But most of the meanings they did eventually assimilate—"removal" of unwanted others, selves, or even thoughts—were in a sense already "there," encoded within a ritual process that inexorably worked to winnow the dead out of society. But Leila's story contradicted this cultural scenario. Instead of mournfully dispatching her husband to the afterworld and accepting her own social death as well, she experienced him materialized in this world on the sixteenth day, and in her very own body. Her "hopping" trance was emblematic of their fusion: she personified Ramesh as she had viewed him in her dream, her feet bound by the same ropes, dramatizing to all how she, too, was entrapped by his fate.

Leila also added a new twist to the dead's "official" departure for the hereafter. Her husband's leaving was not facilitated by any Brahmin priest, or male member of the lineage, but through the timely intervention of two female spirits who escorted him there. And this unexpected feminine intercession naturally created a different cosmology, one in which the dead did not actually depart, as is the case when men officiate, but instead remained with the living as if their demise had never really occurred. After this spiritual manifestation Leila was thus able to resume life as before, with Ramesh still the head of her household. Her unusual "semi-widowed" status was so persuasive to her neighbors that they even invited her to decorate a bride, the ceremonial role customarily performed *only* by married women, suggesting how convincingly Leila was able to elude "normal" ritual arrangements.

But the situation was untenable; one cannot subvert ritual and its intended consequences without paying a price. And Leila did suffer from her idiosyncratic appropriation of funeral processes, as indicated by the fact that eventually she lost control over the timing and place of her trances.[6] At the mere sound of the *pampai* (a not infrequent sound in Tamil villages) she found herself dancing uncontrollably in the streets, giving flagrant, public expression to her corporal fusion with her spouse; worse, her behavior was sexually provocative, for her sari would slip off her shoulder. Whatever feelings Leila may have released through her earlier fusions with Ramesh had now come back to "command" her.

From this situation there was no substantive way out. The only ritualized action that is offered by Tamil society for keeping the dead at bay is the funeral, but she had clearly not allowed (or not wanted) this to "remove" Ramesh from her life. The exorcism known as "making the *pēy* run away" was out of question, for Leila had not ventured in any wasteland landscape, nor invented a fictitious, borderline personality. Quite to the contrary, the spirit who tormented her was real, his identity known to others, and had legitimate sexual claims to his living wife. He could not be expelled like some demon who lacked ontological and moral authority. Tamil culture does not prescribe a therapy for "melancholia" and its painful, bodily side-effects. All one can do is to somehow temper the intensity of one's trances, impose temporal and spatial parameters on the spirit's manifestations, and hire ritual musicians to talk the spirit into "promising" to "dance" only at specific times and places.

At Mēl Malaiyaṉūr in the early 1990s such ritual intervention cost around three hundred rupees. Not in a position to afford the musicians, Leila once again bypassed "normal" ritual practices and pleaded with her husband directly. She seemed to have succeeded, as she again enjoyed some control over her out-of-body states, even if the trade-off, as the diviner suggested, was Ramesh's abiding control over her "intermittent happiness."[7]

But this accomplishment also brought serious consequences. By cutting ties with her husband altogether Leila lost her auspicious status and social protection. She became prime target for slander. As if seeking an alternative mate, it was then that Leila began to "dance" Māriamma.

She first did so at the very place (the Mēl Malaiyaṉūr temple) and time (a new moon day) that the untimely dead are "made to run away," suggesting that she was managing some form of auto-exorcism. But although she was then in the goddess Aṅkāḷaparamēcuvari's abode, Leila had picked Māriamma to succeed to her husband instead. Of course she already had a special affinity for this goddess. It was at a Māriamma temple that she had taken refuge on that seventh day after her husband's death, the same day her widowed status was formalized. It was also there that she had received her first "wake up call." Nonetheless, Aṅkāḷaparamēcuvari would seem to have been the exorcist-deity of choice. We may recall how she single-handedly chopped off Śiva's extra head, the act that restored both his individuality and their marital harmony. So who is this goddess whom Leila chose over Aṅkāḷaparamēcuvari to displace her beloved Ramesh?

Unlike Ramesh, a young *Kavuṇṭar* man whose personal biography was familiar only to relatives and friends, Māriamma is a famous member of the Tamil pantheon, her cultural identity inscribed in ancient myths. The best-known conflates her story with that of the goddess Reṇukā, and Leila shared with me her favorite version of this narrative (see Biardeau 1968; Brubaker 1977; Doniger 1980; Beck 1981; Trawick 1984; Ramanujan 1986; Assayag 1992; Doniger 1995).[8]

> Māriamma was the virtuous wife of a Brahmin sage. She was so devoted to her husband that she would hold in her cupped hands the water he needed for his purificatory acts. But once, at the water tank, she saw the reflection of a handsome bird [Gandharva] and felt pangs of desire. As a result Māriamma suddenly lost her extraordinary powers.

Right away her husband knew what had happened and ordered his son, Paracurāma, to behead her. The son was so angry that he decapitated both his mother *and* an Untouchable woman who had hidden Māriamma in her house.

Later, Paracurāma was full of remorse and obtained his father's permission to bring his mother back to life. But he made a big mistake. He reconnected Māriamma's head to the body of the *Paṟaiyaṉ* woman. Now that she was impure her husband did not want her and sent her to live in the forest. Furious at them both, Māriamma became smallpox (*Ammai*) and covered the bodies of her husband and her son with pustules.

In this story Māriamma emerges as the very antithesis of Aṅkāḷaparamēcuvari. Far from being the prototypical exorcist, she is an ideal candidate for exorcism. Initially she tried hard to be a good wife to her ascetic Brahmin husband. But the dedication proved too difficult to sustain, for she cast her eyes on what appeared to be a more dashing creature. Since "seeing" in the Hindu world is a kind of "touching," Māriamma was in trouble and faced the punishment that befalls women who are accused of having inappropriate extramarital longings: she was decapitated. But unlike the women who undergo this exorcist procedure, Māriamma's body was neither reconnected to her own head, she was not returned to her former marital identity, nor was she reintegrated with her family.

Instead the goddess was transformed in body and spirit. Her very name, "Māri," means "changed," so that "Māriamman," as Margaret Trawick has pointed out, connotes " 'the changed mother' " (1984: 31). And how did Māriamma transform in Leila's story? She acquired a new body, that of an Untouchable woman, a corporality that in Hindu culture is certainly polluted, and somewhat eroticized. She also became smallpox, a rampant force of heat and affliction that is also conceived as a sexual contact. The Tamil word for "pustule" (*muttam*), as previously indicated, is the same as for "kiss," and a doctor of the Gingee Government Hospital once told me that Māriamma personified venereal diseases like herpes. In effect this goddess met the fate of the demon-*pēy* who after his beheading cannot be reconnected to his own body and is instead reattached to a naturally "hot" body. After her physical transformation, we recall, Māriamma's husband exiled her in the forest, in other words, "making her run" to the wasteland, in a final repudiation.

The myth was saying that Māriamma was beyond recovery, that her wifely ambivalences ran too deep. Appropriately, her punishment consisted of a new existence of contradictory identities and paradoxical roles. Split into polarized body parts, her torso was hot, polluted, and dangerously promiscuous while her head remained "cool," pure, and compassionate.[9] Perhaps she was not so much "changed" (as also evidenced by the fact that she kept her head) as "expanded" into her true, original self—a woman who was torn between being free and alive (like the bird whose reflection she "saw" in the water tank) and pure and chaste, a woman too divided by nature to ever become whole.

It is no wonder that Leila identified with this goddess. Like Māriamma she was psychologically tormented and socially ostracized. Like her she could not be exorcised, for that procedure only works on married women who are accused of carrying out fanciful rather than real sexual liaisons. In any case no widow could ever benefit from an exorcism's ultimate objective: Leila' marital identity was gone for good. Much like Māriamma, her initial attempts to repatch her "dead" marriage, to hang on to both her husband and her auspicious status of married woman, had only disconnected her from her body and split her between opposed states of being: life/death, past/present, wife/widow, and happiness/unhappiness.

But Leila identified with Māriamma in another important way: she too acquired a foreign body, which paradoxically helped her become more like herself. At least this was my impression the one time I saw her "dance" Māriamma, shortly after her experience at Mēl Malaiyaṉūr.

The occasion was a familial possession rite (*pūvāṭaikkāri pūcā*) (which I present in full in chapters 9 and 10). This ceremony asks dead parents to return home and bless the coming marriage of their first-born child. To this end the family recruits the services of the ritual musicians to persuade these spirits of the dead to accept their "invitation."

This particular *pūjā* was performed in our village, near the tank. On that afternoon the musicians had been playing for some time without success. This was not unusual; this category of supernaturals are notoriously slow to respond. Upon hearing the drums from the nearby courtyard, however, Leila became entranced. Leaving our house, she followed the sound as if on automatic pilot. At the *pūjā* site, she planted herself in front of the musicians, feet slightly apart and palms joined above her head. Her body undulated and swayed from side to side, mimicking the cobra, which, in turn, is manifested by the South Indian goddess when she wants to communicate to human beings (Meyer 1986: 59).[10] Her face looked serene, and she later described her sensations to me as "bliss" (*āṉantam*). When the ritual musicians pressured this unexpected guest to announce when the spirits of their patrons would arrive, the goddess Māriamma answered through Leila: "They will come within the half-hour." And indeed that was when they came.

Her performance was consistent with her ritual biography; Leila had clearly tapped into this ritual to make her own connections, intercepting this "invitation" in order to communicate her acceptance of ritual logics. Rather than proposing some wild and impossible reunification with the "departed" that discounted death and funerary representations, she was now scheduling the proper timing of the dead's ceremonial reappearance. In other words, she was publicly affirming that relationships with the dead ought to be regularized and formalized. But rather than making this declaration in her own name, she spoke on behalf of the goddess.

It had taken my friend five years to reach this point. Over those five long years she often cried herself to sleep, denied herself food, and sunk into the states that Sigmund Freud would have perhaps diagnosed as symptomatic of "melancholia" (1957). But as experienced by Tamils, they may be more accurately and penetratingly described as the consequences of deep "splits" between the past and the present, between former and new identities.

Now we may appreciate why this untenable predicament cannot be resolved by means of the same symbolic intervention that ended possession by the demon-*pēys*. One can ritually suppress or "behead" an unwanted identity, but no such strategy can repair a "divided self." There is no ritual shortcut for hastening that painful process. All one can do, Tamil culture seems to suggest, is to live with it, or at least to minimize its effects by talking to oneself, which I believe is what Leila accomplished through her monologue to her husband and her "snake dance."

More significantly, if and when one does emerge from the darkness of such "splits," one is irrevocably "changed." This is the most important distinction between possession by the *pēys* and by one's untimely dead. In the former condition, once the surgery has been performed, once that extra demonic head has been lopped off, at least in theory life resumes as before. The whole point of "making the *pēy* run away" is to restore one's previous identity. But in the latter case there is no going back, no husband to reunite with, no married woman status to resume, no whole self to recover. Like Māriamma, one is shattered or torn apart for ever. And like Māriamma, one must reassemble oneself, one must "change," adopting a new physical body, a new social identity, a new personal role, all of which will forever remain somewhat alienated and unincorporated. The widow must accept the inevitable and surrender to liminality. And this was what Leila finally did, *but*—and this is a major spirit-saving validation—at her own pace, and through her own mental and physical participation.

8

FRUIT FROM THE DEAD

By now the reader may have gathered that Tamil initiatory and ritual experiences mostly serve to dissociate people from social and personal identities. We have had ample warrant for such an impression. The *cāmis'* visions of the goddess led them to withdraw from mainstream society and their families. Many of them, in turn, were quick to prescribe "funerals" of debilitating relationships for their clientele. While the ultimate objective of exorcisms may be seen to reunite "possessed" women with their husbands, these reconciliations actually entailed suppressing or "beheading" an inner personality. And while possession by one's untimely dead does not call for any kind of "removal," this is because a more finite separation—death—has already happened. No wonder it can appear that Tamil religious practices lean toward effecting what Luc de Heusch calls "disjunctions" (1981).

But this is only one side of the Tamil cosmological picture and its mechanisms and motivations. Its other "face" is expressed through rituals that incorporate participants into a generational sequence and network of forebears, descendants, and relatives. This body of "conjunctive" rites stands in isomorphic opposition to diagnostic seances, "removals," and exorcisms. A mirrored symbolic vocabulary and identical patterning of actions here are employed to forge a continuity of experience and identity instead of the reverse. Yet, at every crucial step the overlaps and repetitions in these ritual processes are consistent with my deeper conclusion that, above all, Tamil religion works to transform the "inner" self. The difference is that whereas disjunctive practices objectify the "healthy" person as separated from unrelated others (be they "commanding" or alien personalities) conjunctive rituals "prescribe" mingling or even expanding the self into other connected selves.

Before entering this new world of ritual transactions, I might set the tone for the chapters to come by recounting one more diagnostic seance by a recruit of the goddess—a seance of some contrast to those we have witnessed before. It was performed by one of those specialists who could "see" and embody the spirits of her clients' dead relatives.[1] While this female practitioner did not actually carry out the "fruits" she recommended, she brings us closer to the kinds of personal transformations that will now concern us. For her seances made it clear that the good life consisted in establishing a sense of sameness and continuity with related ones—a process, however, as we will subsequently see, which when completed can threaten the autonomy and integrity of the self.

Padmini, Mahentiran, and Rita

A heavy-set woman in her early forties with matted hair, Padmini was no ordinary devotee. Twenty years before at her home in Pollur in the North Arcot district, pregnant and suffering from smallpox, Padmini was "selected" by the goddess Aṅkāḷaparamēcuvari as her "body" on earth. No sooner had she recovered and borne a healthy baby than she proceeded to regularly "decode signs" on behalf of friends and neighbors. In addition to self-induced trances when she became the goddess's mouthpiece, Padmini also enjoyed special gifts for "seeing" the dead relatives of her consultants in the afterworld, and embodying them as well. Twice a week (Tuesdays and Fridays) she communicated with them in her home shrine, but on new moon nights she commuted by bus to Malaiyaṉūr. From dusk to midnight she worked out of the Aṅkāḷaparamēcuvari temple, opening her practice to a wider clientele.[2]

I should say a few words about my relationship with Padmini, because it colored my understanding of her practice and the world that she disclosed. This was the same woman that I recalled in the Introduction bullying me to fund a seance. She was always rough on me and finally I abandoned hope of working with her. From afar she would hail me with her loud, mocking humor, "With all the time you've spent at this temple grounds [at Malaiyaṉūr] you still haven't let Amma into your heart? It's a shame!" hinting that she was not fooled by my devotional posturings. She harangued one of my assistants, in his mid-thirties and unmarried, "If you keep on waiting, no girl will want you!" Yet, one had to admire her gift for exposing hidden agendas and unmasking personal insecurities.

She behaved this way with her petitioners as well. On the five occasions that I saw her in action, her nonstop commentary always ground people down and publicly exposed their nervousness or ineptitude, always accompanied by a series of scornful glances. She seemed to delight in warnings and admonishments. A weakly flickering camphor flame, she was quick to remind her clients, was a sure "sign" that their ties to their dead, their source of protection, had grown tenuous. Unless they fulfilled her procedures to the letter, she threatened, she would not put them in touch with the afterworld. She could be so intimidating that visitors were not infrequently reduced to tears.

Strong personalities are a trademark, almost a requirement, of this line of work. But Padmini was even tougher than the *cāmis*—and two reasons made me suspect that this was a function of her specialized attention to spirits of the dead. The apparition of dead kin into this world was regarded, even by people with great ceremonial experience, as no mean feat. The very idea that human beings who had died as long as twenty years ago might be possessing Padmini (or anyone else for that matter) was always considered astonishing. Of all the categories of spirits whom I researched, these spirits of the dead generated the most incredulity, especially among men. My consultants were willing to concede that possession by the goddess or by the demons could be phenomenologically "real." But several professed disbelief over these communications with the deceased. Perhaps because she faced a much tougher audience, Padmini was more imperious than the *cāmis*.

But another reason was that Padmini impersonated spirits who, on the whole, tended to be more fastidious and demanding than the goddess. At least the goddess's moods fluctuated; she could be unreasonable and distant at one moment, attentive and compassionate the next. But the dead were always disgruntled, full of complaints and recriminations. Their living relatives were always ignoring them, their demands for tangible expressions of love and affection in the form of camphor, food, and cloth were incessant. Perhaps Padmini was so difficult because she had internalized the psychological profile of the dissatisfied spirits she regularly personified.

Whatever the reasons for her browbeating personality, she got away with it because she got results. Her consultants seemed to depart with a deepened awareness of the bonds that were essential to human existence. She even brought me such "fruit," for it was her work during the very first seance I ever saw that persuaded me to shift my research topic from ethnohistory to what I might call her field of practical supernaturalism. Let me introduce the young couple who, on that new moon night, brought their troubles to Padmini.

For the previous two years Mahentiran and his wife Rita, both in their late twenties, had struggled to sustain themselves and two small children, but their fresh fruit stall in the town of Gingee suffered steady losses. Severe headaches also prevented Mahentiran from working on a regular basis. Poor, sick, and demoralized, the couple consulted two *cāmis*, each of whom attributed their misfortune to sorcery. Although entangled in a bitter dispute with Mahentiran's elder brother, also a fruit peddler, over sharing his more advantageous business location, they dismissed these diagnoses. But they did take seriously one of Rita's dreams. Mahendiran's little sister, who had died at age eleven of jaundice, had appeared with a promise to protect them if she was granted a *pūjā*.

To say that this little sister "died" is not quite correct, for in Tamilnadu those who succumb to certain sicknesses personified by the goddess—smallpox, cholera, typhoid, measles and jaundice—actually *do not die*. The Tamil verbs that denote the act of dying (*iṟa*, and *cā*) are expressly prohibited in these circumstances. Instead, these victims, often children or teenagers, are said to "become cool" (*kuḻir*); they merge with the goddess who in her personification as smallpox is known in Tamil, Hindi, and Bengali as the "cool one" (*Māriamma*; *Sītal*ā) (Bang 1973).[3] In other words, they have joined the goddess in the other world; they are now worthy of worship by any living relatives and may become household deities.

This deification process is not automatic, for people's lives have their own momentums and cannot always accommodate cultural scenarios (Sahlins 1985). In our case the little sister's spirit had "cooled" fifteen years earlier, and neither her father, who was then alive, nor her two brothers had found the energy or the money to reincorporate her in household devotions.[4] I also suspect that such deification requires spirit intervention, for the Tamil supernaturals often assume responsibility for initiating their own worship, accosting people and demanding steadfast devotion through dreams. And so shortly after Rita's encounter with her "cool" sister-in-law, the couple decided to reconnect with the child again through the well-known skills of Padmini.

Padmini's Seance for Mahentiran and Rita

That evening Mahentiran and Rita found their way to the open-air shrine, located just left of the main gate outside the Malaiyaṉūr temple, where Padmini conducted her spiritual business. Arriving early, they stood awkwardly at the entrance, waiting for a friend to introduce them. Dispensing with these preliminaries, Padmini brusquely sent off Mahentiran for five rupees of camphor. When he returned she demanded ten more rupees, then impatiently motioned the couple to the floor across her. Padmini faced south, the realm of Yama, god of death. As other clients trickled in, she ordered them to take their places and keep quiet. About thirty people were soon in attendance.

Padmini floated a burning camphor lump on a betel leaf inside a small brass pot filled with water. As it flickered in the fresh breeze, she instructed Mahentiran to add camphor and turned to Rita,

PADMINI: "Hey, you! Does he [referring to Mahentiran] work for the Panchayat [village governing body]?"

RITA: "He is a fruit seller."

PADMINI: "Can he sign his name?"

RITA: "Yes."

PADMINI: "Then he should be a government clerk. Why are you rubbing your hands? What's happening with you?"

MAHENTIRAN [anxiously to Rita]: "Don't rub! Let it be!"

PADMINI [to Mahentiran]: "Who is your family deity?"

MAHENTIRAN: "Māriamma."

PADMINI: "Did you come to ask about your family?"

MAHENTIRAN: "Yes, about my family and my business."

Absorbed by the flickering camphor, Padmini now became oblivious to the couple. She seemed to be seeing the entire host of Mahentiran's dead relatives, and she began picking them out one by one:

PADMINI: "An old man who belongs to your people is standing with tears in his eyes. Who is he?"

MAHENTIRAN: "He is our father."

PADMINI: "Beside him stands an old woman. Who is she?"

MAHENTIRAN: "Our mother."

PADMINI: "Who is that other married woman?"

MAHENTIRAN: "Our aunt."

PADMINI: "And another old man is there. Who is he?"

MAHENTIRAN: "Our grandfather."

PADMINI: "And another old woman is nearby. Who is she?"

MAHENTIRAN: "Our grandmother."

[When Mahentiran neglected to feed the flame, Padmini got testy: "Only if the camphor burns can these questions go on."]

PADMINI: "Who is the child who is there because of the goddess?"

RITA: "That is our little girl (*pāppā*); she [died] from jaundice (*mañcā*)."

PADMINI [snapping back]: "Amma and jaundice are one. Another boy is standing there. Who is he?"

RITA: "Our father's sister's son."

PADMINI: "And who is the other one who died in a dangerous circumstance?"

MAHENTIRAN: "Our elder brother's son."

Padmini was able to "see" these spirits "on" the camphor flame. To Christopher Fuller, this living symbol, which always supports Hindu worship, effects a "transcendence" of the normal divide between divine and human worlds (1992: 73). In chapter 5 the ritual musicians activated Shanti's exorcist trance through drumming and a camphor flame, and in chapter 7 Leila's dead husband required it to communicate with his relatives. Here the burning camphor served as a sort of window onto the hereafter. Although Padmini's fixed stare induced her into a concentration, she still retained self-awareness, as indicated by her swift reproach to Mahentiran when he let the flame falter. Rather than being "altered," her consciousness was more accurately "heightened," since she was able to cross freely over cosmological time and space. Like the classic shaman profiled by Luc de Heusch and Mircea Eliade, her mental powers "increased tenfold" (de Heusch 1981: 153), her visualization enabled a journey to the spirit land (Eliade 1964; Rouget 1985). Yet Padmini neither embodied any supernatural to guide her cosmic search nor gave the impression that she had even left Malaiyanūr. What emanated from her fix on the light was rather a sort of hyperlucidity, purposefully channeled by sheer determination to track down those dead relatives. And she systematically recounted what she saw in the "present world," as if the dead were part of the same uncompartmentalized cosmology—here and now, there and then, everywhere and everywhen, altogether.

Then she switched topics, abruptly asking the couple, she asked, "Who did you have in mind when you asked for the fruit?" Without hesitation, Mahentiran answered, "Our little sister." Shutting her eyes, she chanted the names of her deities, "Oh God! my leader! Ēḻumalai! Caraṣvati! Murukaṉ! Vināyaka! Perumānē! . . . ," punctuating her litany with deep intakes of breath. The invocation ended with the familiar "Kōvintā!" signaling a spirit's arrival, and a good one at that, for demons are incapable of uttering this name of Viṣṇu.

At last it was Minatshi, Mahentiran's dead little sister, who began weeping and wailing through Padmini's body. Her elongated vibrato, which peaked in tearful outbursts, sounded identical to the dirges that women express at funerals. By this delivery, the spirit cued her audience that she was about to bemoan her personal woes. But funeral laments may also communicate women's grievances over their impending widowhood. So just as those protests are directed at male kin, now the spirit addressed her brother, "Are you wondering who I am? Aren't you going to ask the name of our father and mother? Wasn't I born in the same womb that gave you life too? Didn't I leave you soon after attaining puberty? But you are still asking who I am? Don't you understand?"

MAHENTIRAN: [shaken]: "Yes, I understand."

MINATSHI: "I left soon after reaching puberty. I went away wearing turmeric and vermillion powders. Isn't that so? Oh elder brother, where is the cloth you have brought for me? Where is the cloth I used to wear?"

MAHENTIRAN: "Amma, it is not here. I did not bring it."

MINATSHI [ignoring his response]: "You've come to ask questions under the banyan tree of my temple. Oh, elder brother, who used to comfort me and carry me on his shoulders when I would cry."
[At this Mahentiran and Rita both burst to tears.]

MINATSHI: "You were not able to protect your younger sister. You yourself were like a child, but you were older than me. Do you understand? Where is my skirt? Where is the cloth you brought for me? Oh my dear brother! I was precious to you. You would give me foods that I was fond of eating. Where are those delicious foods now? . . . Oh, my brother, how could you have forgotten me?"

MAHENTIRAN: [still crying]: "I have not forgotten you, Amma!"

Still moaning, the little sister now began to give her "fruit" at last:

I shall eat your offering (*paṭaippu*). Place my favorite dishes on a leaf in the domestic sanctuary. Do you understand what I say? Oh elder brother, when I left I shouted "brother! brother!" and I wept. I cried for you like a calf cries for its mother. Do not think that I left the soil where I was born and went to heaven. Do you understand? Today you ask me to protect your family and your wife. The strength of your *pūjā* is proportional to my strength. Do you understand, brother?

In asking for those offerings to be placed in the "middle-house" of her brother's household, Minatshi expressed her desire to return home in the new capacity of a tutelary deity.[5] Her death was no emotional break; she resided in no distant hereafter. But for her presence to extend any sort of protective influence she had to be worshipped. For this Minatshi invoked the fundamental reciprocity of Hindu worship in which a deity's effectiveness is scaled to the sincerity and quality of the *pūjā* of his or her devotees (Meyer 1986: 66). Then the "cool" little sister made some more cryptic demands:

This is what I am telling you. Don't beat her with your hands. Don't kick her with your legs. Don't scold her nor shout at her but put her in school and I will bring prosperity to your family. Present me with a new cloth and give it to that girl who resembles me. Do this every year, do you understand?

RITA: "Who is that girl?"

MINATSHI [irritated]: "*Aṇṇi* [elder brother's wife]! Don't you understand? I am embedded [*pati*] in your body [*aṅkam*] as a god. Is it right for you to interrupt me? Don't you understand? Don't kick her. She is my incarnation. She has my way of walking, my eyes, my ears. Can't you see this? Like me she is a virgin. Why are you hiding? You are asking me whether I can help you or not, whether your business will succeed and I am telling you it will succeed. Don't worry, I promise to protect you."

Then Padmini/Minatshi placed a few margosa leaves in the tail end of Rita's sari and announced in her normal tone of voice, "Elder brother, I may come to your house in the form of a snake. When you see that snake don't beat it. Go to the river bank or the water tank. A railway track will run toward the East or the West. There present me with a *kōriccu*. Now you may go!"

The word *kōriccu* is a cover term for an investiture ceremony whose full name, *kōriccu varutal*, means "the request to come." It installs the spirits of dead relatives in the domestic sanctuary of the household as tutelary deities (*vīṭṭu tēvams*) who are obligated to bless their living descendants. Once the spirit had clearly spelled her desires, she dismissed her relatives and Padmini fainted to the ground. When she came to her senses, the couple joined their hands in reverence, thanking her profusely and departed for home. Padmini immediately moved on to her next clients.

A week later the couple welcomed me into their thatch-roofed hut on the outskirts of Gingee. It was early in my fieldwork and I was still somewhat embarrassed by my professional curiosity. "Did you like the medium?" I finally blurted out to start things. Mahentiran gave a wonderful laugh—yes, of course, they'd been deeply impressed. "She knew nothing about us," he marveled, "yet she clearly saw our dead relatives. She described them without any mistake." And he remembered his sister's words, how she had recalled that he used to carry her on his shoulders, and other details which Padmini could hardly have invented. But exactly how had Padmini so overwhelmingly managed to convince the couple that their sibling, "cool" so long now, had appeared before them?

The Seance Analyzed: Lament, Commiseration, and Reunification

Like the *cāmis* described in chapter 2, Padmini began to yield her "fruit" by imparting visual revelations. But instead of "giving" the goddess for this "darśan" she screened a panorama of her consultants' dead relatives that drew on common knowledge they possessed of the Tamil afterworld. Her far-seeing gaze confirmed that, at death, human beings joined the clan of their ancestors. When she reported seeing spirits with "tears in their eyes" the detail must be understood in light of cultural assumptions that the dead cry over their new anonymity. Padmini's description also relied on common sense, as she always began by describing the elderly. Experience must have guided her too, for like the native sociologist she was she now knew the categories of the timely, untimely, and "cool" dead that constituted a typical Tamil's spiritual kindred.

But unlike the *cāmis* with their ongoing, intimate relationships to the goddess, Padmini was limited in that she had never "seen" these particular spirits before. Since sight was her sole contact, she could only identify them by physical characteristics—age, gender, marital status of women, or the manner of death, as those who had perished under "dangerous circumstances" (like *pēys*) looked different from those who left benignly. But she could not reconstitute their personae, nor discover their relationships to each other or the living. That was left to Mahentiran, only he could chart the full social and emotional relationships among his dear departed and his own position in that web of truly "extended" kinship.

From the outset consultants therefore were far more engaged in what Edward Schieffelin calls "the creation of the reality of spirit presence" (1996: 64–65) than during the *cāmis*' seances described earlier. And since they were indispensable to the conjuring of this involved, interpersonalized "presence," they were also less free to criticize its quality. But such a collaborative evocation of the spirit world was not merely a strategy on Padmini's part to suspend her clients' disbelief. It established subtler connections as well. Her repeated interrogations led Mahentiran to identify *himself* in terms of his relationships with the dead and to learn how what his society already had told him in so many ways was true: they transcended death. Padmini's localization of the afterworld at such a proximate distance also rendered this continuity of bonds quite feasible. The orbit of one's responsibilities was really not that much larger; the dead had always been part of it, but it often took a crisis to remind you of that.

Once she situated her clients at the hub of their genealogies, Padmini strove to personify a spirit of their choice. Here her task was more like that of *cāmis* who put their goddesses in personal contact with clients. But the work was more complex due to the general hesitation to believe in the dead's manifestations in this world, and because these spirits were so well known to her supplicants.

To overcome these difficulties, she first employed the commanding delivery that precluded any questioning of the realities she was to present. Second, she appropriated the genre of ceremonial wailing that is normally used in funeral rituals and obviously demands no verification. The dead are dead, and most of the time that is all there is to it. The very onset of these dirges forces everyone within earshot to surrender to the moment; none can resist the mood of bottomless sorrow they impart. The wails inevitably induce weeping all around. Transposed into the improvisatory flow of Padmini's seance, the genre retained its cathartic properties, engaging the participants' empathies, bracketing their emotions, and cutting short any doubts they may have had regarding its reality. But once again, this was not merely a performative ploy. For all its rhetorical impact, her idiom of expression had a propositional force: the medium was part of the message, of the revelation.

Tamil lament is a vocative language that addresses the deceased from the viewpoint of his or her particular kinship relationship to the lamenter—always a woman. At the funeral of her own mother, for example, a woman is likely to begin each stanza with the words: "Oh my dear mother!"[6] But she is actually addressing an idealized kin as much as a particular woman. What the wording of Tamil laments eulogize to the point of exaggeration is the deceased's conformity to cultural definitions of a good relative. The mourning woman might continue her song by evoking how she used to be loved, even spoilt, by her mother. By tropes of absence and receding landscape, she will make emotional "comparisons" (*oppāri*: the Tamil word for the genre), setting this golden past against the desolate present where she is devoid of a mother's emotional involvement in her life. The Tamil lamentation is a language that communicates to the dead and to any living person who listens painful feelings of loss for a kin relationship that was fulfilling, centering, and which grounded the self.

Yet in Padmini's seance it was a "cool" woman who reversed this pattern by bewailing the fact of her living relatives having let *her* down, as if they were really the ones who had "departed" from this world. And this deceased lamenter was entitled to such a moving "comparison," for she was evoking the most idealized bond in Tamil family life, that between an elder brother and younger sister. As the Tamil scholar Indira Peterson (1988) has recently shown, the plots of South Indian myths, films, and novels all agree that there is no stronger love (also see Trawick 1990a; Nuckolls 1993).[7] This is why the spirit had pulled out all the emotional stops, remembering how Mahentiran lavished her with gifts of favorite foods and clothing as a child. Those reminiscences of a blissful time when she felt safe under his love and protection only intensified her "comparisons," the emotional oblivion to which he had abandoned her since her "death." It was no wonder that the girl's anguish brought Mahentiran, Rita, and the surrounding crowd into a shared outpouring of grief.

Whereas the *cāmis* produced a goddess who was so distant and aloof that clients had to plead for her sympathy, Padmini yielded spirits who, although dead or "cool," were emotionally full of life and need. They strenuously coerced the living to empathize with their suffering, resorting to the "Tamil psychology of interaction," so nicely captured by David Shulman: "What counts is, first and foremost, the inner emotional reality, which abrogates the normative divisions between living beings. Shared sensation, especially of great intensity—especially sensation focused on or derived from loss and separation—becomes a form of self-transcendence" (1993: 14). The little sister was using all her skills to make Mahentiran suffer her sorrow and to experience the state that, as Shulman points out, Tamils often refer to as emotional "melting" or "liquefaction" (*urukkam, urukutal*) (ibid).

She had insisted on this catharsis from the beginning. How could her brother have failed to recognize his sibling? Had they not shared the "same womb" (*cahōtarar*), a term that glosses as "the state of being brother and sister?" As if this symbiosis was still not close enough, she offered the obscure revelation that she was even "embedded" in his wife's body: "She is my incarnation, she has my way of walking, my eyes, my ears. . . . Like me she is a virgin."

On our first postmortem, Mahentiran and Rita told me that they understood Minatshi to mean their own daughter, who was then eight years old.[8] The message was not merely that the living and the dead were related through kinship ties but that they were fused into one genealogy, one womb, one body, one child. In losing touch with their dead or "cool" relatives, the living had lost touch with themselves as well.

If the *cāmis* were prone to advise people to undergo a "funeral" to objectify the "transformed" self as a free being and ritually "remove" them from "commanding" living relationships, Padmini was adding that a healthy life depended on renewing ties to the dead and attending to their living expressions. This was why she invited her consultants to "see" and emotionally revivify their former neglected kinship connections. It was why her chosen instrumentality was a mortuary practice—lamenting—that was conspicuously absent from the *cāmis'* countersorcery rites. And it was also why she recommended that the dead be reincorporated in her brother's domestic sanctuary by means of a ceremony, which as we will see in the next chapter, is modeled after marriage, the central metaphor for intimacy, self-transcendence, and fusion in Tamil society.

What was striking about this particular seance was that Padmini had not determined its outcome. The spirit whom she mediated scheduled the time and place of her return. Mahentiran and Rita would recognize her in the form of a snake that in Tamilnadu, as Eveline Meyer observes, "often serves as a means of communication between the goddess and the devotee" (1986: 59). Upon seeing it, the couple should head for a water source where investiture ceremonies, which the spirit requested, are usually performed. The *pūjā* should also be near a "railways track running from East to West" but no one, including the medium herself, could explain this reference. Padmini had not fixed anything, she had entrusted the couple to "read the signs" and interpret them on their own. Their self-transformation was in their hands.

Allowing such initiative contrasted with the *cāmis'* more controlling style of *kuri*, which generally specified the prescribed courses of action and the time when people ought to undergo "removal." It was as if Padmini was advising that a reunification with a "cool" little sister, a reconstitution of the self, should not be planned or rushed. Such linkages, such transformations, were quintessentially liminal, subjunctive, and relational. All she was willing to do was open the door, show people what to look for (a snake), and empower them to make the journey themselves (a railway track). Perhaps she was also suggesting that the experience she had imparted had made that process irrevocable and irreversible. They were already on their way.

I came to suspect that the entire experience was meant to remain unfinished, open-ended, without any ritualized closure. At least this was the case for Mahentiran and Rita, who, upon each visit I paid them over the next ten months, would say, "We still have not seen the snake. Our little sister will let us know when to do the *pūjā*. She is not ready yet." Although they felt confident that Minatshi was already protecting them, I also got the impression that the original rationale for their consulting the medium—the couple's unsuccessful fruit vending business, Mahentiran's headaches—had lost its importance. They still seemed under the sway of the intense "comparisons" that had been made by their little sister.

Since Padmini left it up to her customers to complete her revelations it would seem that "fruits" from the dead are those of personal resolution and gradual acceptance instead of the dramatic, durable transformations obtained from the goddess. This may be true if the spiritual communication began, as was the case here, in times of misfortune. But Tamil culture also provides institutionalized opportunities through which this "little sister," and Leila's husband of the last chapter, all dead, can indeed return home at last. Identifying and analyzing those opportunities return us to prescriptive rituals and mandatory reconstitutions of personhood.

9

THE RECAPITATION OF YOUNG GROOMS

The ceremony that incorporates the newly dead into Tamil household devotions should become familiar since it is structurally identical to the *pēy*-exorcism discussed in chapters 5 and 6.[1] From beginning to end, it exploits the same tripartite core sequence of actions, the same linguistic and bodily enactments, and is likewise performed by the ritual musicians, known as *pampaikkārar*. But since these family dead are honored guests whose presence is highly desired, their intervention is invested with contradictory significance; the structure of their ritual operations and their objectives stand in binary opposition to those that "make the demon-*pēy* run away." Rather than working toward the separation, or what Luc de Heusch terms, the "disjunction" of human and supernatural spheres, their objective here is to achieve the fusion or "conjunction" between the living and the dead (1981: 213).

In presenting this opposition this chapter will depart from the mode of narration one finds throughout the rest of this book. Rather than describing a particular enactment by specific protagonists in an actual context, here I construct an abstract performance, divorced of social processes and personal interests. I do this because it was when I reduced this ritual to its bare essentials and compared it to the exorcism that I came to grasp its symbolism and the full significance of its climactic sequence. As we will see, such comparative perspectives clearly highlight the fact that this ritual ends up enacting personal transformations that are alike in all ways to those affected by the exorcism except that they are opposed. They also suggest that the ceremonial incorporation of the dead in the household is just as prescriptive and just as coercive on the Tamil self as the ritual which expels the demons from this world.

Household Deities versus Demons

In the abstract Tamil human beings are said to become demon-*pēys* if their lives have abruptly ended due to accident, murder, or suicide—those deaths that thwart the "fate" written by the creator Brahmā on people's "heads" at birth. So it is not surprising that the death that deifies those who once lived among us is said to have been ordered by gods. The typical family deity, I was always told, is the spirit of a human being, who like the little sister in the last chapter, is recalled by the goddess through her special manifestations, particularly smallpox. In real life, however, the same logic that led my consultants to deny that their untimely spirits became demons overrules this cultural scenario. All dead relatives have the potential to come back "as gods," even those who died like *pēys*.

The crucial term that designates these deified spirits is *pūvāṭaikkāri*, which means "the woman who wears flowers" (*pū* = flowers, *āṭai* = dress, (k) *kāri* = feminine person). The word evokes the epitome of the virginal bride who is sent to her husband wearing a crown of interwoven jasmine blossoms in her hair, and who thereafter proudly wears flowers as the insignia of an auspicious wife. Perhaps this is why in the ethnographic literature *pūvāṭaikkāri* have been understood literally to describe the deified spirits of married women or young virgins who also can wear flowers in their hair.[2]

These spirits may appear to be ideal prototypes for deified relatives (Dumont 1986; Reiniche 1979; Jacob-Pandian 1975; Harlan 1992), but my documentation suggests that not all *pūvāṭaikkāris* turn out to be the spirits of married women, or of virgins, nor are they necessarily female. Only five of the rituals I recorded installed the spirit of a mother (and of those two had *not* died in the married state). Three were actually held to honor a father, five were directed at both mother and father, one was for a male elder sibling, and the last addressed paternal grandparents. Despite its feminine connotation, therefore, the term *pūvāṭaikkāri* can apparently designate any and all deceased close relatives who had undergone this investiture. To one consultant the word simply meant "the one who died and come back to us as god."

It is partly because such spirits reenter this world in the structural position of legitimate brides that they are opposed to the demons who return as spurious husbands. The archetypal *pēy*, we have seen, is the spirit of a man who took his life because he was prevented to wed, or because his marriage did not work out, and who henceforth "catches" other men's wives. The *pūvāṭaikkāri* stands for the probability of marriage ("she" is readied with flowers for it), but the *pēy* symbolizes its obstruction and desecration.

This explains why these categories of spirits have such different rapports with sexuality, reproduction, and rationality. The demon is said to engage in wild copulation that renders women infertile and crazy; the *pūvāṭaikkāri* is known to protect marital procreation, ties of filiation, and the continuity of parental reason. Such associations are also suggested by their different environments. The *pēys* inhabit a wasteland which—whether filled with tamarind trees, stagnant pools, movie theaters, or bus stands—lack those features essential for normal social life. But the *pūvāṭaikkāris* dwell amongst cultivated fields, in a domesticated landscape that is incorporated and indispensable to the reproduction of the household and Tamil society.

These representations highlight one more critical distinction between demons and household deities. The *pēy* represents a generic, timeless entity, a "departed" who cannot change nor grow. His arrested development is suggested by his cosmological predicament: stuck on earth he cannot transit to the other world. The "woman who wears flowers" also evokes a classificatory and fixed status, that of a bride, but one that is regularly invested with a new, specific identity. For every one or two generations this tutelary deity is personified by a recently deceased family member who is known by name (also see Moffat 1979: 227; also see Jacob-Pandian 1975: 73). One explanation for these successive investitures emerged from a musician when I asked about the tutelary function of such spirits: "*Pūvātaikkāri* is to bride what mud is to gold. There is no strength in the soil. The plants soak it up. This is why we need to put mud or manure in the field over and over again. Likewise, both *pūvāṭaikkāri* and bride bring growth."

His analogy indicated that, like crops, the family could not reproduce itself; one cannot secure procreation from a mother, father, grandparents, or siblings. Incorporation of an outsider is essential, a bride, who enters the household as a daughter-in-law. And much like those specific women who regularly enter the house "with flowers" to introduce the missing ingredient that grants generational continuity, newly dead relatives periodically "come home" as *pūvāṭaikkāri* in order to ensure succession.

Generally, they are "invited" to do so during auspicious moments of transition, such as the move to a newly built house, a birth, or most especially, the marriage of a child.[3] Indeed, all of the ceremonies I recorded were held one or two days prior to a marriage, usually of a first-born son who had lost either his mother or father or both.[4] And the repeated reason I was given as to why people held it was quite simply to "invite [a<u>l</u>ai] the dead parents to the marriage of their son."[5]

Glossed in common parlance as *pūvāṭaikkāri pūjā* for the basic reason that the dead whom it installs in the domestic sanctuary are henceforth dubbed *pūvāṭaikkāri*, this ritual is generally performed by all non-Brahmin castes at the peak of the marriage season, during the Tamil months of *Vaikāci* (May/June) and *Āṉi* (June/July) when the time for sowing new crops still lies ahead. Since it is conducted by households on agricultural fields privately owned by family members, it unfolds outside the domain and control of village religion. Its beneficiaries are those patrilineal kin who live under one roof, eat food cooked in a single kitchen, worship and hold property in common, and form the "joint family" of Indian society.

Comparison of the "Marriage Invitation" with the Ritual That "Makes the Demon Run Away"

Tamil exorcisms begin at the threshold of a communal sanctuary, such as the Aṅkāḷaparamēcuvari temple, where around mid-morning the demons are "warned" to "meet" later, "outside," on the cremation ground. The *pūvāṭaikkāri pūjā* begins with the same kind of "notification," albeit in the most sacred part of the domestic arena.

The "family" for this auspicious occasion usually includes all those who ever lived with the deceased—parents, siblings, children, and in-laws. Around mid-morning they gather in the ritual center of the household, the *naṭuvīṭu* (literally "middle-house"), which is usually located near the cooking hearth in the northeastern corner of the house.[6] An air of gravity pervades; all watch attentively as the senior married woman lights the auspicious lamp[7] and waves a camphor flame around the ritual space; the spirit(s) who currently personify the household deity are invited in.

When these old *pūvāṭaikkāris* are provoked to "dance" or possess someone by the sounds of the musicians' drums, they are asked to "meet" later with the new guest(s) of honor. One may be instructed, "Go to the grave [*kiḻkkarai*: literally "the edge of the pit"] and bring back all who have died in this family." Another may be requested to specify the direction in which the wedding party is supposed to "meet" its newest *pūvāṭaikkāri*, a query often phrased as, "A man has died in this family. In which direction should we go to get him to speak to us: north, east, west, or south?"

The spirits respond by designating the "meeting place" through the pointing fingers of their mediums. The question is generally rhetorical, since the family has already decided on where to look. But as a musician told me, one must ask because "the *pūvāṭaikkāri* is our father and our mother. When they were alive we consulted them on important matters. We must still defer to them and give them the power of decision making. At the beginning of our invitation we show special respect or the spirit won't come."

If the family is landless the *pūjā* is performed near a communal water source, such as the village tank. Or they proceed to their cultivated fields where spirits of dead kin are known to reside beside the irrigation well. "Our parents have worked that land all their lives," one farmer said. "It is now like their palace [*māṭam*]." Most people agreed that spirits were fond of the fields that sustained them when they were alive, but another man gave a different reasoning for having the ceremony outdoors. "In the house there is pollution," he said. "The spirits are reluctant to enter it. Beside the house may not evoke good memories to the spirits. Friction and disputes linger. The field is a more neutral ground to call our *pūvāṭaikkāri*."

At exorcisms the "warning" of the demon establishes both the means and ends of the ritual. It is at that point that the *pēy* demands the "life" that he eventually receives in exchange for leaving this world for good. His demand for "life" is also a green light for the exorcism to proceed, for according to the musicians, it confirms the *pēy*'s consent to "meet" again at the cremation ground.

This "notification" of the old household deity also anticipates the immediate and central aims of the investiture. Now this tutelary is asked to nominate someone to carry to the fields the basket containing the ceremonial pot that serves as the vehicle for carrying the new *pūvāṭaikkāri* back to the domestic sanctuary. The spirit's nomination of its carrier and "her" placement of the basket onto the head of that person—usually a woman—also launch the ritual, for it is said to ratify "her" willingness to "bring back" the newly dead to the water source where the core of the *pūjā* is to be held.[8]

Led by the musicians who sing praises to various tutelary deities along the way, the wedding party walks single file on a narrow path that usually borders their rice paddies. Behind the appointed basket carrier follow the family's married women with big baskets enclosing ceremonial cooking pots balanced on their heads. Then trail the children, with the men bringing up the rear, and the groom last in line.[9]

At exorcisms the preparation of a ritual space is minimal. Since the demon is already "on the head" of the "caught" woman, the musicians do not seek to embody him in an icon. They simply scratch a circle into the cremation ground to "arrest" him in place. At the final destination of the wedding party, however, these same musicians must provide a proper receptacle for materializing the *pūvāṭaikkāri* into this world and transporting "her" back home. To this end they ready the ceremonial pot known as *karakam*, which will stand for the "woman who wears flowers."[10]

About this corporal symbolism the musicians are quite explicit. The yards of white thread that they continuously wind around the unglazed pot in a tight, criss-cross net are said to be "like veins and arteries that nourish and vitalize the body." The outer surface, which is smeared with turmeric paste and daubed with five large vermillion dots, is likened to "the skin of a married woman." Water is poured in because, I was told, "it makes up most of our human body." Turmeric powder, milk, yogurt, cow urine are added "to purify" this "human body." A rupee coin is dropped in to "give it life" (*uyir koṭu*). To ensure that the spirit of the deceased successfully possesses the pot, mud from his or her grave is added as well.[11]

To further the deceased's transformation into the symbolic and functional equivalent of an auspicious *pūvāṭaikkāri*, long branches of margosa leaves are inserted into the pot. Then it is entirely wrapped with spiraling bands of white and orange jasmine blossoms so that the finished *karakam* resembles a two-and-an-half foot, flower-swathed cone. Last, strings of yellow marigolds fall "like a skirt," as one musician phrased it, around the base. Underneath this "skirt" is placed a small pendant of turmeric root, a common ritual substitute for a woman's *tāli*, or marriage insignia, which is fastened, as are real *tālis*, by a turmeric-dyed string.[12]

To regale the honored guests who are expected to "come down" into this flowerpot, women gather firewood for boiling raw rice into the sweet milky-white *poṅkal* ("boiling"), which according to Anthony Good, is "the epitome of prosperity for every Tamil" (1983: 235; also see Beck 1969). His observation that this ceremonial "boiling" often signals the ritual prelude to a more desirable state of being is also relevant. For here it announces an imminent, if temporary, progression from death to life—a transition that the musicians facilitate by gently transporting the decorated pot to a bed of raw rice, where it is laid to rest facing to the east. Immediately the lamp of the domestic sanctuary is lit, pots of *poṅkal*, as well as fruits and sweets, are generously displayed, and burning camphor invites the spirit to "descend" into the flower-wrapped pot.[13]

At exorcisms, once the demon and his victim are enclosed in the ritual circle, the musicians' drumming and singing entreat them to "dance" and speak. At these investitures, too, when the "woman who wears flowers" is contained in the *karakam* pot "she" is asked to possess one of "her" relatives so that a dialogue can ensue.

For this communication the preferential mediums are the agnatic group's unmarried sons, especially the groom. Returning from purificatory ablutions at their agricultural well, these candidates who may be as young as four or five, line up before the pot. With the groom conspicuously positioned in the middle, the lead singer swipes sacred ash across their foreheads to consecrate them as suitable vessels for a possible possession. The musicians split into two groups, framing the *karakam* pot with the chosen young men in between them. Behind them stands the rest of the family, in a watchful semicircle.

Securing divine "protection" through a formulaic praise to both the great Hindu gods and key deities of the local pantheon, the lead singer hurls all his vocal talent into inducing the "woman with flowers" to appear. Addressing the deceased directly, his entreaties will swell with rhetorical intensity and dramatic sequencing (as we heard during Shanti's exorcism in chapter 5).

> Chaste woman! we have not seen you since your death. Beautiful lady! This is the right time for you to come. From the place where you died, get up and come down!

Or the singer may shift to a more cajoling, personalized tone of voice:

> Though you may have had quarrels with this family, come here today. They are waiting for you. Come, come on the hair [like demons, these spirits are believed to penetrate the body through the hair].

And if this still fails to stir "her," the singer may start to beg:

> We have not done anything to you, why don't you speak?

Then he may sermonize:

> Don't you have a duty to take care of your poor and powerless relatives? They have spent a lot of money on these offerings, aren't you going to come now? Are you going to let them down?

At the fourteen *pūvāṭaikkāri* "invitations" (*alaittal*) I documented, the musicians had to play for many tiring hours before contacting these spirits. If anything, the *pūvāṭaikkāris* were more difficult to rouse into motion and verbal action than the demons, but for opposite reasons. *Pēys* are slow to "dance," I was told, because they resist a process of dance and dialogue that will inevitably cause their departure. In the binary logic of "invitations," the "woman who wears flowers" is slow to dance because "she" may have reservations about "coming home." "The *pūvāṭaikkāri* is *āvi* [or "soul"]," a musician said, "It was not born as a god. These spirits may not feel like coming as gods to their relatives."

Since the *pūvāṭaikkāris* are "good" spirits whose presence is highly desirable, the musicians cannot adopt the kind of verbal abuse and physical threat that work with *pēys*. They can only create the maximum ritual conditions and meet all technical requirements to the letter. The invitation must be performed at the same place and preferably the same time as the spirit's own death so the *pūvāṭaikkāri* will be sure to "hear" the family's call. Camphor lumps must burn throughout the musicians' invocation to keep open the channel of visual communication open with the other world. All ritual protagonists must prepare their bodies as suitable vessels for their immaculate, deified relative, by ritual bathing and adornment. These encounters are not the place to tinker with traditional usages; conservative *pūvāṭaikkāris* do not like change.

The most dramatic example of a ritual that was delayed because of a grievous lapse in protocol occurred at a *Paraiyan* (untouchable) *pūvāṭaikkāri pūjā* that I witnessed nearby my village. When the guest of honor, the groom's deceased mother, descended on her daughter, "she" rushed to hug her two sons, the groom and his younger brother. But then the latter was abruptly entranced by his paternal grandfather's spirit, producing a situation of double possession.

At this the "mother" began sobbing so loudly that everyone was moved to wailing as well. In this midst of this outpouring, the lead singer implored, "We don't know why you are crying. Please don't cry. Talk to us! One or two words are enough." Instead of replying, the "mother" spirit ran stumbling toward the cremation ground about a kilometer away. When the family caught up with her, she was prostrate on her own grave, gripping fistfuls of dirt. "You have not put the mud of my grave in the *karakam* (the ceremonial pot)," she cried, "My name is Tagarammal and I want my mud in the pot." Immediately her own brother added mud to the *karakam*, but it took many apologies before she forgave her relatives. The omission was not frivolous, for without precious mud from her own grave the woman was incapable of personally reincorporating into the *karakam*.

But mere ceremonial exactitude was not enough either. The specialists always emphasized that neither the timing nor the nature of a *pūvāṭaikkāri*'s manifestation were entirely in their hands. The critical ingredient, all of them agreed, was the power and sincerity of relatives' love (*aṉpu*) and affection (*pācam*). "If the dead were not loved during their lifetime they won't come," one said. "It is love that makes them come back as gods."[14]

A dancing *pūvāṭaikkāri* does not signal her identity by wildly swinging "her" head around as with a demon-*pēy*'s arrival. Instead, staring at the *karakam* pot, "her" medium usually takes a halting, half-step forward. At that barest hint the musicians and the family suddenly huddle in, pleading for the person to surrender to the drum, nursing this promise of fusion with the spirit into a full-fledged trance. In a minute or two the dancer's body jerks convulsively backward, he or she reaches into the air as if grabbing for balance. Their screeching cry, "Kōvintā!" announces that the spirit is about to switch to a linguistic manifestation. Without hesitation, the lead singer initiates a dialogue with the question that also frames communications with the demon: "WHO ARE YOU?"

Unlike exorcist dialogues, however, there is little effort to reconstruct the existential or psychological realities of these spirits. Even eliciting their name is not central here, and even after such a disclosure, it was my observation that the living often insisted on other sorts of identification. What seemed uppermost in their minds was verifying the spirit's kinship pedigree. Questions regarding genealogy—"How many children do you have?" "What is the name of our father?"—peppered the dialogue. The living needed persuasive evidence that the spirit was someone willing to subordinate his/her individual identity to the larger set of relationships that constituted the family.

Generally these *pūvāṭaikkāris* castigate their relatives for any failure to recognize them and to appreciate their anonymity and loneliness in the afterworld. "Are you asking me who I am? Don't you know?" they often reply to the musicians' interrogations. And they refuse to be defined in terms of structural categories or roles. Instead they insist on individual commemoration, demanding tangible evidence of love, such as daily offerings of camphor, favorite foods, and clothing before they respond to genealogical inquiries. "I will tell you the name of our father," one spirit said, "but first you must clean and spruce up my grave." It is as if these incoming household deities, supposedly protectors of the family, have a hard time accepting a generic kinship pedigree and affirming any ties of filiation that might efface their distinctive personalities.

This apparent need for personal and emotional recognition might also explain why they infuse their revelations with autobiographical reminiscences. And as these spirits unhesitatingly unload their pent-up resentments, the *pūjā* organizers take considerable emotional risks and are almost always in for unpleasant surprises.

Spontaneous, even bitter exchanges are commonplace. At another *pūvāṭaikkāri* ritual in a different *Paraiyan̠* (or Untouchable) village a groom's dead mother "came on" her son only to berate her surviving husband, "*You* didn't treat me well," she said, "I didn't like being married to you." When the lead singer tried calming her, she only added to her widower, "You never told me the truth of your own heart. Why should I tell you my name?" Speaking on behalf of the husband, the singer protested, "What have I done?" Pointing to her husband, the spirit replied, "Ask him, he'll tell you."

She yelled so loud and long that her embarrassed husband asked the musicians to call her back on someone else. But the spirit interrupted, "You think you can order my coming and going. Do you think that if you play your instruments I'll come on a different person. This I want to see. Come on, play!" Then, she lamented, "My girl is missing!" and she accused her husband, "You let her elope, you did not arrange for her marriage. Nobody is here to protect my children." As she moaned, her younger sister, who also happened to be her husband's new wife, was moved to reply, "Don't cry! I am here to look after them." The spirit retorted, "Why did you let the girl run away then?" As the husband was pushing her away, the spirit said to her sister, "See how he has always separated us!"

These sudden, emotion-laden declarations of unrequited love and allegations of abuse or neglect also contrast the *pūvāṭaikkāri* with the *pēy*. For the demons are characteristically shy and slow to reveal their personal problems. The reason for this nonassertiveness is that they are not exactly sure who they are; the musicians must tease out the bare facts of their lives and even their names. With the *pūvāṭaikkāri* there is no hesitation and a strong, usually wronged, sense of self. They are only too ready to pour out their hearts to the wedding party.

But families do not really want to get entangled in the spirits' emotional dilemmas. At times relatives may commiserate with the spirit's lot in the hereafter, but never for long. "Tell us why you are crying in one or two words," the family told the dead mother. "Don't make a big deal about it," they seemed to be saying. The living even pressure the dead to delete traumatic life events from their memories. "Don't think about that now," they advise, cutting short their testimonies and urging them not to be so self-centered and disruptive.

Whereas at exorcisms the musicians encourage full expression of the "ego" who is speaking through the woman, and listen with a relatively sympathetic ear to its problems so as to better exorcise it, at familial investitures they seem to inhibit manifestations of individuality. This may sound contradictory, since the *pūjā*'s goal *is* to invest the household tutelary with a new identity. But these dialogues indicate that a standard rather than distinctive successor is desired for that post, someone who will inconspicuously blend with its previous occupants. What is wanted is a generic human bridge between the generations: a bride, a woman who will reproduce the past in the present.

If they cannot behave like proper conductors of lineal continuity, there are two ways to expel these spirits from the scene. The family may ask the musicians to terminate the trance so that a different medium may find a less self-absorbed manifestation of the dead relative.[15] When this strategy does not work the family can openly question the spirit's identity and the medium's legitimacy. Both are put to a test, which is exactly how Tamils phrase this procedure, using the word *pariṭcai* ("test") or simply the English term.[16] The singer may line up a lime, a betel leaf, and a bidhi (rolled tobacco leaf/cigarette) before the ceremonial pot. The spirits are then asked to select which of the three their living kinfolk have in mind. What is wanted is evidence of some psychic or cognitive contiguity between the dead/medium and the family. If spirits cannot prove a telepathic affinity they (and their mediums) are promptly evicted. But as Eveline Meyer points out, "These tests very rarely fail" (1986: 237). Perhaps because they realize that not accepting this "marriage invitation" will make their death an ultimate finality, nearly always the spirits pick up the right object.

Once the exorcists have secured a demon's self-identification, they place the *pēy* on oath "to leave the girl alone and never come back." Likewise at these investitures the musicians extract a pledge from the *pūvāṭaikkāri*, but to the opposite effect. After the family is convinced that a manifestation of "father" or "mother" is before their eyes, they plead: "Tomorrow we are going to hold a marriage, will you come? Do you promise to come?" Since the invitation should be extended to all known dead members of the family, they may add, "Is our little brother with you?" Tamed and conciliatory after their individualistic outbursts the spirits now respond, "All [*mottam*] *pūvāṭaikkāris* are here."[17]

At most exorcisms the demon's mere promise to depart is never enough, so the musicians pressure it to commit in the same way that earlier in the ritual he had confirmed his vow to show up. Demanding a "life" had pledged him to participate in his own exorcism, taking a "life" then guarantees his exit. This was evidenced by the musicians' swift retort to the reluctant demon in chapter 6: "If you don't take this life, who is going to believe that you are leaving?"

In similar fashion the *pūvāṭaikkāri* must confirm "her" promise to attend the wedding by the same verbal and bodily enactments with which "she" had originally agreed to usher the newly dead to the family well. Then she was expected to appoint the bearer of the "unmade" pot to the ritual site; now "she" chooses the individual to carry the "made" flowerpot back to the household. Previously she designated a woman, but invariably the *pūvāṭaikkāri* now points to the groom: "He should carry the *karakam*!"

After taking the "life," the demon loses his personality, turning into an inert "weight," the heavy round rock which the musicians place in the woman's hands. She is compelled to "run away," the exorcism climaxes with her dropping the rock by a tamarind tree. Once her task of appointing the groom is done, the new *pūvāṭaikkāri*'s individuality likewise merges with "her" predecessors who are collectively recognized as "the woman who wears flowers." Then, "she/they" lifts the ten-pound vessel containing them all onto the groom's head. This crowning arouses a heightened alertness in the family, the drumming intensifies, cries of "Kōvintā!" punctuate the air. Upon coming into physical contact with the pot, the groom's body "shakes" with involuntary force, and he is instantly in trance (*āṭṭam*).[18] His glazed eyes lock on some imaginary point, as if he is stunned by the multitude of manifestations and implications riding on his head.

The exorcism concludes when the musicians nail the woman's lock of hair into a tamarind tree and exile her demon to the wilderness. This "marriage invitation" ends with the opposite scenario: reincorporating the "woman who wears flowers" into the domesticated hearth.

The procession goes back to the village, led by the musicians' drums, and recovers a definite calm and formality. Everyone clusters behind the groom, still in a state of ecstasy with one arm steadying the "made" *karakam* pot.[19,20]

Once in town, the crowd halts at each crossroads, the musicians proclaiming their success at winning the *pūvāṭaikkāri's* blessings and singing "her" praises. It is now that one can sense how this ritual has successfully transformed the host of family dead into the embodiment of the ideal Hindu wife, or the *cumaṅkali* (Harlan 1992; Reynolds 1980). Once a returning procession was halted by a cluster of married women, one of whom addressed the *karakam* carrier: "If you are a *pūvāṭaikkāri*," she said, "you must protect our *tāli* [marriage insignia]. Give us your powerful *maṭipiccai* ["alms"]." As requested, the spirit tucked the protective margosa leaves into the folds (*maṭi*) of all their saris, indicating that these spirits, like brides, should selflessly devote themselves to perpetuate the family, symbolized by the *tāli*.[21]

At the threshold of the ancestral home, the family's *cumaṅkali* performs a small rite to deflect any malevolent gazes that the procession may have attracted while negotiating the village's narrow streets. As the groom stoops so the pot can clear the low jamb, the drum beats accelerate. At last inside, with extreme care, he lifts it onto a bed of rice in the north-east corner (*caṇi mūllai*, or the "corner of Saturn"). With one voice, everyone shouts, "Kōvintā!" signifying the dead's reincorporation into the household. Camphor is lit and waved around the pot, relatives line up to prostrate themselves before their living ancestors, and for the next two or three days this *karakam* will be worshipped continuously.

Following the wedding, however, the pot is carefully dismantled, its margosa leaves and flowers thrown into a nearby stream, and the liquid poured into a brass pot, the *kalacam*, which represents the more permanent locus of domestic worship (Moffat 1979: 227–228). Here the preceding household deity loses its specific identity and "merges with the new one," as Michael Moffat was also told in the Chengelput district (1979: 227). For it is the groom's deceased father or mother (or both) who will now personify this family's *pūvāṭaikkāri* along with all previous occupants of that vessel.[22] He or she has thus become installed as the tutelary deity who is now obligated to bless a new generation of devotees, so that Henry Whitehead's observation in 1921 that in Tamilnadu "it is easy to observe a deity in the making even at the present day" still applies in 1991 (1988: 20).

Summary of the Ritual Oppositions

I have tried to show how this household deity investiture follows a remarkably similar processual structure to that of an exorcism. Both begin in an inner space with a "notification" intended to elicit a spirit's commitment to "show up" in an outer space, where the ceremony will be held. The attempts to "arrest" or enclose the spirit, whether in a circle or flowerpot, suggest that this movement through space also corresponds to an objectification of ritual goals. Subsequent requests that spirits incorporate themselves in human bodies and identify who they are indicate that participants need to subjectivize these goals. In both instances, this possession phase ends when the spirit is asked to swear "his" or "her" consent to live by the central objectives of the ritual. Finally, the respective and contradictory purposes of these two rituals are enacted. While the *pēy* is "made to run away" and symbolically married to the tamarind tree in this no-man's land so that his woman can resume life with her true husband, newly dead relatives are granted a permanent return to the living, wearing all the paradigmatic insignia of married women, and henceforth dubbed *pūvāṭaikkāri*, or the "auspicious wife wearing flowers."

Clearly both household deities and wilderness demons are absorbed into or expelled from domesticity by way of the same covenants that forge or end intimate relationships between a woman and a man. The investiture of the household deity consecrates a "marriage" between the living and the dead, the exorcism effects a "divorce" from a demon-lover.

But this comparative analysis also suggests that these parallel processes of union and separation encode a more fundamental opposition between family gods and demons. This opposition surfaces most clearly during their liminal phase, when spirits are made to "dance," speak, and identify themselves. It is then that the *pūvāṭaikkāris* contrast most strikingly from demons. The demon presents himself as an apathetic and inchoate figure who needs help to recover his specific personality and particular problems. The recently deceased reveal themselves as uninhibited and self-centered individuals who must be talked into forgetting their personal traits and emotions. And indeed the ritual succeeds at doing just that. Initially the newly dead "may not feel like coming as gods to their relatives" because they are reluctant to accept this irrevocable reincarnation as a structural category. But by the ritual's end, they pass the "test" and agree to merge with and represent the anonymous collectivity of previous brides.

These existential meanings reappear in the core episodes of these two rituals: the dropping of the stone at the exorcism, and the crowning of the groom with the ceremonial pot at the investiture. They are key sequences because at this point in both rituals the mood dramatically shifts to a new register; the main participants, both "caught" woman and groom, enter trance states that are different from the states of possession enacted during the dialogue. In both instances some kind of intense, nondiscursive communication with the self seems to be taking place.

If the falling of the stone symbolically effects both the beheading of the demon and the decapitation of the woman's unsuitable personality, the crowning of the groom constitutes a "recapitation": the rereunification of the disembodied parents, "heads of the household" (*talaikkaṭṭu*) to the bodies of their "headless" child.[23]

But the groom is now subordinated to someone else: his mother or father or both, who extends above his head as if in completion of himself. The implications of this enhanced self come to light when we realize that the pot and its embodied spirits stand in a synecdochical relationship with the young man. Citing Hayden White, Valentine Daniel explains that "in synecdoche . . . , it is not merely a case where the part stands for the whole in which the whole is reduced to one of its parts, but *the part selected to represent the whole suffuses the entire being of the whole that it represents*" (1984: 107, emphasis mine). The crowned groom is "suffused" by his parents' "heads," whose identities and generic attributes of authority, influence, and the like now imbue his person.

Now the opposition between these two rituals is complete. Both enact similar, albeit opposed, personal transformations. Whereas the woman possessed by a *pēy* is forced to give up an unwanted personality and satisfy cultural expectations of the "good wife," the groom is pressed to abdicate his personal identity, to detach from himself, and become, as good sons should, the living embodiment of the parents who are attached to him. This "recapitation" is also just as mandatory and unavoidable as the "decapitation" of "caught" women at exorcisms, as suggested when one man referred to his ceremonial pot as *muttirai*. This word literally means "a mark," "an impression made by a seal," and I have already compared the way in which exorcised women are linked up with the goddess by means of an old initiation rite, also known as *muttirai*, which marked the *tēvatāsi*, or temple courtesan (Kersenboom 1995: 186). According to Saskia Kersenboom, "branding" her upper arm with a burning trident committed the *tēvatāsi* to her marriage to the god (1995: 189–190). Likewise, placing the pot on the groom's head "impresses" on him the consequences of his dedication or union to his dead parents: he is to perpetuate them through his being and life experiences; he must complement them, he can only expand himself through them.

10

WHEN PARENTS ARE UNSUITABLE BRIDES

We have just seen that the investiture of the family deity climaxes with the crowning of the groom with the flowerpot. Comparison of this ritual with the exorcism has allowed us to discern that this crucial sequence enacts a symbolic "recapitation": dead parents, heads of the family, are affixed to the groom's body in proper conjunction.

It is critical to never forget, however, that despite the tidy, depersonalized framework offered in the last chapter, whatever relevant representations this investiture might encode for any given body of participants are constructed on the spot, during actual performances. Ritual meanings do not exist independently of specific people's actions and agendas. They are created, recreated, or modified in the course of any given ceremonial process. The cosmology that is articulated through any of these "decoding" seances, countersorcery rituals, exorcisms, and instances of spirit possession has neither reality nor efficacy apart from social and personal investments. Most especially is this the case for the investiture of household deities, whose success, as we have seen, is held to depend upon the "love" and "affection" of the family. The question, then, is do participants themselves arrive at the meanings which are suggested by the comparative approach we have just read?

I say "arrive" because I do not think that the wedding party departs with the intention of "marrying" their dead or investing the groom with the identity of recently deceased kin. The common reason I was given as to why people held this *pūvāṭaikkāri pūjā* was simply "to invite dead parents to the marriage of their first child." This explanation grew out of a firm belief that for any wedding to establish a first line of descent it must have a parental blessing. Not even death can interfere with this rule. My consultants never said that this *pūjā* actually culminates with a marriage to these honored guests. Nor did they ever state that its purpose was to install these spirits as new "heads" of the household. They did not even define this ritual as an investiture of a new family deity.

So the reader may rightly object that any meanings that have emerged through my tortured comparative analysis have little or no value; since they are not formulated by participants, they do not constitute valid representations. And numerous anthropologists would endorse the position that only conscious, verbal explanations ought to be counted as ethnographic meanings.[1] But as Victor Turner forcefully argued, the methodological stance of studying ritual via "the native's point of view," "emic" statements, and so-called "experience-near concepts" (Malinowski 1984; Geertz 1979) can be "equally one-sided," as suggested when commentaries offered by specialists and lay people are contradicted by ceremonial behaviors (1967).

This was my experience, at least, for my consultants' explanatory concept of a "marriage invitation" was not corroborated by their own actions. As the ceremony unfolded, for example, deceased guests of honor who joined the living through the medium of trance-possession were not treated with the deep respect one might expect. Their requests were often unheard or ignored; they were never asked specifically to bless the coming alliance; and if the dead ever expressed disapproval of the union, I was assured the marriage would take place anyhow. This was attested by the *pūjā*'s timing only one or two days before the wedding, when everything was in prearranged motion. More puzzling was the fact that the whole purpose of the invitation was rarely spelled out; the spirit was usually asked: "Will you come home? *From now on, will you stay home and look after us?*" (emphasis mine).

Even more confusing than these discrepancies between "exegetical" and "operational" meanings (Turner 1967) was my discovery that, in their own way, specialists and lay people alike were not oblivious to the transformation of dead into brides. In the last chapter, we heard one musician venture the equation that *pūvāṭaikkāri* was to bride as mud was to gold. Now let us hear a woman explain the meaning of the *tāli* (marriage necklace) with which the wedding party encircles the rim of the flowerpot: "In order to get a girl in your house you need to put a *tāli* around her neck. Likewise we need to put a *tāli* around the neck of the pot to get our *pūvāṭaikkāri* to join us."

Although bridal symbolism kept reasserting itself in these Tamil interpretations, no one ever stated in so many words that the *pūjā*'s purpose was to return the dead as brides. The overall symbolism remained unformulated and very much alive, not "added up." This was curious in light of the fact that obvious metaphors of sexual and marital union organize so much of Tamil devotion.

It may be that the main objective of the *pūvāṭaikkāri pūjā* remains muffled or unstated because its naked purpose—to "seal" parents onto their living sons—might cause understandable resistance on the part of young men—one more cultural strategy for the subordination of the self. But I believe that there are two other plausible reasons for why the wedding party is reticent to declare that their "invitation" culminates with the marriage of the children to their dead parents.

What Men Think of This "Marriage"

The first explanation is hinted in a chartering myth for the central icon of these "invitations," the *karakam*. This narrative associates the "flowerpot" (*pūṅkarakam*) with the goddess Śakti and is a folk variant of the well-known story of Śakti's marriage to Śiva (see Shulman 1980: 167; Meyer 1986: 6–9; Nuckolls 1996: 153–162). As I heard it from a singer of the *Paṟaiyaṉ* or Untouchable caste:

The Story of Śakti's Marriage

Four *yukams* ago [a cosmic unit of time] there was a ball [*uruṇṭai*]. It burst. A woman named Śakti came out. She had three eyes, the third was placed in the middle of her forehead. She was alone.

She thought she needed a man so she made Ganesh, Viṣṇu, Brahmā, and Śiva. She wanted to marry Śiva. But Viṣṇu warned him that Śakti's third eye was very dangerous. "If she opens that eye in your presence you will die."

Convinced of the danger, Śiva told Śakti, "Give me your eye and I will call you wife [*peṇṇē*]." Śakti accepted. But when she placed her eye on Śiva's forehead, he opened it. Śakti burned on the spot and Śiva lamented the death of his wife.

Viṣṇu proposed a plan to bring Śakti back to life. The three gods, Śiva, Viṣṇu, and Ganesh, made a *karakam* [the ceremonial pot used at these investitures] and respectively played the *pampai* [drum], *uṭukkai* [drum], and *cilampu* [brass rattle]. With their music they tried to wake her up.

Śakti came back in the *karakam*. As soon as she had contact [*aṭai*] with the flowers [*pū*] she returned to life. She was the first *pū*-[*v*]- *aṭai*- *k*- *kāri* [in this folk etymology the first "woman who came in contact with the flowers"].[2]

This story opens up the possibility of transforming dead progenitors into a "wife." But it also suggests that this transformation is problematic to "sons," who in this narrative initially resisted their mother's wish to marry one of them. Their reaction is reminiscent of the *cāmis*' initial reluctance to "follow" their sexually enticing goddess. But here Śakti's sons did not capitulate so easily, and in fact turned the violence around: rather than being coerced into an intimate relationship, they burned their mother-goddess to death. What was it that they resisted so forcefully?

In our story one of Śakti's children contended that their mother was dangerous and could kill her son/groom. But in another version collected by Eveline Meyer, we hear a different argument. Viṣṇu says, Śakti "is the one who created us . . . , she should be considered as our mother, how can we take one who is our mother as our wife? We should burn her" (1986: 8). The children refuse to ratify an incestuous marriage, which involves partners so closely related that it will only produce dangerous repetitions and death.

It may be that offsprings participating in a ritual enactment of this myth are also troubled by these ramifications of the *pūvāṭaikkāri pūjā*. For the "woman who wears flowers" stands in the position of consanguineal kin, principally mother and father, people with whom sexual union is of course forbidden.[3] Perhaps the incestuous connotations of this alliance, sure to arouse feelings of horror and revulsion, inhibited my consultants from stating that they "invited" the dead to marry the living. Perhaps, they adhered to the notion of a "marriage invitation" in order to deny its very problematic resonances altogether.

My consultants' disinterest in articulating the bridal symbolism of this *pūjā* may also stem from the formidable problems that the prospect of any "marriage" presents to a Tamil family. In South India marriage and its key symbol, the bride, represent what one might call a "kinship of division." For this rite of passage is paradoxically the mechanism through which, over time, the joint family will formally "split" into separate, autonomous households, as brothers set up their own hearths. Hence the arrival of a new daughter-in-law is to some degree a threat to the integrity and continuity of the joint family.

Likewise the "woman who wears flowers" symbolizes the forces of structural opposition to the unity of the joint family. "Her" investiture formalizes the fragmentation of this kinship group into separate ritual constituencies, for as Michael Moffat also noted, "one of the first acts in establishing the new household of the divided family is the installation of a new *kalasam* pot . . . to the family god" (1979: 228). However I must emphasize the strict rule that *so long as their father lives*, sons who have partitioned the ancestral home are forbidden from inviting a new household deity. Instead, they "divide" the identity of their father's tutelary and worship "her" in their separate households (ibid). Only after their father's death will they call in any new *pūvāṭaikkāris*.

These investitures institute other kinds of distinctions as well. Because of his seniority, it is incumbent upon the elder sibling to install his dead father or mother or both in his household, to connect the past, present, and future generations in a bilateral "line" of descent (*varicai*). But in doing so he irrevocably cuts off occupants of his household, both human and spiritual, from those of his younger brothers, who often reconstitute their families by inviting a nonparental *pūvāṭaikkāri*, for example, the spirit of a deceased wife, an unmarried daughter, or a "cool" little sister as Mahentiran (of chapter 8) may do one day. In this way, over time these sacramentalized unions between the living and the dead subdivide the family into smaller, separate, and mutually exclusive ritual collectivities.

We need not be reminded of the hardship and suffering that separations place on the Tamil "self." Walking away from one's family, disjoining from one's lover and one's dead husband almost literally tear a person apart, as suggested by pervasive references to bodily piercing, decapitation, and reattachments to wrong heads. "Even from a demon," a Tamil adage emphasizes "parting is painful" (in Trawick 1990a: 100). Likewise I suspect that these ceremonialized "divisions" of the household deity take a considerable toll on the family, particularly on any male siblings who end up being "cut off" from the parental line. Perhaps, then, the wedding party covers up the "real" purpose of the *pūjā* and serves to downplay the incestuous and divisive implications of these marriages with the dead. Couched as an "invitation to a marriage" is a way of providing it with the alternative, uncontroversial cast of an all-inclusive, all-encompassing celebration.

If participants do not join the *pūvāṭaikkāri pūjā* with the intention of marrying their parents, however, over the ritual's course they will feel compelled to do so, as was Śiva's experience in the chartering myth. At first he was reluctant to marry his mother, but no sooner had she died than he immediately felt a longing compulsion to merge with her. Members of the *pūvāṭaikkāri pūjā* are also driven by circumstances to discover their bride on the spot. Critical to their search are the mediums who personify the "woman who wears flowers."

What Women Do at This "Marriage"

We should remember that in Tamilnadu the critical mission of searching for a suitable bride customarily requires the involvement of mediators. Parents request relatives or friends to be on alert for a proper mate for their son. When they finally decide on a likely candidate, they first dispatch someone else in reconnaissance. If this initial report is favorable, they send that intermediary to "request" the permission to "see" the bride (*peṇṇai pārkka*), even going through this formality when they are perfectly well acquainted with her family. At all these preliminary stages one must behave with utmost respect lest the bride refuses to see the groom.

In the context of these household deity rituals, the wedding party likewise entreats specific emissaries to negotiate on their behalf. In the house, prior to the departure for the fields, the musicians first request the spirit(s) who currently personify the old family tutelary to "search" for the new *pūvāṭaikkāri*. The possessed individual who looked for this "guest of honor" was always a woman who could be father's sister, an elder-sister, a younger-sister, or a mother. In real life these paternal aunts, sisters, and mothers would similarly play a central role in arranging a young man's marriage. According to the preferential Tamil practice of bilateral cross-cousin marriage, they would be either potential bride-givers or critical links to bride-givers (see Dumont 1983; Good 1991; Trawick 1990a). A man may wed his father's sister's daughter and in some caste-groups even his own elder sister's daughter so long as she is younger than he. He, of course, would be barred from marrying the daughter of his mother who stands in a sister relationship to him, but he can wed his mother's brother's daughter. Thus one correlation between the function of these house spirits and that of the individuals who represent them may be that both deliver the bride. In fact, they literally deliver the bride as they jointly hand the basket containing the unmade flowerpot to the individual—generally also a woman—who will carry it to the field.

The mediums who eventually produced the *pūvāṭaikkāri* at the family well were not chosen at random. Unlike the "warning" in the household, where the medium's role appeared open to any and all family members, the marriage party had specific candidates in mind. Preferential hosts were the unmarried sons of the agnatic line who lined up in front of the pot. Generally the families discouraged participation by unmarried girls. Or if they did (as I observed on a few occasions) join their brothers and male cousins, the young women behaved shyly and stood some distance from the *karakam*.

Young men were preferred, I was told, because unresolved friction might linger between adults and spirits that could inhibit the trance, whereas personal grudges were unlikely here since the deceased were especially fond of male descendants. The very sight of "their" young men was sure to attract the *pūvāṭaikkāri*. A second reason for this premium on young males had to do with the spirits' insistence upon purity. Undefiled by sexual intercourse or menstrual blood, their bodies were best suited for hosting these pollution-conscious tutelaries.

Yet the unfolding of the actual ritual contradicted these explanations. Out of twenty-six instances of these possessions that I personally observed, nineteen *were* actually fulfilled by women, ten of whom were married. Of the seven trances that were staged by men, five were instigated by supernaturals other than the household deity. Only twice was the optimal candidate, the groom, actually picked by the targeted *pūvāṭaikkāri*.

Women coopted the ritual. From beginning to end they arranged these marriages between the living and the dead. In the house they volunteered to "go and get" the bride. Then they graciously delivered "her" by carrying the "unmade" pot to the ritual site, where they produced the new "woman who wears flowers" before the family. Finally they handed "her" over to the groom by crowning him with the flowerpot.[4]

Throughout the proceedings women also ensured that the "bride" stayed under their control. In the house female mediums nominated a woman to carry the ceremonial basket, in the field they promoted each other as spokespersons for the *pūvāṭaikkāris*. I often witnessed how women, usually elders, such as paternal aunts, "danced" the old family deity or lineage tutelary simply to predict that the new *pūvāṭaikkāri* would soon descend on a younger woman, and they were almost always right. When young women were possessed by the *pūvāṭaikkāri* and unable to answer some genealogical question, they were often rescued by an older female relative who quickly entered into trance and provided a close male ancestor's name for her. A solidarity of women never seemed to allow the "bride" out of their grasp.

This strong degree of female participation can be disconcerting enough to a wedding party that did everything in its power to make sure that its young men took center stage. But the family is in for more surprises when it finally "meets" the dead parents. They prove to be extremely fussy, making all kinds of excessive demands and accusations, exhausting everyone. The family is in a state of shock, for these spirits are truly behaving much more like brides than parents. When I asked a musician why their verbal interactions with these spirits were so fraught and cranky he said:

> The *pūvāṭaikkāri* cry a lot because they died and left the house. They are like a girl. At her marriage her father will provide her with so many things but still she won't be satisfied. She'll keep asking for more. It is the same for the *pūvāṭaikkāri*. We may offer *vaṭai* (a food delicacy) and camphor everyday, but they are never happy. They'll keep asking for more.

The profound trauma that is shared by both new brides and the deceased is that of being forced into anonymity if not oblivion after exclusion from their natal household. So it seems fitting that it is predominately women who are chosen to voice the spirits' demands for individual commemoration and continued emotional involvement.

But the wedding party ignores these pleas for undying love and personal attention. Strongly uncompassionate, they urge the dead to identify themselves not as sensate individuals but only as figures in the family stream, as children of parents and parents of children. The spirits who speak through the mouths of their female mediums are just as stubborn and vigorously refuse to be reduced to filial roles and kinship identities. They remain intensely self-preoccupied and constantly assert that they are unrelated, different, and special.

This back and forth is not merely over whether the dead should enter as kin or affine. That has been decided: as suggested by the flower symbolism and ritual terminology, they are returning as brides. Instead, this conversation points to a larger argument over the ultimate meaning of marriage. For men it serves to reproduce the family, duplicate the parents in the children, and ensure generational succession. But women, reinforced by the dead, reply that marriage is to renew the family, differentiate generations, and ensure personal continuity. For men marriage must promote a comforting structural sameness and rigid kinship, for women it should create complementarity and affinity.

It is as if the women are striving to create a deeper awareness of family as a cluster of unique individuals with special needs beyond which any rigorous system of kinship roles alone can address. It is also as if they are struggling to articulate what they also try to, but cannot, communicate at *pēy* exorcisms. This is that marriage and intimacy are not to be taken for granted, which is why they now urge men to look after their wives and to properly arrange the marriage of daughters and sisters.

Women do not completely get away with their critique, however, for men attempt to interrupt, silence, or even "test" their spirits. And women will ultimately lose this struggle, as they and their spirits relapse into a generic identity and the relative anonymity of structural roles. But in this ritual context they must be momentarily heard because marriage and its key symbol, "the woman who wears flowers," are indispensable to biological fertility and family reproduction. Without marriage, without a bride, without the fact of difference, in other words, there can be no continuity, no filiation, no replication of the parent in the child. This is why this ritual identifies the household tutelary—protector of generational continuity—with a "woman who wears flowers" and why it construes "her" investiture as a family wedding. It is also why women actively participate: they ceremonially mediate between parents and children because that is what they do everyday. Moreover, their message of love and "family values" is essential to a healthy, fertile, and prosperous household. As Margaret Trawick has eloquently demonstrated, in Tamilnadu *aṉpu*, or "love," is the emotional foundation of marriage and family organization (1990a). If there is no love between husbands and wives, women identify with the wrong "guys" and go crazy. And as we will now see, without love between fathers and sons, the goal of this particular marriage (the *pūvāṭaikkāri pūjā*) cannot be achieved.

A Father's Rejection, a Son's Emancipation: The Case of Saravana

A Tamil (Untouchable) friend told me a long, funny story about a wedding party. En route to the marriage grounds it ran into so many problems that the ceremony never took place. First, a flooding river delayed the family, then a fish swallowed their cargo. A king's fisherman retrieved it but now the king invited his court to the marriage where his greedy minister ate the entire feast. The family cooked another batch of food but by then, tired of waiting, the bride's father called off the marriage. "What is the moral of the story?" my friend asked, and answered himself: "It is not until the marriage is over that it is over." He was confirming what we already know, Tamil rituals do not always go according to plan. But he was also stressing that marriage was an especially precarious transaction, and of all Tamil rituals, it is by far the most difficult to successfully conclude. Grooms are reluctant, brides are fastidious so that the risk of offense is ever present, and the recent inflation of dowry has only increased the probability of cancellation.

It is much the same for marriages of the dead. No matter how hard the musicians try to pacify everyone, something can always go wrong, for the emotions, frustrations, and revelations released by this ritual cannot remain in their hands. Nor can women entirely control or direct the proceedings, because the critical ingredient of this *pūjā*, what truly transforms a newly dead relative into a familial bride, is emotional involvement. "If the dead were not loved during their life time they won't come," I was told before. "It is love that makes them come back as god." With this key ingredient in mind, let us hear about the *pūvāṭaikkāri* ritual of a twenty-four-year-old *Paṟaiyaṉ* (Untouchable) man named Saravana.

When I met him in his native village of the South Arcot district, this well-groomed young man, dressed in modern attire, had just arrived by bus from Madras with his brother, his sister-in-law, and nephews. All had returned to the ancestral home, where their widowed mother still resided, to "invite" their deceased father to Saravana's forthcoming wedding.

> I never got along with our father. When he died seven years ago we were not even on speaking terms. I did not want to invite him. Why should I? He had no affection for me. This *pūjā* was my older brother's idea. His wife worried that if we didn't call our father people would talk. I don't care. I don't even believe in all that. It is village custom. This *pūjā* is important to my older brother, that is why we are here today.

The *pūjā* was "important" to Saravana's elder and only sibling, Mukan, because, as the first born son, he was expected to bring his father back home. And Saravana had accepted the role of surrogate groom for Mukan's "marriage" to their father because he owed him his current good fortune. Through shrewd maneuvering of the government's policy of granting educational and employment concessions to "backward castes," over the past twenty years Mukan had entered the middle class. He had resettled in the state capital, Madras, subsidized Saravana's education, devised his admission into the air force, and then arranged his marriage. Now in his early forties, Mukan held a prestigious government post, spoke English fluently, and had three healthy teenage sons.

Later that night the family was joined by the dead man's four younger siblings—three brothers and a married sister, together with their spouses and children. Though each resided in a separate household (and the sister in an entirely different lineage) and would not install this particular *pūvāṭaikkāri* in their own hearths, at one time they had belonged to an undivided family together with the dead. Out of this loyalty, affection, and respect they had convened for their older brother's return.

On the morning of the *pūjā* the entire family prepared to host the father: women put on their finest silk saris and jewels and braided the hair of little girls, while younger men made countless errands to the local store for last-minute essentials: camphor, flowers, more vermillion, and turmeric powders. But Saravana kept his distance and refused to take part, even abstaining from greeting the *Paraiyan* musicians who had bussed from Gingee town to serve as masters of ceremony.[5]

When the "notification" rite in the household yielded no spirit, the family was not surprised. It had been over forty years (during the marriage of Saravana's father) since they had sponsored such a *pūjā*. All agreed with Mukan that "it has been too long since we have invited our *pūvāṭaikkāri*," who until now had been personified by the two brothers' deceased paternal grandmother (their father's mother).[6] Without evident disappointment, Saravana's sister-in-law hoisted the basket containing the ceremonial pot onto her head, and the family proceeded to their millet fields about two kilometers away. Saravana not only brought up the rear, as he had to be, but he trailed way behind everybody else, walking reluctantly.

At a lovely and secluded grove, all welcomed the shade of a large banyan tree. The family's pleasure at visiting a familiar refuge was palpable, but Saravana stayed glum. He did not help in preparing the ceremonial pot nor in laying out the offerings, and seemed openly resentful about having to line up with his cousins before the decorated *karakam*. Since this son made no secret of his misgiving about the entire "invitation," and the two had not been on speaking terms, one could understand why the guest of honor was unwilling to heed the musicians' call. For at least two hours they played without success.

So the family directed the lead singer to appeal to their lineage goddess, Aracāttā. Words of praise were hardly out of his mouth than Saravana's body stiffened, he commenced to shake, and as if to release the tension he flung his arms over his head and yelled, "Kōvintā! Kōvintā!" confirming the arrival of an auspicious supernatural. All joined palms in prayerful postures of devotion and respect. To the question "Who are you?" Saravana immediately answered, "I am the lineage deity, Aracāttā." At this the family burst into a welcoming "Kōvintā! Kōvintā!"

But to the singer's next question, "Will the *pūvāṭaikkāri* come?" the goddess was mute. Abruptly Saravana fell to the dusty earth and began to crawl like a snake.[7] The young man who only the day before had flaunted his disbelief in "village stuff" was serving as both the human and animal vehicle of his lineage deity. Propelling himself along the ground in a sinuous motion by arms pressed to his sides, he inched towards two sacred margosa trees in the grove where his embodied goddess was said to reside. Stones were hastily cleared from his path, at regular intervals bowls of milk were placed, which he lapped up with a darting tongue. After encircling the two trees, he crawled back to the *karakam* pot where he stopped and fell into apparent unconsciousness.

The musicians resumed their invocations, but by five o'clock no *pūvāṭaikkāri* had showed up. Frustrated, they took a short break. When one of Saravana's uncles proposed again calling Aracāttā, the singer complained that the lineage goddess was not cooperative, "She just came as a snake without saying anything." Another uncle suggested that if they held the ritual at its customary location, on a flat next to the grove, the spirit might feel differently. This seemed promising, and the musicians moved their operations.

But as we have seen time and again, an unexpected supernatural visitor arrived on the scene. When the wife of one of Saravana's paternal cousins entered a trance and was given the usual identificatory drill, she claimed to be "Celliammā, the lineage deity." Everyone protested, Celliammā was not their goddess. "She belongs to the girl's natal house," someone shouted. But lacking any other link to the spiritual realm, the musicians asked whether she had any idea if the *pūvāṭaikkāri* would ever show. When Celliammā answered positively, one musician begged to know, "On whom will it come?" And when the goddess designated the wife of Saravana's elder brother, the lead singer warned, "You have five minutes to call the *pūvāṭaikkāri*. We have played for a long time, we are tired. Bring the spirit *now!*"

Everyone's attention immediately turned to Saravana's sister-in-law who, as if on command, began to stare at the *karakam* pot. After she and her spirit "danced" to the sound of the drums, the singer halted the music, asking: "WHO ARE YOU?"

The spirit's subsequent answers were typical. "What can I say?" he replied at first, "You did not put my mind at ease." As if offended on second thought, he lashed out, "You know who I am. I am Kuppaṉ! [Saravana's father]." At a trial question about his family, he got angry, "Don't you know I have three children? Why are you asking me?" and absolutely refused to give the name of his own father. But then he relented, so long as his grave was first cleaned and decorated. He accused his living relatives, one brother in particular, of neglecting him. "You are not really thinking about me. You don't pray or light camphor for me. Go away!" But the younger sibling tossed back, "If you had blessed me, I would have sponsored the *pūjā*," insinuating that a *pūvāṭaikkāri's* blessings were preferential.

The dead father did not hide his preference for his first son. Stepping before Saravana's elder brother (the possessed woman's husband), he cried, "You alone love me. Except for this boy, no one else cares for me." But the spirit never even acknowledged Saravana's presence, and the spirit's widowed wife, who had remained silent, began to sob audibly.

In the end the dead man accepted the invitation, saying, "My mother is with me too. I will bring everybody." And he even walked toward Saravana, apparently intending to crown him with the ceremonial pot. But at this crucial moment, Saravana was suddenly reentranced by the lineage goddess and glided on the ground like a snake away from his sister-in-law (and her embodied spirit), who was left waiting for him for a good twenty minutes, swaying from side to side with the heavy pot in her hands. When Saravana dragged himself back to the ritual scene, he was crowned with the *karakam* at last and his relatives set up a cheer.

The ritual did not seem to reconcile the father with his younger son; if anything it had revived the tensions between them. Three times the dead man rejected Saravana, by delaying his arrival, publicly stating that he was in no hurry to accept his son's invitation, and favoring his elder son. Right until the end the dead man's estrangement from Saravana remained in evidence, for it was not the spirit (or more exactly his host) that installed the pot on this groom's head but the musicians.

So understandably Saravana tried to avoid being burdened with his father's identity as symbolized by the ceremonial pot. At the moment he was to be crowned the young man for the second time spontaneously crawled away. In a similar ceremonial context my friend Leila also took on the body of a snake in order to express that she was "changing," that she was shedding off her past identity. Likewise I suspect that through his snake-trance Saravana was communicating his autonomy, his independence from his father. And since in Indian culture the snake also symbolizes immortality I wonder whether Saravana was not also boasting to his father: "You need me to be reborn in this world but I need no one, I'll live for ever, I'll always be myself."

But Saravana's snake trance was actually an established lineage tradition, and the last person reportedly to engage in one was, ironically enough, Saravana's father. On three separate ear-piercing rites his young son had personally witnessed the man writhing on the ground and drinking like a reptile. So the entranced Saravana seemed to be expressing a degree of filial piety that the "conscious" son would have disdained. But he had modified the ritual to maintain some distance, preferring to identify with his father's "liminal body" rather than his "head." Much as David Shulman argues in his analysis of the *Brāhmaṇa* narrative of Śunaḥśepa, "The father's rejection thus becomes, in effect, his truest gift to his son" (1993: 102). The dead man's snub freed his young son from the obligation to replicate him in his life and person. He might *be like* his father, but he did not have to *merge with* the man.

The power of these complex, interfamily psychodramas is due to the contribution of the possessed individuals whose personal investments are permitted considerable play. It is not enough to say that the dead prefer to possess people who can empathize with their existential dilemmas in the afterworld. They also possess those who resemble them emotionally and share their feelings. It was no wonder that the daughter-in-law was selected to express the father's rejection of his younger son, for she was also not on speaking terms with Saravana. In fact, she saw him as a spoiled young man who was unappreciative of all that her husband (the "good son") was still doing for him. She was also a natural to voice the dead man's approval of that senior son, for Mukan was her beloved husband.

Without the wholehearted efforts of the wedding party, no matter the emotional toll, sacramentalized unions between the living and the dead cannot reach closure. This is because without love and affection the groom cannot fuse with his parents into a single organism and identity. In this sense the ritual echoes the message of Padmini's seance in chapter 8: reunifications with dead kin and acquisitions of their identities are not matters of command and will. Such linkages, such personal expansions, are quintessentially subjective.

Yet these marriages with the dead do not exactly unfold to the wedding party's unanimous consent or delight. They turn out to be everything the participants find abhorrent or threatening: they are dangerously incestuous, even beyond the obvious mythic influence of Śakti's marriage with her own son. In coming back to life in the person of his son, a dead father turns his wife into his own mother.[8] The potential for improper unions only increases during the ritual, as he may "enter" his living mother, wife, sister, daughter, or daughter-in-law in order to be reborn.

Marriages with the dead are also divisive and especially can exacerbate relations between brothers. Furthermore, they are coercive, as bridegrooms are usually transformed into compliant initiates who are obediently "completed" and "sealed off" by their parents' "heads."

But the biggest problem that this marriage presents to the family is that it cannot last. Like "real" brides, "women who wear flowers" come and go. Whatever they accomplish is ephemeral: the reign of these particular parents as tutelary deity will only survive as long as their child lives, then they will be replaced by that dead son, who too one day will be replaced by his own deceased offspring, all of them absorbed into the generic anonymity of familial ancestorhood. The underlying revelation of this *pūjā* is that marriage establishes a personal continuity, which paradoxically is tenuous and impermanent, and decays as rapidly as the flowers that are its key symbol. This is poignantly voiced by both the dead and women who share a fear, with good reason, of the loneliness and oblivion that will ultimately follow their wedding into the family. Now let us see how males, however, manage to avoid that fate.

11

FROM FEAST TO SELF-SACRIFICE

By concentrating on religious experiences that concern individuals, couples, or families, this essay has remained within the confines of the particular, the private, and the domestic. This focus made me aware that the symbolism of marriage (and its counterpart divorce) threaded through much of Tamil religion. But as the preceding chapters suggest, marriage is generally employed for transforming a situation of disunion [usually: absence or death] into one of lasting or surviving intimacy between goddesses and male initiates, for example, or dead and living kin. For effecting "crossings" with gods and others who are already connected with one's self, Tamil religion offers another model: sacrifice.

In exploring the transformations that result from sacrifice, these final chapters will take us outside the ritual practices that are bounded by individuals and their households. This is because sacrifice is not a private endeavor but always a collective one. Accordingly, the remaining pages of this book expand into the realm of lineal worship, which might be seen as the next tier of religious activities, falling somewhere between rites of the domicile and married families and those of village temple worship. For in rural Tamilnadu a key ceremony for descent groups is their sacrificial offering to the lineage deity (*kulam tēvam*), in which all lineage members must have a "share" (*paṅku*).

Three Western Interpretations of Tamil Sacrifice

Although Western scholarship has neglected the ritual realm of exorcisms and investitures described in these pages, much has been made of "village sacrifices" and the non-Brahmanical deities who accept blood. Most explanations contrast sacrificial practices (*bali*) with nonsacrificial worship (*pūjā*). A consequence of this comparison is that sacrifice and non-Brahmanical deities are commonly characterized in the negative, a point-of-view that can be traced at least back to the writings of the Dutch Calvinist, Abraham Roger, who from 1632 until 1642, served as chaplain in Paliacat, north of Madras.[1]

Since his perspective remains influential, let me extract some key points in Roger's treatise on Tamil religion (1670).

His account details the Brahmanical beliefs and practices that he researched through a Vaisnava Brahmin informant named Padmanabha. Tucked within his text, however, is a firsthand account of a village festival honoring a popular goddess named "Ganga," which ends with an anthropologicallike interpretation of Tamil sacrifice.

Roger contrasts offerings that were presented to the high gods Śiva and Viṣṇu with those that were given to village deities such as Ganga. While no blood was shed before the male gods, he personally witnessed immolation of "sheep" and "buffalo" during Ganga's festival. Then he points out that this ritual polarity was also common to Greek religion, which Roger studied at the University of Leyden (Dharampal 1982: 208). And the Dutch priest proceeds to expose the Greek philosophers' explanations of this double standard in ritual practices.

It was Porphyrius, Plato, and Plutarque who first distinguished these major categories of worship. They extolled the first as beneficent, for it consisted of securing the assistance and blessings of benevolent gods by means of vegetarian offerings. But they branded sacrifice as malevolent, as it aimed to prevent the affliction of malignant forces by means of blood. "These [Tamil] heathen authors are of the same opinion," wrote Roger, "they worship some gods to obtain profit and advantage, but they adore this Ganga and her counterparts so that neither will cause harm" (1670: 253; trans. mine). After many examples of the prophylactic nature of Ganga prestations, Roger concludes, "In everything they undertake they are always worried that Ganga will afflict them with some misfortune or injury. . . . To this end they use any means to please her" (1670: 253–54; trans. mine). As in Greek religion, the Tamil solution for taming this dreaded supernatural was blood offering.

The good priest was aware that his interpretation rested on frames of meanings that were foreign to the people whom he observed. But Roger's dichotomy between orthodox Hinduism (a worship of benevolent/vegetarian gods) and popular village cults (a propitiation of frightening/bloodthirsty devils) still hangs on in ethnographic representations of South Indian religion. When compared to the "great" vegetarian deities, the "little" gods who accept sacrifices are portrayed as "malevolent," "fierce," and "angry" powers who require blood so that they will leave human beings alone. As Peter Claus has lamented, "Western writers . . . have concentrated solely on the negative and punitive aspects of these deities, despite the fact that the people themselves insist that these same deities protect the village" (1973: 231).

Recently, however, Christopher Fuller has revisited the relationship of *pūjā* and sacrifice that have long been part of Hindu studies (1987; 1992). Drawing on Henri Hubert's and Marcel Mauss's analysis of Vedic animal sacrifice (1964), and his own ethnographic research on vegetarian worship in the Madurai's Mīṉaṭshi temple, Fuller presents *pūjā* and *bali* as structures of communication with the supernatural world. For Fuller the best evidence that *pūjā* is " 'a positive' ritual . . . [that] serves to bring the deity and the worshipper close to each other" is found in the consumption of *prasāda*, the food that is returned to devotees after worship (1987: 23). As a consequence, Fuller sees those types of non-Brahmanical animal sacrifices where *prasāda* is produced as having "a positive aspect as well," as they bring "deity and worshippers closer together" (1987: 24). But where the flesh of sacrificial animals is not cooked, or transformed into meat that is consumed by human beings, *balis* become " 'negative' . . . rituals of propitiation, appeasement or exorcism, which serve to separate the worshipper from an angry deity or a malevolent demon" (ibid).

In a general way Fuller's distinction between "negative" and "positive" sacrifices conforms with my observations. At rituals that aim to dissociate people from unwanted supernaturals such as demon-*pēys*, the "life" does not become human food (although I was told that nonrespectable exorcists might consume the chicken). At ceremonies that express devotion to lineage or village tutelaries, however, sacrificial flesh is shared, cooked, and eaten. But the *pūvāṭaikkāri pūjā* presented in the last two chapters also expresses devotion. So if both the investiture of the family deity, a *pūjā*, and the sacrifice to a lineage or village deity, a *bali*, have "positive," or to use de Heusch's terminology, "conjunctive" power (1981: 213), one might still ask why they are practiced under different circumstances and moments on the ritual calendar. Or why does *bali*, as Fuller himself discerns, sometimes occurs "in conjunction" with *pūjā*? (1987: 23). And in the light of current campaigns to suppress ritual killing in India, why do sacrifices continue to be necessary, albeit with less frequency than in the past?

Not all current attempts to explore *bali* in relation to *pūjā* fall back on the thesis that sacrifice is a process of separation or communion between humans and gods. The French anthropologist Louis Dumont radically shifts the terms of this question when he explains the relationship between two Tamil deities whose icons are often found combined in village temples; Aiyanar, a vegetarian god, and Karuppan a meat-eater (l970). Since these dietary practices contrast Dumont's deterministic binaries of purity and impurity, which he maintains underlie caste hierarchy, he concludes that Aiyanar is "pure" and therefore "superior" to "impure" Karuppan (1970).

But any proposition that the Tamil pantheon "purely" and simply mirrors social representations, and caste distinctions in particular, renders negligible too many ethnographic facts and contextual imperatives (1970). To reduce the relationship between demon-*pēys* (who request "life") and household deities (who only accept vegetarian food) to an opposition between impurity and purity explains nothing about other fundamental differences between these spirits, about their respective associations, for example, with infertility and fertility, madness and reason, divorce and marriage, etc. Nor does Dumont's overarching explanation—we will soon see—shed light on the relationship between the vegetarian family deity and the meat-eating lineage god.

The stubborn, myopic tendency to define sacrifice only in relation to vegetarian cults also willfully ignores the wealth of religious meanings and ritual dynamics of Tamil sacrifice. Proponents of this perspective simply refuse to read the rich vocabulary of representations that are linked with and exhibited by actual performances involving sacrificial offerings. They do not account for the manner in which the animals are killed, nor for the energy released on the immolation. Since they are fixated on diet rather than ritual enactments they cannot appreciate Tamil sacrifice in its broader structural and psychological contexts.

Yet what is needed is precisely a broader comparative perspective. This was made clear to me when I recorded the system of worship (*kumpiṭal*) associated with the lineage god named Periyāṇṭavar (literally "the Great Lord"). The striking characteristic of this ceremonial complex is that it is structurally identical to the "invitation to the marriage" and is also glossed as an "invitation," albeit to a "feast" (*viruntu alaittal*), for it climaxes with a sacrifice. Since the "invitation to the marriage" is itself structurally opposed to the ritual that "makes the demon run away," the system of sacrificial worship linked to Periyāṇṭavar is also structurally connected to the Tamil exorcism. In fact, it stands in binary opposition to both the investiture of the family deity and the exorcism of the demon-*pēy*. From beginning to end it exploits the same core structure and the same tripartite sequence of actions, albeit for contradictory purposes. This last ceremonial complex studied in this book thus presents us with the opportunity to analyze sacrifice in a more congenial frame of reference than the old juxtapositions of *bali* and *pūjā*. And when we compare the "feast" to these rituals, focusing on its relationship with exorcism and investiture, we must discard the notion that Tamil sacrifice is a "prophylactic," "negative/positive," or "inferior" form of worship. Let me briefly characterize these lineage cults.

Lineage Worship in South Arcot

The supernaturals who assure a descent group's health and fertility are different from household deities in that they tend to be members of the local pantheon with fixed personalities and individual myths of origin (Reiniche 1979; Beck 1972; Moffat 1979; Dumont 1986). One man summarized the distinction when he said that whereas a family tutelary was *āvi*, or "spirit," the lineage deity was *āti*. Literally this means "origin," and in this case signifies, said my friend, that a lineage deity "has been a god since the beginning."[2]

Unlike the family deity who is personified every one or two generations by a different spirit, the lineage deity never changes of identity but is maintained and kept potent through successive generations of patrilineal kinsmen. He or she is not some elusive, ephemeral other, like the "woman who wears flowers," but an older, and more familiar acquaintance, a "regular guest in our households," the same man added. Furthermore, the relationship of the *tēvam* ("deity") and its *kulam* ("lineage") is territorially based.[3] Gods and devotees reside in the same site, having adopted each other, in some cases, many centuries ago. But the deep importance of these common regional roots becomes clear whenever lineage members migrate; the immigrants refuse to worship their lineage deity anywhere but their native village. Once a year they board buses or ride bullock carts back home to honor these tutelaries (Diehl 1956; Kjaerholm 1990; Burkhart 1987).

A lineage deity is worshipped by kinsmen who trace lineal descent to a common male ancestor and identify themselves as *vahairā*, which Louis Dumont translates as "and those of the same kind" (1986: 184). For the most part this group is not as genealogically deep as their own representations would suggest. Usually it consists of those kinfolk who trace common descent through the male line up to the third or fourth generation, including their wives and unmarried daughters. Nor is this group very corporate. Most lineage members reside in separate households, do not eat food cooked in the same hearth, and do not hold property in common. In fact, their "partnership" is pretty much limited to the ear-piercing ceremony for children, a rite of passage that in Tamilnadu is conceived as a "thanksgiving" (*nanṟi collutal*) for the lineage deity's "gift" (*koṭai*) of children and lines of descent.[4]

Another contrast between family and lineage tutelaries concerns their differential involvement with village ceremonialism. A member of the Tamil pantheon whose biography and exploits are rooted in a specific landscape, the supernatural who protects the descent group is often a village deity as well. So if lineal members do not collectively have their own shrine, which is usually the case in South Arcot, they will time their private celebrations to coincide with communal festivals at the village temple.

What is unusual about the lineage god Periyāṇṭavar introduced in this chapter is that he has no permanent shrine or icon (this also holds for his female counterpart, Periyāyi). Born for but one cosmic mission he is only a minor figure in the Tamil pantheon. He plays no role in communal religion, and only takes center stage during the ear-piercing rite for first-born children, which is celebrated at intervals of several years on a fixed date, usually in the month of *Āṭi* (July/August) when the early southwest monsoon brings light summer rains, ending the hot season and announcing a new agricultural year.[5]

Serving as masters of ceremony for the festivities intended to "thank" Periyāṇṭavar for the birth of children are the same musicians who officiate at exorcisms and investitures. But here their operations are more elaborate and costly.[6] For one thing Periyāṇṭavar is not reincorporated into a mere flowerpot; he requires a massive, twenty-five-foot anthropomorphic effigy that the musicians usually fashion of mud on agricultural fields owned by a lineage elder. And to please Periyāṇṭavar calls for expensive offerings: a hundred and eight banana leaves piled with various vegetarian delicacies, the same number of helpings of sweetened rice, and three sacrifices of a rooster, a goat, and a boar, of which the pig most completely expresses the lineage's "gratitude" to its deity.

The Invitation to the Feast

We have seen how both exorcisms and household investitures open with a preamble intended to "warn" demons and family deities of the coming transactions. Similarly, here, the musicians "alert" Periyāṇṭavar of his coming "feast," but first they must obtain divine protection (*kāppu*). This also occurs at exorcisms and investitures, when the great deities are invoked to "make sure," as one musician put it, "that nothing wrong happens." But rituals involving sacrifice are said to release tremendous, potentially dangerous energy and call for extra safeguards.

One additional piece of protection is an amulet, colloquially known as *kāppu*, which is tied around the right wrists of ritual officiants (Hiltebeitel 1991: 79–116; Meyer 1986: 107–9; 234–235; Beck 1981: 110–11). For Periyāṇṭavar worship, the amulets are obtained from the sacrificer's family deity (the *pūvāṭaikkāri*) who, anyway, has to be consulted before any family centered ceremonial transaction. So the evening before the actual "feast" the musicians request this *kāppu* in the sacrificer's house. Usually the "woman who wears flowers" responds immediately to the musicians' calls, authorizing the procedures through "her" medium's voice, often a woman. With the amulet around the sacrificer's wrist, the god Periyāṇṭavar can be formally "alerted" about what is to come.[7]

Whereas we have grown accustomed to witnessing these sorts of ritual "warning" around mid-morning and in an indoor sanctuary (be it communal, such as a goddess temple, or private, a family's "middle-house"), the lineage god Periyāṇṭavar is "notified" just before dawn and outdoors, on the privately owned agricultural fields of lineage members where its mud effigy will be built, for he enjoys no permanent shrine.

Usually a truckload of wet clay has already been dumped on the ground. After testing its consistency, under flickering oil lamps the musicians, together with the sacrificer and his close male kin, shape four earthen cones about fifteen inches high. Starting at the northeast, they position them at the four corners of the heap of mud, then link them with a white, cotton thread. This "arrests" (*kaṭṭu*) the god and functions much like those space-enclosing perimeters (*cakkaram*) that prevent demons from escaping.

Since the notification takes place right here, and Periyāṇṭavar is now "tied down," the god is not requested to "meet" somewhere else. After waving camphor above the enclosure, the musicians break the predawn stillness by singing:

> Please come down and be seated here!
> We will be coming back today to worship you.

> Today we are holding a feast in your honor.
> Please wait for us here!

They do not press the god to reply or commit himself to "coming back." This is not a tense, insecure proceeding; they make their invitation and return home to rest for the busy day ahead. Their calm demeanor suggests that they enjoy a certain rapport with this deity, as if they are confident of his susceptibility to human aspirations.

Not until mid-morning does the god signal his acceptance of the "invitation," by allowing the consecration of the central offering. If for some reason Periyāṇṭavar does not wish to attend, it is said the pig will not cooperate; and if it frantically runs around, "something will go wrong with the worship." In that case it is prudent to reschedule.

Blessing the animal usually takes place in the sacrificer's rear courtyard, where he smears turmeric paste over its body. As Brenda Beck noted in her study of South Indian color symbolism, turmeric is strongly associated with "cooling" away pollution and "is often placed on animals before they are sacrificed and on new clothes before they are presented as gifts" (1969: 559). On the animal's head and flanks the sacrificer daubs huge dots of bright vermillion powder. "Red," Beck tells us, "is the colour of vitality because of its association with blood. It is appropriate where something important and life-giving is about to occur" (1969: 554). It seems particularly "appropriate" here since the coming sacrifice is premised on the idea that life, in this case that of children, is "thanked" for with death. The sacrificer finally garlands the swine with jasmine flowers, a common offering to gods or deified ritual protagonists such as grooms, brides, and corpses. Worthy of sacrifice at last, a camphor flame is waved over its snout.

With the pig's compliant behavior signaling the god's acceptance, lineage members defile to the spot where earlier in the day Periyāṇṭavar was told to "wait." The procession is quite ceremonialized. First strides the sacrificer who parades his offering trotting beside him on its leash. There is no doubt that he, or more exactly his pig, occupy what Oliver Herrenschmidt calls the "place of honor" (1982: 45–49; in Hiltebeitel 1991: 449). Then come what Herrenschmidt calls the "carriers of symbols," women with ceremonial baskets on their heads containing the raw, vegetarian offerings of their respective households (ibid). In contrast to their fast-moving, somber single file, the remainder of their lineage, which may include up to 200 or 250 people, stroll and converse at a leisurely pace in small groups.

It usually takes virtually all morning for the musicians to mold the mud into a four-armed figure. Lying on its back, the effigy measures approximately twenty-five feet from head to toe. Without discernible gender or sexual attributes, its feet are splayed apart, two right forearms are raised above the elbow, two left ones rest along the torso. As the musicians smooth its surface, they cover its large eye-sockets with half-eggshells so the effigy seems to be staring through goggles. Drooping down its chin, a clay tongue is smeared with bright vermillion. In the figure's two right hands they model two musical instruments, the hour-glass drum and brass rattle. In the two left hands are two emblems of the goddess, the trident and the sword. The figure is finished with a bright yellow cloth extending from its knees to its shoulders.

Save for its size the effigy is reminiscent of sorcery dolls. But its context is unmistakably that of one who invites worship, for the body is circumscribed by a familiar sanctuary. Enclosing the reclining deity is a superstructure of one hundred and eight mud cones, which replicate the basic architectural plan of a South Indian temple and its ramparts. Approximately ten inches high and linked by a white cotton thread that droops from cone to cone, they represent guardian-deities, called *kāval* ("watchman") or *piḷḷaiyār* ("children") (Fuller 1984: 2).

Interrupting the thread barrier are four gateways (*vācal*) that lead into the sanctum where the god stretches out. Flanking them are taller cones, presumably imitating towers (*kōpuram*), which, as Fuller noted for the great Mīṉāṭshi temple in Madurai, "straddle the gateways in the outer walls and are visible for miles across the plains surrounding the city" (1984: 2). To the west, at the effigy's feet, is the main entrance. A participant faces the head upon entering and notices nearby a two-foot-high mud cone wrapped in a turmeric-dyed towel, which a Tamil man explained to me represents "a sort of power control." This is also consistent with temple iconography, where enshrined deities are positioned before opposite forces, often animals, known as *etiruṭaiyāṉ* ("the one who stands on the opposite side"), which can dampen or modulate their excessive energies.[8]

Within the sanctuary, the musicians place three additional large cones at the northeast corner: the *trimūrti*, or three gods, of Brahmā, Viṣṇu, and Śiva. They also sculpt a tortoise, symbol of the goddess, as well as a Śivaliṅkam that represents Lord Śiva's erect penis—all subsidiary images that are indispensable features within most South Indian temples.

To regale this Periyāṇṭavar requires an intricate spread of offerings. Before each of the 108 cones and along the contours of his body are always placed two large plantain leaves. The first contains generous heapings of hot, sweetened *poṅkal* rice that women, crouched under nearby trees, have "boiled" on open hearths. The second holds the customary array for a temple deity: split coconut, flowers, incense, betel leaf, araca nut, banana, as well as a small lamp made of flour dough, puffed rice, peanuts, and raw rice mixed with brown sugar. As a final touch, the musicians scatter the entire ritual grounds with big lumps of shiny camphor, which they will light during the actual sacrifice.

With his sanctuary ready, Periyāṇṭavar's divine essence (*mūrtiharam*) is transferred to the earthen body through an "eye opening rite" (*kaṇ tiṟappu*). Beyond a cloth screen a musician paints with black charcoal the pupils of the god's bulging eyes.[9] When a camphor flame is waved before his face, the crowd cheers "Kōvintā! Kōvintā!" the cry that always greets the reincorporation of gods in human bodies. Now that the god can "see" his devotees he is expected to talk to them in the same personal, possessed manner that we have heard demons and household deities speak.

Both boys and girls are elected to serve as mediums, and to maximize their chances of being "entered" by Periyāṇṭavar, they line up before the main access to his rudimentary "temple." After applying sacred ash to their foreheads, the musicians urge the children to stare at the god. Everyone else crowds around the temple "ramparts" to watch.

But before invoking Periyāṇṭavar, the musicians first secure the "protection" of the great Hindu gods, then call on the village deity (*kirāmatēvatai*). This protocol reminds everyone that the lineage is incorporated within a larger territorial entity to which it owes civic and religious loyalty. Almost immediately the village deity "comes on" the lineage headman (*talevar*), an elderly man who usually serves as medium on such occasions, which is not surprising for both roles are responsible for the community's welfare. Their common duties are suggested by the ensuing dialogue, as the lead singer asks the god, (who is intimately associated with rain and agricultural fertility) "Will the rain come?" "Yes, it will rain within the next five days," the deity may answer. Satisfied, the singer then orders, "Go and get the *pūvāṭaikkāri*."

When the *pūvāṭaikkāri* comes on a child, usually a girl, there is no attempt to identify it, because in this context "the woman who wears flowers" represents not a particular deceased member of any single household but the combined dead of the entire lineage who belong to a common pool of ancestors. But the impatient descent group shows little interest, urging the *pūvāṭaikkāri* to "bring back our lineage god, Periyāṇṭavar."

Periyāṇṭavar's prompt and positive response to the musicians' calls is one of the most outstanding aspects of these "invitations." He readily divulges his name, whereupon the lineage shouts its approval, "Kōvintā! Kōvintā!" and no one demands corroboration.

"The lineage deity is under the obligation to protect us," one woman told me. "It is like our slave [*aṭimai*, also meaning "devotee"]. It ought to respond to our call and stand beside us at all times." Since it is the reason for Periyāṇṭavar's very existence to guard his constituency, his devotees do not hold back when he fails at his duties. At one ritual, a man accused his Periyāṇṭavar, "I am so poor, why aren't protecting me?" to which the god replied, "What can I say, you never listened to my advice! I told you to go back to your village. There you'll be all right"—a reminder that lineage deities always advise people to return to their roots.

Such an easygoing discourse, in which one can negotiate the terms of divine protection, hardly matches the descriptions of meat-eating gods. Periyāṇṭavar is considerably less ferocious than the "woman who wears flowers," a strict vegetarian deity, who places stern conditions on "her" protection and never hesitates to threaten "her" constituency when "she" fails to get her way. "The lineage deity," on the other hand, as a musician once told me, "is not greedy, we give as best as we can, and it is enough." And while a family deity may move relatives to cry, argue, and fight, Periyāṇṭavar evokes a casual, almost absentminded stance among his devotees, and neither his possessed arrival nor his transmitted words appear to arouse any great emotion.

There are some issues that can drive Periyāṇṭavar to get stiff with his devotees. These involve any threats of lineage fragmentation, interfamily conflict, or disunity of their constituency. This seems pure self-interest, for without pooling the entire lineage's resources, individual householders cannot afford the homage to him described in this chapter. This was why Periyāṇṭavar warned members of one descent group, "If you don't settle your differences and collectively worship me every year, I'll make you all sit in the house [meaning: "I'll make you sick"]." But the lead singer threw the challenge back to the god, "You have to make them cooperate. You must bring them together. They may have different feelings among themselves, but you have to lead them." Even Periyāṇṭavar's threats were seized as opportunities to admonish him; the god seemed more vulnerable to devotees' criticisms than they to his.

We can guess what is to come. For we have seen how after such self-identifications, the musicians press possessing supernaturals to pledge their endorsement of the ritual. As Periyāṇṭavar is formally petitioned to accept his "feast," the singer inquires: "Are you pleased with the *pūjā* [or vegetarian offerings]?" "Will you protect their children?" Without a fuss the god embraces their sacrifice.

Although he is not forced to swear, the lineage god is expected to ratify his positive answer by means of some bodily demonstration. While musicians light the hundreds of camphor lumps, the sacrificer purifies his animals (chicken, goat, and pig) with turmeric water. This is the god's response, or "test" (*pariṭcai*), for if the victims produce a visible shiver when the water hits them, the sacrifice has been accepted (also see Fuller 1992: 84). But since Periyāṇṭavar has plainly agreed, little attention is actually paid to this sign-communication, and it is always interpreted as positive.

Tied up by their feet, the animals are placed close to the prostrate god and in his line of sight. Their sacrifice constitutes the ritual climax and an expectant mood takes hold. Encircled by an advice-giving cluster of elder, male relatives, the sacrificer waves a camphor flame before the animals and in a fast movement he bites into the chicken's neck, tearing off its head. Seizing a sword (*aṟuvāḷ*), with one strong stroke he severs the goat's head. To kill the pig he grabs a long spear (*vēl*). As the squealing animal is held by other men he pierces its throat.

Suddenly his own body stiffens, his eyes widen and he stares straight ahead. Thrusting his arms toward the sky, for a second it is as if he too had been impaled. As he leaps into a run he is quickly pinned down by his companions.

Regaining consciousness a minute later, he sprinkles the mixed animal blood into a clay pot containing cooked rice. Then he paces around the sanctuary, throwing balls of bloody rice (*rattam cōṟu*) to appease any demons (*pūtam*) who might be attracted by the scent. Breaking into another trance he again begins to run but is restrained and slumps into unconsciousness. By then the scattered camphors have flickered out, the effigy is divested of the god's life-force, the worship is over.

Our exorcism concluded when the musicians expelled the demon-lover and returned his married victim to her husband. The "marriage invitation" ended with the incorporation of not just one but two "women who wear flowers" into the household: a dead one and a live one. This worship associated with Periyāṇṭavar closes with the ceremonial incorporation of children into the lineage.

The formal trek home from the "temple" grounds is accompanied by drumming; on their shoulders the sacrificer and his male relatives carry wooden poles from which the three dead animals hang upside down. Later all vegetarian offerings (coconuts, ceremonial rice, peanuts, etc.) and each butchered animal are divided into equal portions among the different "branches" of the lineage in order of seniority. The heads are the sacrificer's "share." Since neither the meat is cooked nor eaten that day, this distribution concludes the second day's activities.

But on the ceremony's third and final day its symbols reach some sort of final clarifying expression. Around the middle of that morning, all eligible children of the lineage undergo their ear-piercing ceremony (*kātukuttal*). First a barber of a nearby village tonsures the children. Then a local goldsmith perforates (*kuttu*) their ear lobes (the right ear for a boy, both for a girl). The puncture is reminiscent of the manner in which the pig was sacrificed and likewise dedicates the children to Periyāṇṭavar. In the case of first-born boys and girls, this consecration actually began at birth, for they are commonly named after the lineage deity himself (also see Dumont 1986: 262). It also demonstrates an ultimate sort of reciprocity: in exchange for his enabling the successful bearing of their children, the lineage now symbolically offers the god these same offsprings. To express their total gratitude the ceremony concludes by feasting the god with the sacrificial meats. Now members of the lineage have properly "thanked" Periyāṇṭavar for his "gift" of life.

Tamil Sacrifice in a Positional-Contextual Frame

The "invitation to the feast" belongs to the paradigmatic ritual pattern that includes the exorcism and investiture of family tutelaries. Although it adds a sequence, the initial procuration of the family deity's "protection," it follows the same process: a "warning," a god's acquiescence, an incorporation into an icon and human bodies, a self-identification, and an affirmation of the ritual objectives. But here its symbolism and values diverge from the other two rituals. Rather than being asked to "leave the girl" or "come to the marriage," a supernatural is asked to accept a "feast." Sacrifice remains the characteristic means by which devotees transact with Periyāṇṭavar.

Yet the same preoccupation with the head, particularly loss of head, also resurfaces at this "top-end" of the intimate, family-oriented spiritual operations that we have previously explored. All three rituals climax with symbolic or literal enactments of decapitation and recapitation. In the case of our "feast" the head of a chicken is "bitten off," a goat is beheaded, a pig is "pierced" just below the head. And these dramatic actions occasion the same transformation of mood and peculiar form of trance. I say "peculiar," for the behavior seems qualitatively different from that induced by the musicians' drumming. Participants do not dance or utter a word, and nobody expects them to serve as mediums between cosmic orders. My suspicion is that they are in fact not "possessed" by a known supernatural, for they fail to exhibit the characteristic traits of demons or deities. Rather than an impersonation of a specific divine, their behavior better fits Rouget's definition of "communial trance," which emphasizes a more amorphous "encounter" and "a revelation, or an illumination" (1985: 26).

In the case of sacrifice, the trance appears to move through two kinetic phases. First is an immediate, jolting body spasm and then a rigid paralysis, which seems to dramatize the sacrificer's own death. Next, comes the frantic urge to leap up and run, the diagnostic reflex for what one might call a "sacrificial trance."[10]

Even the demon-*pēy*'s behavior suggests this double-reaction process, when he bolts into a blind run after the chicken sacrifice that anticipated his own symbolic decapitation. The difference is that the *pēy* is being forced to run; the whole purpose of the exorcism is to "make him run" until he falls from exhaustion. The sacrificer's mad dash is restrained by supportive comrades who are posted to grab him and help him recover his senses.

This ceremonial flight is known in Tamil as *marul̠ oṭutal*, meaning "running in a state of confusion or frenzy." The *pēy* is bewildered because he has forfeited his own head and any consciousness of self. He runs much like the proverbial chicken with its head cut off, out of a last desperate surge of physical energy. I suspect that at the "feast" the sacrificer takes off for the same reason. He has just surrendered his identity, enacted his own symbolic decapitation (as evidenced by his initial reaction to his treatment of the three animals), and is in such a state of complete confusion that the musicians told me that he was in danger of becoming mad or dying.

This final sequence has nothing to do with propitiation of a "fearsome" or "inferior" god. It has everything to do with a transformed identity, or more accurately, with a loss of identity. All three rituals, then, effect deep "inner" changes, dispossessing participants of their former sense of self. The exorcism beheads and expels a foreign personality who is responsible for the madness and infertility of a married woman—a process that suppresses her own subjectivity. The investiture of a household deity "seals" the groom with his parents head—the act that takes away his own individuality. sacrifice enacts a total, albeit momentary, self-negation whose motivations, meanings, and consequences will be explored in the final chapter.

Lay these rituals and their patternings side by side and we begin to discern that Tamil religion is a religion of repetition and inflection, of variations on a common, underlying theme: Whether preoccupied with individuals, household, or corporate groups, the work of these Tamil ritual symbols almost always aims to transform "inner" selves and create more socially appropriate persons, usually by means of all the force and commitment that ritual participation can summon forth.

12

BEYOND PROCESS AND SEPARATION

Of all the rituals explored in this book, the sacrificial complex of the last chapter is the most violent. It climaxes not with a "funeral" of past relationships, not with a "beheading" of a demonic personality, not with a "stamping" of parental identity on a son's head, but with a bloody impalement. As we have just seen, such transpiercing is no symbolic enactment, the pig is no mere surrogate victim. The sacrifice is carried through, in all its brutality, upon the sacrificer who dies, if only for a few minutes. What is the rationale for such violent deed?

Anthropological Explanations of Sacrifice

Very different answers have been given to the question of what motivates human beings to sacrifice an "offering" to a deity (see surveys by de Heusch 1985; Valeri 1985). One was developed a century ago by Henri Hubert and Marcel Mauss when they analyzed ancient Vedic and Hebrew rituals of sacrifice (1964). We are already familiar with their main premise, for Christopher Fuller's analysis of Tamil sacrifice reviewed in the last chapter built from it (1987; 1992). But Hubert and Mauss did not limit sacrifice to a matter of entering into, or terminating, contact with the divine; they discerned other forms of communication as well.

Based on ancient Sanskrit texts, Hubert and Mauss's study was nonetheless context sensitive. They noted, for example, that Vedic animal sacrifices "released an ambiguous force—or rather a blind one" (1964: 34). Such observations led them to reject Edward Tylor's gift theory (1871) according to which a sacrifice was a business transaction of *do ut des* ("I give so that you will give in return") without subjective investments on the part of givers. To Hubert and Mauss, on the contrary, sacrifice was neither a rational or mechanistic affair but a deeply transformative experience, it "modifies the condition of the moral person who accomplishes it" (1964: 13). This was because the sacrificer came to recognize the presence of collective forces represented by the "sacred" (Evans-Pritchard 1965: 70).

In René Girard's more recent formulation sacrifice has very different functions (1972). Girard builds his argument around his conception of human relationships. In brief, he contends that human beings always compete for the same things and resort to force and violence in order to get what others possess. To him sacrifice is a safe outlet for pent-up rivalry and aggression that are redirected at a scapegoat victim, generally an outsider. Such focused violence is cathartic, saving society from the war against all and from total collapse (also see Burkert 1972).

But for Maurice Bloch (1992) sacrifice does not end violence: if anything it starts it. This must be understood in the light of his general theory of ritual (1992). In almost all societies ritual denies the transience of life and of human institutions through a two-stage process. In the first phase participants are the "prey" of violent power—ranging from bodily mutilations to symbolic "killing"—and are forcibly driven out of society into a "world beyond process," a space of transcendent power that is external to social and political relations. The second stage begins when ritual participants somehow acquire (often by acts of consumption) this power. It ends when they reenter society as "changed persons," as aggressive consumers of their new vitality. In Bloch's view, then, sacrifice does not function to recall to individual consciences social forces or to reharmonize society but to conquer life that is not subject to natural processes of growth and decay.

In his recent work, however, Bruce Kapferer argues that sacrifice is concerned with creating representations of life that affirm rather than negate everyday understandings (1997). The sacrifice performed during the Sinhalese Suniyama exposes the ways in which human beings constitute their daily, existential realities. Much like sorcery—whose dynamics of creation and destruction make it possible for people to maintain or radically change the circumstances of their lives—sacrifice is creative power. Its basis in cosmogonic and ontogenetic dynamics actually makes it "*the* total act which condenses . . . the generative processes constitutive of human beings and their life worlds" (Kapferer 1997: 187; emphasis his).

All these perspectives are of interest because they explore the relation of sacrifice to social processes in general terms. But how do the arguments that sacrifice serves to connect individuals to society, purge innate aggressiveness in humans, secure permanent vitality, and remake personal situations explain our Tamil "feast?"

The Story of Takkaṉ's Vow for a Daughter

To begin delving more deeply into the meanings of this sacrificial ritual, let me present its chartering myth. I am referring to a tale that is well-known throughout India. It begins with the desire of King Takkaṉ ("Dakṣa" in Sanskrit) to father Śiva's wife and climaxes with his failure to invite the god to his sacrifice. The version that I recorded is a folk variant of the Kantapurāṇam, held by David Shulman as "the main Tamil version of the (Dakṣa) myth" (1980: 338; for other Tamil folk variants see Meyer 1986: 231–34; 238; Beck 1981: 107).[1] Shulman translated and interpreted this text (1980: 337–46). Here I do not offer an alternative reading, but at the risk of oversimplifying Shulman's argument I will suggest how his analysis brings out homologies between the world of mythic actors and the ordinary lives of some of the ritual protagonists I met.

My narrator was an old man, belonging to the *Kavuṇṭar* caste, who in his prime was director of a *terukkūttu* ("street drama") troupe. On many occasions he had staged the story of Takkaṉ's sacrifice and kindly agreed to recount his version. I recorded him on a boulder-strewn hillside while the effigy of his lineage god, Periyāṇṭavar, was being constructed. His words drew a large audience of elder people and children, and produced an impromptu, subsidiary performance in the unfolding ceremony.

Before telling his story this man lit a camphor and joined hands in the *namaskāram* gesture, thereby placing his narration under the "protection" (*kāppu*) of the gods.

> Takkaṉ was the greatest man on earth. He wanted to obtain a boon [*varam*] from Śiva. He wanted Pārvatī [Śiva's wife] to be reborn as his daughter so that he could marry her to Śiva. He began a penance [*tavam*] and Śiva granted his wish. The goddess was reborn and brought up as the king's daughter.
>
> One day after she reached puberty she was picking flowers in the garden. Śiva saw her and said to himself, "Pārvatī is my wife so I must take her back home. I have the right to do so, why should I bother asking Takkaṉ?"
>
> When Takkaṉ learned that Śiva had eloped with his daughter he grumbled, "This beggar [*iravalar*] has taken my daughter without my permission!" For years he refused to visit the couple. Finally, persuaded by the gods who argued that it was no dishonor to have a daughter abducted by Śiva, the king agreed to see the couple in their abode on Kailasa.
>
> When he drew near neither Śiva nor Pārvatī made a move to welcome him. They continued to dispense alms as if he was not there. An angry Takkaṉ left Kailasa, ranting, "Not only has this beggar eloped with my daughter, but now he is insulting me and she is rude to me as well." On his way back he stopped on the banks of the Vaikai River and began this *pūjā*.

[At this point the narrator pointed out the similar ceremonial preparations that were then taking place right in front of us].

> Takkaṉ sent an invitation to Pārvatī that said: "On the bank of the Vaikai River I am going to hold a *yākam* [sacrificial fire], please come!" As soon as

she read the scroll, Pārvatī asked for Śiva's permission to attend her father's *pūjā*. Śiva said: "I don't see what good could possibly come of your going. When your father came to visit us we did not welcome him. You should not go." But she kept begging and Śiva gave in, warning her that she would suffer the consequences.

When Pārvatī arrived at the site of Takkaṉ's *pūjā*, she found out that thirty thousand crores of gods, sages, and angels were also present.

[Here, again, my narrator pointed to the 108 clay cones (*piḷḷaiyār*) that surrounded the effigy, saying, "You see these cones, they stand for the assembly (*kūṭṭam)* of these beings. There ought to be 1,008 cones but there is no time to build that many."]

Takkaṉ welcomed his daughter with a slap on her cheek and scolded her, "You took a beggar for husband and you don't even respect me anymore. What are you doing here?" He slapped her again and Pārvatī fell unconscious on the ground.

[My attention was distracted by a child motioning frantically at me. One of our listeners, a woman, had thrown her arms straight ahead, fists clenched, eyes wide-open, seemingly in pain. The child giggled and whispered to me, "Cāmi!" (literally "God," but here more, "unspecified spiritual power"). Our narrator ignored this intense reaction to his dramatic tale and continued.]

From Mount Kailasa, Śiva could see Takkaṉ abusing his wife. The god assumed the disguise [*vēṣam*] of a buffoon [*kōtāṅki*] and quickly reached the scene. In the river he drowned the four guards that Takkaṉ had posted around his sacrifice [*yākam*] and took Pārvatī back to Kailasa. Since the king had already received the gift of invulnerability against Śiva, the god entrusted Ganesh [his first son] to cut off Takkaṉ's head and destroy his sacrifice. Alerted, Takkaṉ used his magic power [*vaciyam*] to create a spread of Ganesh's favorite sweets [*koḻukkaṭṭai*]. The trick worked and on the way Ganesh stopped to eat the sweets. Śiva then charged Murukaṉ [his second son] with destroying the *yākam*. Again Takkaṉ used his magical power and created two beautiful dancers who distracted Murukaṉ from his mission.

When Śiva realized that his sons had failed him he became so angry that he broke into perspiration. From the sweat on his forehead he created Vīrappattiraṉ (also known as Vīrabhadra) with a thousand heads and two thousand hands. "Father! why did you call me?" Vīrappattiraṉ immediately asked. In response, Śiva ordered him to destroy the sacrifice and behead the arrogant king.

Vīrappattiraṉ did as told. He also killed this *cāmi*, [my narrator now pointed toward the effigy that was then in the making] the demon (*pēy*) that came out of the sacrifice to assist Takkaṉ. If not stopped he would have killed the god.

Vīrappattiraṉ brought the king's head back to Śiva and the god was satisfied with his mission. But Pārvatī was upset and lamented the death of

> her father. She threatened Śiva that if he did not bring Takkaṉ back to life she would leave him. After giving thought to her warning, Śiva gave his wife a rattan reed [*pirampu*] and some water. "With this stick sprinkle the water on your father," he told her. She followed his instructions and Takkaṉ came back to life and Śiva sent him to heaven.

Let us examine this narrative more closely. It opens with the king's desire to father Pārvatī. As my narrator made clear, Takkaṉ intended to return the goddess by making her Śiva's bride. But the nuptial transaction that he sought rested on a ludicrous claim. As David Shulman points out, "[Takkaṉ] fails to see the absurdity of giving Śiva something that is already Śiva's" (1980: 342). Indeed, in our version the god did not feel he had to request the king's permission to reclaim his own wife. "Why shall I bother asking Takkaṉ," he asked himself.

The problem arose when Takkaṉ took offense. And as the divine couple resumed their lives in their heavenly abode ("as if he was not there"), the king felt additionally snubbed. Clearly, Takkaṉ was not subscribing to the Hindu marriage sacrament, which, according to Ralph Nicholas, stipulates that "the father or other male masters of the bride [*kanya*] should make a selfless 'gift of the bride' [*kanya dan*] to the groom with no expectation of return" (1995: 141). In fact, this father even attempted to retaliate against the groom, by organizing a sacrifice to which he invited all cosmic beings save for the god. The insult was flagrant, for in Hinduism Śiva rules as "the indispensable lord of the sacrifice" (Shulman 1980: 341).

To my narrator, Takkaṉ's transgression connoted the perversion of royal power and the dark side of sacrifice. He compared the king to a "sorcerer," and his *yākam* to "an act of magic [*vaciyam*], the first act of black magic [*pillicūṉiyam*]." Perhaps unsure whether I would comprehend the full implications of his remark, he added that "the purpose of the *yākam* was for Takkaṉ to take revenge and kill Śiva." His comment accorded with what we learned in chapter 3, namely, that alleged sorcerers seek to exclude or even eliminate anyone who ignores their claim to whatever they think they deserve. So it was not surprising that the god ordered Takkaṉ's death in retaliation, for as countersorcery rites also suggest, violence and killing are appropriate punishments for those who try to take "command" of others (see chapter 4).

Now let us inspect the denouement. Takkaṉ's offense actually brought him what he wanted so desperately. First came recognition from the goddess who, strangely enough, accepted against Śiva's wishes her "father's" invitation to his *pūjā*, thereby suggesting that in myths as in rituals such preliminary entreatments are binding. Then, like a dutiful daughter, she lamented his death and even warned that Śiva's failure to resurrect Takkaṉ would constitute grounds for divorce. Now she was willing to sacrifice her marriage for the life of her "father," confirming that decidedly in Tamil myth one discovers kinship relationships in their absence (see Śakti's myth recounted in chapter 11).

But in this story Śiva turned things around and transformed Takkan̲'s death into a sacrifice. The king was revived with water, a rite that in "the invitation to the feast" purifies sacrificial victims and signals the deity's approval of their immolation. In accepting Takkan̲'s death this way Śiva made it plain that one should return a gift to the god, in this case a daughter, much as one should perform a sacrifice without expectation of worldly return. Any intent to use the initial gift as a means to bind the god into a reciprocal obligation was wrong, for the covenant specified no further exchange but the gift of one's self. Such self-sacrifice was the ultimate transaction for uniting the god to his devotees, as indicated by the fact that now the king was sent to "heaven."[2]

The myth then is clear. Vows related to the birth of children should not be made with the hope to strike a kinship with the gods or to obtain any kind of material reward. Instead the payment of such vows entails the complete surrender of one's identity, of one's head, as evidenced by the fact that in another version of this myth that I collected, the king's decapitated body was reconnected to the head of a goat, a common sacrificial animal in Tamilnadu. But the narrative of Takkan̲ also emphasizes that initially such surrender of one's self is unanticipated and perhaps even unwanted. We remember that the king is ambitious, his yearning to father Pārvatī only a pretext for satisfying his greed for earthly power. And it is despite himself that he relinquishes these goals and becomes a devotee. With this in mind let me introduce the main character of this chapter, a thin man in his early thirties, actually a relative of my narrator, whom I will call Perumal.

Perumal's Vow for a Son

During our first conversation on the front porch of his home in his village near Malaiyan̲ūr, this is what Perumal told me,

> When I got married I made a vow [*pirāttanai*] to our lineage god, Periyāṇṭavar. I pledged that if my wife gave birth to a boy, I would sponsor a feast on his behalf. So when my son was born I went to purchase the piglet which we will offer at the worship of our god. Now it's time for me to fulfill my vow. When we request Periyāṇṭavar to bless us with a son, we must pierce the pig during the third month of *Āṭi* [July/August] after the child's birth.

After relating this, Perumal dispatched his cousin to bring out a fat pig. Perumal tapped the animal fondly on its rear, exclaiming, "I raised this Antavar like my own child!" Then he called for his boy who was standing in the threshold of the house with his mother. When the toddler stepped forward, he too petted the pig without any fear. Perumal nodded approvingly, "The day after we pierce the pig, this boy will undergo his ear-piercing ceremony."

In South Indian ethnographies, practices related to vow-making are often discussed under the heading of "individual devotion" (see Dumont, for instance, 1986: 455). There is warrant for this categorization, for as Dumont rightly points out, here the individual "is the one who chooses to perform a certain rite or a certain observance in relation to a certain deity" (1986: 455).[3] But Perumal's offerings necessitated the approval and ritual contribution of all his agnatic kinsmen who too had a "share" in the worship of the lineage deity. More than a simple transaction between two independent partners, Perumal's vow became the pivot for a complex system of life-giving exchanges between the god and his many relatives.

Perumal's lineage was divided into three *kottus* (literally a "bunch" or "cluster"), each of which represented the descent line of three brothers at the third generation. His particular *kottu* embraced seventeen households (*talaikkaṭṭu*). Each head of these nuclear or joint families (*kuṭumpam*) had to contribute a "share" of 100 rupees. For when a member vowed to sponsor a sacrifice to the lineage deity, all others (regardless of whether male births had occurred in their own families or not) had to pitch in that sum. In the second *kottu* of Perumal's lineage Periyāṇṭavar had answered another man's plea for a son. He too was expected to present a pig, a goat, and a chicken to the god. All fifteen householders of this second "cluster" likewise donated 100 rupees. No one in the third *kottu*, comprising eight households, had made such a vow. Yet, each family provided 50 rupees. Altogether the forty householders of Perumal's lineage raised 3,600 rupees for the coming festivities.

Of the seven Periyāṇṭavar/Periyāyi rituals that I documented, this was the only one triggered by personal vows. All others coincided with ear-piercing ceremonies for first-born children of the lineage and were officiated by the oldest male (or another particularly authoritative elder) of the descent group. Adding the institution of the vow, with its concomitant stipulation that the debt had to be paid three years later, dramatically altered the terms of worship. This was first made clear to me when I compared the frequency rates of these rituals. One consultant whose relatives performed them in the more perfunctory manner that I have described in the last chapter, reported that over his fifty-five years of life, his lineage had celebrated the Periyāṇṭavar worship on only three occasions. By contrast, Perumal, the main protagonist of this chapter's case-study, who was merely thirty years old, had participated in seven such rituals. When instigated by a vow, therefore, the ritual was no longer the mechanism by which all householders were punctually united for the ceremonial initiation of children while affirming the leadership of their senior members. Instead, the ritual authorized young men, like Perumal, who were beginning their reproductive years, to pressure their kin to let them serve as the leading officiants.

The pledge to father a son from Periyāṇṭavar thus expressed individual motivations and interests that ran counter to the ideals of sameness, unity, and respect for the authority of elders associated with the Tamil notion of descent. When granted, it further distinguished vowers like Perumal from "all others of the same sort": their prayers for progeny had been personally answered by the god. And from what I observed such divine recognition and the ritual privileges that it conferred could get to the head of vowers, like Perumal.

The festivities were launched one Saturday night of the month of *Āṭi* inside Perumal's domicile with the rite whose purpose was to seek the "protection" of his household deity. It was then that I began to realize that this young man was not exactly without personal ambition. Soon after his marriage, five years previously, Perumal had "separated" from his elder brother. But instead of moving out of the ancestral house, as he should have done since he was the younger sibling, he had managed to evict his brother who now resided with his family in a recently built addition in the rear of the house, an unusual arrangement for the first son should inherit the domestic sanctuary of his father. Since their father was still alive, the two brothers still worshipped the same family deity, personified by their deceased mother, both in the "old house" and the "new house."

For her invocation all those who at some point had shared living quarters with the dead mother—including her elder married daughter (Perumal's sister) and her brother—gathered in Perumal's domestic sanctuary. No one seemed particularly surprised that in this case the spirit wasted no time in responding to the musicians' call. Five years earlier, at Perumal's marriage, she had undergone the same sort of investiture ceremony that I have described in chapters 9 and 10. As already mentioned, newly consecrated *pūvāṭaikkāris* are known to come on quickly, especially in the domestic domain of their jurisdiction. Moreover, this spirit chose her married daughter as her host, a somewhat safe and predictable personification since at the marriage invitation rite she had already graced this individual, and together the mother/daughter had crowned Perumal with the ceremonial pot.

Still, we may recall how ritual exchanges with *pūvāṭaikkāris* often revive old intrafamily resentments, and it was much the same here. No sooner had this *pūvāṭaikkāri* arrived on Perumal's sister than it suddenly raced out of Perumal's quarters and settled in the ritual hearth of his elder brother, located toward the rear of the house, ordering that the *pūjā* be conducted "right here." This was the spirit's way, I was later told, to put Perumal back in his proper place and remind him that the "new house" was where he belonged. In other words, the *pūvāṭaikkāri* was scolding him for having appropriated his grandfather's home to which, in role of younger brother, he was not entitled.

Perumal stuck up for himself, "That [pointing to his own room] was our grandfather's house. This [his brother's home] is the new house. The *pūvāṭaikkāri* must come to my house. I won't accept her in the new house." The musicians tried to negotiate, saying, "It is all the same." But Perumal was now incensed, "She should come to our grandfather's house. Otherwise there is no need to call her. I don't want this *pūvāṭaikkāri*!"

Eventually the musicians coaxed the spirit back into Perumal's quarters, whereupon the singer threw out the key question, "Tomorrow we are going to hold a worship. We cannot make a mistake (*piḻai*). Will you see to it?" Somewhat mollified, the *pūvāṭaikkāri* agreed that nothing wrong would happen. But Perumal still harbored resentment at the spirit's accusation and whispered to the singer that he had to be sure of its identity. As we now know his concern was understandable. Those who have been publicly chastised by the "twin performance" of *pūvāṭaikkāris* and their mediums often retaliate by attacking the spirit's credibility. When the musician made the desired inquiry, the spirit replied, "I am the one who died, I am the mother." This satisfied the rest of the family, who cheered, "Kōvintā! Kōvintā!"

Still disgruntled, however, Perumal yelled in a loud voice, "WHO ARE YOU? WHAT IS YOUR NAME?" At this the spirit turned coy. To Perumal this behavior was proof that his sister was possessed by a demon, and he demanded of the singer, "How can a *pēy* know my mother's name?" This was a clever move, for in Tamilnadu, as we have seen in chapter 5, married women are well known to be prone to capture by the untimely dead. Such susceptibility often provides a convenient pretext for discouraging their participation as ceremonial mediums or, as was the case here, for silencing their judgmental spirits.

Yet Perumal's suspicions did not convince the musicians, who argued that no malignant spirit could penetrate the sanctity of the family's ritual space. At this Perumal simply brushed their interrogation aside and harangued the spirit directly, "Say my mother's name. If you can't, get out! Don't dance here!" Without waiting for a response he pushed his sister out of his house and forcibly expelled the spirit as well. His erratic behavior cast a pall on the scene, and no one seemed surprised that when the musicians resumed their invocation no other candidate came forward to act as medium.

For at least an hour they played to no avail. Hungry and exhausted, the musicians proposed to try again in the morning, but Perumal ordered them instead to call his favorite deity (*iṣṭa tēvam*)—the god Murukaṉ.[4] This strategy worked. Murukaṉ immediately "descended" on his devotee, openly identified himself and authorized the coming sacrificial rites. In the end then Perumal had succeeded in muting the objection of his own household deity. In fact, he had single-handedly divested his *pūvāṭaikkāri* of any authority and promoted his personal deity as the legitimate patron of his ritual performance, thereby verifying David Shulman's insight that one can achieve "earthly power through devotion" (1980: 321). Now the musicians tied the string amulet dyed with turmeric around Perumal's right wrist and did the same for his father and brother. This signified that Perumal and his kin were eligible ritual officiants under divine "protection."

The next morning, I found Perumal in the rear courtyard of his house readying his main sacrificial offering. Here I must say that the consecration had actually begun long ago, for Perumal had already named his pig "Antavar" after his lineage deity (Periyāṇṭavar). Over the past two years, he had even trained the animal to daily circumambulate "on its own" around a nearby Ganesh temple in his village. Furthermore, in Perumal's opinion the pig had already communicated its awareness and acceptance of its sacrificial fate. He told me that earlier in the day it had refused its food. "Our pig has voluntarily taken on a fast," he said. "You'll see. It will go of its own to the sacrificial altar [*pali pīṭam*]. Our pig has devotion [*bakti*] for the god. If something goes wrong with the *pūjā* it will cry, although it may also cry because it is going to die."

In a final consecrative gesture Perumal waved a camphor flame before the swine. At this moment Perumal apparently absorbed the pig's divine essence, for his body registered a strong physical shock. He threw himself into his house where he disappeared for at least forty minutes. When he emerged Perumal was wearing the same skirt of colored paper strings and conical crown of bright paper maché that devotees commonly put on to fulfill vows in the nearby Aṅkāḷammaṉ temple of Mēl Malaiyaṉūr (also see Meyer 1986: 257–258). In his hand was a leash for tying his pig. Apparently in the personification of the goddess he prepared to lead his lineage in procession through the village to the ritual grounds.

Once underway, however, the actual walk cast some doubt on Perumal's faith in the voluntary surrender of his offering. Panicked by the crowd of onlookers that swelled along their route, the pig began dashing from left to right in a zigzag pattern. When Perumal grew angry and yelled for the path to be cleared ahead, the animal froze, refusing to budge in any direction. But with much goading from the crowd, Perumal and his frightened sacrifice finally reached the ritual grounds.

It was customary for this particular lineage to hold this ritual not on any privately owned lands but in the center of the village. The site was nonetheless secluded as it was partitioned from the residential area by down-sloping banks of huge, odd-shaped boulders that formed a natural amphitheater. What looked like a stage was blocked off from the main road by two large banyan trees underneath which women began cooking ceremonial rice, while children played hide-and-seek among the surrounding boulders.

Once on the site Perumal's pugnacious personality resurfaced. Pacing back and forth around the large effigy, he criticized the musicians' work and ordered them to redo the god's torso. Then he aggressively demanded that I pay him a thousand rupees for recording the ritual. But when I explained that I could not give him that kind of money, he practically ordered me to stay and photograph him in the illustrious company of a number of important politicians from nearby Gingee whom he had invited to stop by while the effigy was in the making. I also suspect that at this point he was afraid that my departure might cost him the pictures of his pig procession. For despite the confusion, this had been a great moment for Perumal. In front of everybody he had been the main facilitator and conduit for ritual exchanges between his corporal group and its deity.

When in mid-afternoon members of the some forty households that constituted Perumal's lineage convened around the effigy, Perumal remained near the musicians to monitor dialogues with the five supernaturals who within the brief span of forty-five minutes, successively appeared. First came the village deity and the "woman who wears flowers," and since both stated their satisfaction with the proceedings, the musicians next called the lineage god. But at that point, as has occurred on other occasions in this book when these specialists were playing their music, an unexpected visitor descended on the scene.

Suddenly a young woman entered a state of trance, swirling her head around and weeping copiously. Despite the singer's repeated encouragements, her occupant refused either to provide the divine password, "Kōvintā!" or to identify itself. Almost in agony, the woman eventually cried out, "A *Paraiyan̲* [Untouchable] is on me," which indicated that she had been "caught" by the spirit of an outcast man who had met an untimely death. This also caught everyone's interest, and now all followed the exorcist interrogation most intently, as the singer began to ask of the spirit the usual questions: "How did you die?" "How long ago?" and the like. But Perumal intervened, objecting to any discussion with the uninvited *pēy*. "Send him away," he cried, and handed a whip to the musicians who began chasing the demon around the sanctuary. As he leapt ahead of the lash, his whining for mercy delighted members of the descent group, especially the giggling children. Finally, the *pēy* was evicted, his woman lost consciousness, and the musicians returned to their main task.

The lineage god successively appeared through the persons of three young girls. But it was not until he came on a twelve-year-old boy that the descent group actually asked Periyāṇṭavar to protect the children. After he did so, the god was requested to call "Amma," the goddess Aṅkāḷaparamēcuvari, who "came on" a young woman and also expressed her satisfaction with the "*pūjā*." Since communication with all these deities proved to be positive, Perumal could then proceed with his sacrifice. As the musicians lit the hundreds of camphor lumps previously scattered around the effigy, the expectant mood picked up again. The time had finally come for Perumal to pay his debt to Periyāṇṭavar.[5]

The Feast Analyzed: In the Heart of Descent

Three years before, Perumal had vowed to sacrifice a pig if his lineage god was to give him a son. Actually he had obligated himself to give "three" lives, for the protocol of worship required that he kill a chicken and a goat as well. But Perumal's transaction with his lineage deity was not simply about securing biological reproduction. His pledge had been initiated at his wedding, prior to obtaining proof that conception would not naturally ensue from the coming union. And if he had merely wanted to overcome infertility other procedures would have done just as well, such as tree-worship, recitation of certain mantras, or dietary prescriptions. No, Perumal had deliberately obligated himself to what was a risky commitment, since failure to repay his debt (in this case a sizable amount) could yield terrible consequences, even the death of his child, in order to obtain a son issued from his relationship with Periyāṇṭavar rather than with his wife. Like the king Takkaṉ he wanted what we may call "divine progeny." And this is what lineage members want from Periyāṇṭavar and why when they beget children they treat him to a "thanksgiving feast."

This reproductive principle is entirely different from the sexual or marital procreativity that is bestowed by the family deity. The *pūvāṭaikkāri* is connotative of biological fertility and continuity of bilateral ties of filiation. But "she" is also suggestive of decay, impermanence, and replacement. *Pūvātaikkāris* are dead, and like real brides come and go, following one after another—a process that parallels the child's succession to his parent. Finally, these spirits fragment the descent group into separate households and represent the particular interests of their family. In short, then, these family tutelaries symbolize a continuity that prevails through dynamics of obsolescence and individuation.

Lineage gods also bequeath a life that is premised on death. They grant birth to children on condition that they will be symbolically killed. But such sacrificial death, and its attendant violence, is meant to re-create a life whose basis is external to, and unconditioned by, the inherently imperfect life-giving potential of sexual/marital generativity. This is a death that ends death itself, a destruction that wins "true" permanence befitting of lineage deities. These tutelaries have been around since the "beginning" of time and are passed down, unchanged, from one generation of devotees to another. Since their continuity is assured by constituencies who identify themselves as "co-sharers" (*paṅkāḻi*), "and others of the same sort" (*vahairā*), they symbolize a perpetuity that is sustained through sameness, unity, and corporateness.

The system of representations associated with sacrificial lineage cults is therefore inimical not merely to the *pēys*' wild and unprocreative sexuality but to the *pūvāṭaikkāris*' domesticated reproductivity. Its antagonism to marital fertility is evidenced by the fact that throughout Tamilnadu, worship of the lineage deity is usually celebrated in the month of Āṭi (July/August) when marriages are expressly prohibited (also see Reiniche 1979: 46; footnote #8).[6] Moreover, a marriage transaction is not the operative metaphor that organizes relationship with a lineage god. The chartering myth for Periyāṇṭavar worship proposes that the wish for such an alliance might even lead the devotee on the wrong course.[7]

All this boils down to an opposition to women who personify both the *pēys*' barren libido and the *pūvāṭaikkāris*' bridal fecundity. This explains Perumal's aggression, demonization, and eviction of his sister-mother manifestation as family deity and his subsequent treatment of the "caught" woman. But ritualized hostilities toward women particularly surface at the main possession phase of the "feast" for Periyāṇṭavar.

At the ceremonial investiture of the household deity, the *pūvāṭaikkāri*'s insistence on ritual purity was grounds for barring young girls from the medium function. Yet, those "women who wore flowers" had minds of their own, often preferring to be represented by women who could best empathize with their emotional predicaments. This connection seemed to have been tacitly understood, for participants neither denied nor aborted women's trances. By contrast, however, here at the worship for Periyāṇṭavar, girls of the descent group were invited to serve as mediums for the lineage god. But I often observed that if Periyāṇṭavar favored these young women, the remainder of the lineage who were positioned around the "ramparts" of his temple actively contested his choice, refusing to transact with his female mediums.

At Perumal's ritual, for example, Periyāṇṭavar successively appeared through the persons of three young girls. However these manifestations did not provoke the gratification that I anticipated, and adult members of the descent group made no effort to conceal their disappointment over the god's choice. "We spent so much money for this *pūjā*," someone complained, "we want our *cāmi* [here, "god"] to come on a boy." It was as if women were invited to participate for the sole purpose of being excluded, as I too personally experienced when Perumal abruptly told me to pay his fee or else leave. Actually in one extreme case, at a *Paṟaiyaṉ* (Untouchable) "feast," women were altogether strictly prohibited to host the lineage god and relegated to stand out of his sight, actually behind his effigy. This is not to deny that women entered trancelike states, but no sooner did they begin to "dance" than they were forced out of the ritual grounds.

Women's "removal" from the "feast" is fitting with Girard's idea that sacrifice is a process whereby internal, destructive forces are blamed on a scapegoat who is violently expunged. In this ritual context women are held responsible for all that is inherently negative and disruptive for the descent group—biological fertility and the particular interests of the household—and must be put down when they manifest themselves. Their treatment is also consistent with Bloch's notion of "rebounding violence," the notion that the ritual acquisition of "external vitality" turns participants against the bearers (for example, domesticated animals and women) of "home-grown vitality."

But Girard's and Bloch's theories only throw light on what we may call the "side effects" or the "secondary consequences" of the Tamil "feast." They fail to explain its two main clauses. A sacrifice to Periyāṇṭavar, or any lineage deity for that matter, cannot be made without subjective, emotional investments. This was made clear to me during my first conversation with Perumal. His constant reminder that he had raised his pig "like his son" and his genuine affection for the animal suggested that he was not about to merely trade a life for a life but to surrender his most precious possession, his symbolized offspring, his own son, and therefore his own extended self. The second Tamil clause to ritually constituted vitality is that in the context of the "feast," at least, sacrifice cannot solely be made in the name of private interests—the procuration of self-immortality, for example.[8] It must benefit all members of the descent group who too have a "share" in the worship of the lineage god.

These two clauses differentiate the "invitation to the feast" from the *pēy* exorcism. Rather than giving his own "life" so that his kin can obtain more of it, the demon takes "life" out of no other concern than himself, which is why he is then ostracized from both societies of the dead and the living. By contrast, the sacrifice enacted at the "feast" is intended to forge social and personal connections. That is, of course, what marriage tries to do too. But as both the *pūvāṭaikkāri pūjā* and the Takkan myth make clear, marriage is an interested transaction that over time produces differences between self and connected selves: individuated filiations, "splits" from brothers, expectations of personal benefits, etc. Sacrifice, on the other hand, is meant to abrogate any and all distinctions between self "and others of the same sort."

The Tamil "feast" therefore does not so much connect disparate categorical domains—profane/sacred, individual/society—as Hubert and Mauss generalized of Vedic sacrifice, as create an irreducible unity of experience and identity with forebears, contemporary selves, and descendants. In enforcing the sentiments on which the descent group depends, the "feast" also creates the feeling of participating in the continuity of an entity that transcends the flux of life. But, once again, the condition of such ultimate experience is that sacrifice remains outside the realm of particular instrumentality, calculated reciprocity, and singularity. This is why it is carried through, in all its violence, on the sacrificer who dies for his god and kinsmen.

What is strange, of course, is that in both myth and ritual Tamil sacrificers enter the realm of sacrificial action with contrary dispositions, with assuming almost "commanding" attitudes,[9] so that they are in for some surprises. But this is consistent with what we have learned about revelations in the Tamil world. So far we have noticed that human encounters with gods, spirits, demons are rarely announced or anticipated. The goddess recruited her initiates when they least expected it; the demon-*pēys* surprised their victims; and the dead husband abruptly "woke up" his living wife. Even when such encounters are planned or initiated by human beings, they may still produce unforeseen consequences. Tamil rituals have a way of shocking participants into new states of being. The seance with the "cool" little sister swept her surviving brother with emotions that stunned him. The "marriage invitation" reunified the living and the dead against their will. This tendency toward unintended transformations applies to the "feast" as well.

No sooner than Perumal had pierced the squealing swine in the throat than his own body stiffened, as if he too had been impaled. His impulse to run was quickly checked and left him hovering between the exertions of his killing and the languors of his mad flight. When he was signed to follow his companions back home, he held himself at a distance with none of the braggadocio he had displayed on the way to the ritual site. Nor did he seem interested in talking to me, when I went back to his village three weeks later to give him the pictures. His welcome was oblivious and remained so even after I told him that this was my last visit, for I was soon to leave the field. He barely responded to my greetings and maintained an absent, day-dreaming look throughout the exchange. He refused to comment on the photos, pretending he needed to rest.

In the end, I must once again qualify Bruce Kapferer's proposition that practices such as sorcery or sacrifice are creative manifestations of human power in the world (1997). There can be no doubt that the "feast" is an "act of (re)origination by means of which human beings radically reconstitute, remake, or maintain their life and its circumstances" (Kapferer 1997: 187). It is also probable that this Tamil sacrificial ritual is "a primordial act, an act of instantiation par excellence, . . . a total act" (Kapferer 1997: 189). At the very least, the "invitation to the feast" is a profoundly imaginative way to transcend life—its divisions, transitions, and finality. But we must never forget that the vitality it confers depends on throwing out constitutive elements of nature (sexuality, biological procreativity) and culture (alliance, reciprocity, and difference). It also requires the exclusion of women, the death of animals and sons, and above all the destruction of individuality. The basis of sacrificial efficacy—that human power over life and death—is the total abnegation of the I.

CONCLUSION

One moment above all stands out with signal clarity from my fieldwork in Tamilnadu. That is when the medium named Padmini "saw" the dead relatives of her clients, Mahentiran and Rita, in the afterlife, as described in chapter 8. Her vision was also my first introduction to this world of connections and disconnections between gods, other people, and the self. Everything about my ensuing investigation was, in fact, born in that moment: my concern for people who were having it rough, as well as my sympathy for supernaturals who also seemed to wrestle with life and death issues in ways that made them virtually indistinguishable from human beings. It was then that my unusual "field" began to take shape: my routine of venturing outside the well-trodden paths of the ethnographic itinerary to pursue esoteric practices and their social linkages that fell somehow below or beyond village religion and its better-documented inter- or intracaste ceremonies. My schedule revolved around Tuesdays and Fridays, new moon and full moons days, when I visited homemade sanctuaries and the Mēl Malaiyaṉūr temple, along with marriages and children's ear piercing ceremonies, when I walked to my consultants' agricultural fields and witnessed their "invitations." Over time I began to discern that this low-visibility world had a coherence of its own.

Perhaps, out of a sense of duty to make the most of my privileged time in Tamilnadu, I observed and recorded too many rituals. Perhaps I should have spent less time following the "chain" of symbolic enactments that did seem to possess so many cross-references. Perhaps I should have been more willing to know one ceremony truly well.

On the other hand, I do not believe that a more fashionably experiential approach to my fieldwork would have deepened my understanding of this somewhat marginalized or liminalized Tamil world. I could never have freed myself from my own system of cultural meanings, which is why I declined Padmini's offer to put me in touch with my dead relatives. In my case, I would also have had little in common with any of them and had no business, unfinished or otherwise, to transact. Furthermore, after witnessing how people could be psychologically manipulated while they "danced," I acquired none of the fascination that anthropologists working on possession sometimes develop for states of trance (Desjarlais 1992; Gibbal 1994).

This distance brought teasing from the Mēl Malaiyaṉūr musicians who, based on their encounter with some tourists, assumed that all foreigners would pay "good money" to get lost in their drumming. When it became clear that I had neither the gift nor inclination to enter trance, one of them reasoned: "There are three kinds of human beings. The first are endowed with *tēyvakuṇam* ["divine nature"]. They will dance the gods quickly. The second are born with *maṉuṣakuṇam* ["human nature"]. They too will dance the gods, but it takes longer. The third are afflicted with *rakṣhasakuṇam* ["demonic nature"]. They never dance the gods." Given all the hours of drumming I had heard without falling into "god-dancing," the man logically concluded that I was probably of the demonic persuasion.

Perhaps. But I subscribe to Olivier de Sardan's point of view that, in any ethnographic project, "to understand belief is not to believe" (1986: 150; trans. mine; also see Geertz 1979). Quite simply, an outsider's comprehension must begin with a search for the categories of meaning that social or religious representations have for participants. Above all, I felt obliged to recover my consultants' knowledge and experience of their cosmology and to contextualize the expressive idioms that linked them to their spirits, in both social and symbolic contexts. By attending to the imaginative, lived forms of this particular skein of Tamil beliefs and practices I tried to partake of its subjective reality. But I could never internalize that reality, and in my case, felt it would be false, presumptuous, even transgressive, to try.

Not that eliciting the so-called native points of view, "emic" representations, or "experience-near" concepts was easy (Geertz 1979). Padmini the medium completely shunned me; I never obtained her justifications for or interpretations of what she was doing. I felt "lucky" when people spoke to me, but what they said did not always conform, or even contradicted, what they did or what others said. Often I felt that the direct search for meanings was an elusive, even fruitless, pursuit. Ritual participants could not remember what they felt or did during altered states of consciousness. The communicative link between deeply felt experience and descriptive language was tenuous and called for the special skills of a natural storyteller, which few of my consultants were.

But the reverse was also true. When people were able to articulate their extraordinary emotional states I had a hunch that something important was lost in the process of explanation. As Michelle Rosaldo (1984) and Arjun Appadurai (1990) both argue, emotions in any cultural setting can have a secondary linguistic life, but they have a deeper basis in what these authors term, "embodied experience." To listen to people talk about feelings can be quite different from grasping their full, abiding experiential impact.

At times I stumbled on what anthropologists call "blocks in native exegeses" (Turner 1967: 38; Obeyesekere 1981: 20). Participants simply had nothing further to say about a particular ritual sequence. This was even the case with those ritual specialists who had pondered long on the mysteries of their own cosmology and who decoded other ceremonies for me, volunteering commentaries on unsolicited details, parenthetical explanations, and fully consistent glosses. In this book, however, I have tried to suggest that what we have here is more than an indication of some sort of difference between more and less *meaning-full* rituals. We are actually witnessing two kinds of ritual processes. Some are free-form, open-ended, and invite reflexivity. Others exploit techniques, such as formulaic speech and bodily states like trance, that may hinder interpretative engagement. In these processes, at the same time, lie different forms of ritual effectiveness. Countersorcery rituals "remove" spells by letting participants "perform" their own solutions to personal dilemmas; the exorcism "makes demons run away" by "prescribing" both predicaments and resolutions.

In the absence of readily available or reliable exegeses, I often resorted to local myths to "crack" the ritual code, as Victor Turner might have said. This was not an arbitrary move, for when working with what I have called "prescriptive" rituals myths were often handed to me in lieu of personal commentary.[1] But myths are not shortcuts to rituals, and they could even complicate the interpretative task. Usually, I was unfamiliar with the forms and codes in which they were given; I had no studied feel for the relationships between their surface actions and exegetical subtexts. They were also deceptive: one moment they simply appeared to echo and restate the problems presented in rituals; the next they seemed to be "thinking among themselves," as Claude Lévi-Strauss says. I was never sure whether to read myths as rejoinders to rituals or as separate entries in a covert conversation. But my friend Leila taught me how Margaret Trawick is on the right track when she claims that Tamil people "live" their myths and "take them to heart, so that a person's life may become an enactment of a story and vice versa" (1990a: 24). In this respect Tamil myths do function much like these ritual forms which, as we have seen, have no "self-existence" outside of the human predicaments they address and need just as much "flesh, matter, circumstantiality, to give them shape, to make them real" (Trawick 1990a: 23).

I have also tried to show that another reason Tamil rituals have no "self-existence" is that they are not autonomous. They always exist in relation, or more exactly in opposition, to others. Countersorceries, exorcisms, investitures, and sacrifices are linked not merely by common metaphors and dynamics but by a system of oppositions, a structure of dynamic tensions that gives meaning to those who participate in a given ritual.

The problems of analyzing just what was involved in the "meaning" of this structure preoccupied me throughout the writing of this book. No single consultant, I was well aware, not even a ritual specialist, would lay it out the way I have. Fieldwork taught me how prone are ethnographers to construct configurations that cannot be found in other peoples' knowledge of their world. Before leaving the field, for instance, I showed to my friends in the nearby village of Mēlaccēri the admirable video that Alf Hiltebeitel edited of their famous eighteen-day-long festival for the goddess Draupadī (1988). Their reaction was instructive. "This is what women do?" or "I did not know that. . . ." They only possess a fragmented view; none seemed to know the festival in its entirety. It was their tradition only as an assemblage of many different, self-centered, and implicated perspectives. Hiltebeitel's film seemed to be showing it as a single, cohesive performance to them for the very first time.

So why hang on to wholes? Why connect everything to everything else, or at least try to do so? The query is all the more pressing when so much of current anthropology has exposed how the construction of coherent cultural orders is at best provisional and illusive, at worst arrogant and hegemonic. It suppresses the boundless, shredded, plural, and ever-changing dimension called "context." To the clamor of contemporary consensus on this position I can only respond: not so fast. Let us not assume that our postmodern tastes for unfinished narratives are shared by other peoples. Tamils may not always "see" the larger wholes they construct, but they nonetheless create them and dearly enjoy doing so. This "*desire* for wholeness" was also noted by Margaret Trawick, who has argued that the "patterned systems" into which Tamils organize their families and larger kin groups "have a kind of real beauty" and "give their creators pleasure" (1990a: 117).

How Tamil people in South Arcot derive deep aesthetic satisfaction from stylized forms can be seen when women draw with rice flour intricate *kōlam* designs before the threshold of their houses every morning. It can be appreciated in the highly logical structure of their language. It can be understood in the always-systematic presentation of their offerings to gods. It can be sensed in the way that each supernatural carries something, by means of oppositions, of the attributes of the other supernaturals. Tamil culture is founded on the all-encompassing message that this world is a world of connections, or as Louis Dumont says "a world of relations." This message need not be verbally explained to be comprehended; its significance is instilled at preconscious, unconscious levels and is as much a part of Tamil existence as the air they breathe.

But the most arresting quality of this village cosmology is not that it repeatedly communicates that life with others is all there is. What came to fascinate me was how much it underscored the fact that personal relationships are paradoxically dangerously encroaching, even physically threatening, to the Tamil self. One of the common propensities for all of the protagonists of this book was to "run" or "crawl away" when they felt that their parents or spouses were neglecting their emotional needs, or else to recriminate and remonstrate against their kinfolk. Some seemed to completely "forget" their kinship identities, others resolved difficult relationships by performing "removals." Not all of the spirits we met bore grudges, some actually liked family life: "I don't want to leave my wife and children," one yelled in despair to his living brother. "I want to go home," was another's plea. Spirits who could not cope with spouses in life even longed to be married in death.

But to say that one cannot live in the afterworld without kin is not to say that one can live *with* them in this world. No sooner than were these spirits reunited with their living relatives that they inevitably cried out for individual recognition and personal attention in the form of "love" and resisted being appended or conflated with them. All these spirits, and their human hosts, appeared to contend with what Sudhir Kakar identifies as "the essential psychological theme of Hindu culture" namely, "the polarity of fusion and separation . . . a dynamic counterpoint between two opposite needs, to merge into and to be differentiated from the 'Other.' "(1981: 34, in Mines 1994: 17).

In day-to-day life and death, I suspect, Tamil people haphazardly swing back and forth between these extremes. But the Tamil world of ritual is much more stark and absolute: you either fuse or separate. If you have been persuaded or "invited" to do the first, you can rarely evade the process which "warns" you and infuses you with the value of connecting, so that you end up "promising" to make it yours. In the event you have not quite internalized the "truth" of returning to your husband, of reproducing your dead parents, and sacrificing yourself to your lineage as your own, your tongue will be pierced, your head will be cut off or replaced with that of another. As a consequence you become a compound of disparate entities, which both are and are not organically united; you are and are not yourself, you are and are not someone else. The body does not merely become a "natural symbol" for such a paradoxical state, it is the site par excellence for literally experiencing the split self in all its ambiguity.

The alternative to relational identities is hardly less brutal. One can preserve some sort of individuality and integrity by extricating or, as the Tamils say, "removing," the self from the excessively demanding or "dead" relationships. But as we have seen, in this process one must endure the emotions of unsettling "fear," the risk of bodily pains and cuts, the deeply troubling experiences of sexual aggression and disempowerment, the terror of funeral rites and even death. The main difference is that now the violence is self-inflicted. The prime victim of such scenarios is, of course, the individual who becomes a demon-*pēy*. Unable to bear the pressures of social existence, he takes his own life.

But the *cāmis* and some of their patients also leave the world of intimate relationships by undergoing a similar kind of traumatic self-extinction. This makes sense. In a world in which life with others is all there is, life without others must become a form of death. Nor is the path to individuality easier than that to sociality: you remain less divided to be sure, but you are still essentially alone. Moreover, there are hazards: solitary young women, for example, always run the risk of being "caught," pronounced mad, and forcibly returned to reason. Finally, to gain any kind of social reality you must latch onto strangers and frustrate their own dreams for personal freedom or, on the contrary, liberate them from the trappings of relationships. Either way one is now the conduit for more violence against the self.

Yet the Tamil theory of ritual is not entirely deterministic. First and foremost, what counts are personal, inner dispositions. If fathers and sons have no love for each other, the investiture ceremony will fail to reunite them. If a young wife still loves her deceased husband, a funeral will not succeed at separating them. Participant investment might be said to constitute the critical glue of Tamil rituals. This is what makes them so dramatically intense. For inner dispositions are variable, never wholly foreseeable, even from the perspectives of the persons most concerned. Anything can happen, and may very well happen, in the unpredictable unfolding of these Tamil rituals. Some have an uncanny way of even engaging "innocent bystanders" especially at the point when insiders themselves are slow to get the action moving. (As if there were such a category in a Tamil village as the "innocent bystander.") The goddess may invite herself to an exorcism or an investiture, or a demon might unexpectedly show up at a sacrifice. Although such intrusions are never exactly wanted, they testify to the degree to which the ritual process can catalyze unexpected individual investments and make sudden contact with the wider logic and full personnel of a spirit world that remains very much involved with the workings of "this" earthly existence.

Finally, for all the systematic analogies and structural oppositions that scholars love to puzzle out, we must never forget that the Tamil cosmology is not closed. There are always escapes hatches, safety valves, loops out. The cases covered in this book rarely constituted a one-time, all-or-nothing, finite experience. Once a supernatural barged into an individual's life, he or she opened up a line of communication that could, in turn, lead to other sorts of connections.[2]

For such a fluid and dynamic cosmology, neither a "hierarchy of purity and impurity" (Dumont 1980) or a "ladder of command" (Moffat 1979) seem to be the right models. The Hindu world that I have tried to describe in this book is more like a "busy intersection," as Renato Rosaldo once commented about ritual in general (1984: 190). But perhaps it is even better characterized as a road, on which the gods, the demons, and the dead all travel at different speeds, sometimes getting stuck, sometimes making wrong turns, sometimes taking terminal exits, but always aspiring to get back on. For this is the ritual's road of life, the road which "crosses over," leading them back into human existence in all its emotional entanglements, social dramas, and personal obligations. This is why the *pēy*, the demon, the dead one, the true protagonist of this study always cries out: "I want life."

NOTES

Introduction

1. In Tamilnadu such lunar days allow for what John Stanley calls "the special accessibility of power at certain times" (1977: 27). As he notes, Indian astrological theory regards new moon nights as inauspicious and polluting but also a time when power is "doubly heightened," "fluid," "accessible" (1977: 29–30) and therefore propitious for beginning or ending relationships with spirits of the dead. But such transactions can also be performed on full moon days, for they often require the assistance of the goddess who, like other Tamil deities, at those times achieves "completion, fulfillment and total maturity" (Clothey 1982: 167).

2. A term introduced by M. N. Srinivas (1969) to describe the process by which middle and low castes emulate and adopt the behavior and values of Brahmin castes.

3. Victor Turner's premise partially endorsed the French sociologist Emile Durkheim's proposition that ritual is a powerful device for organizing categories of understanding and perceptions of nature and society that are felt by the participants to be absolute and hence obligatory (1965). I say "partially" because Turner repeatedly emphasized that ritual is not an epiphenomenon reinforcing the primary social order that it reflects but always a "process," in which Van Gennep's second and transitional stage is of critical importance. On the basis of intensive fieldwork among the Ndembu of northwestern Zambia, Turner noted that this phase of the ritual process is replete with symbols of death and decomposition, or gestation and parturition. To him such symbolism was suggestive of the ritual condition that Van Gennep had called "liminality." And he too concluded that at this point participants are "betwixt and between," neither here nor there, no longer children, in the case of initiation rites, and not yet adults (1969). But Turner also observed that far from dissolving human bonds among ritual participants, leaving them by themselves and separate from one another during this formative transition, the liminal phase reconstitutes those bonds (Torrance 1994: 12). Such liminal relationships contrast with those formed in regular, day-to-day life (1969: 95–96). As Turner explained, "the [model] which emerges recognizably in the liminal period, is of society as an unstructured or rudimentarily structured

and relatively undifferentiated *comitatus*, community, or even communion of equal individuals who submit together to the general authority of the ritual elders." To him the ritual process permitted initiates to experience a form of human interrelatedness that is actually opposed to the social model of structured, differentiated, and hierarchical roles. And it is this experience, rather than social life and its divisive categories, that creates in human beings a deep awareness of society as a shared human need (Torrance 1994: 12). What Turner, then, so powerfully documented was that ritual is not merely a "passage" but a process that encourages participation in sentiments of mutual concern necessary for social life—a process, in sum, that creates the very basis for society. Even when he saw rituals as forums for antistructural feelings, in dialectical tension with structural norms, he still interpreted them as having positive functions, as mediating contradictions and conflicts of the social order (1957; 1968).

4. For an excellent discussion of the shift from an analytical focus on symbols and meanings to an investigation of performance and practice, see Bell 1997: 61–90.

5. His argument was strongly criticized by David Scott for positing that "subjectivity" and "experience" are existential givens, ontologically prior to certain cultural realities (1995). But a case can be made for contending that Scott himself relativizes these categories too much. At the very least he seems strangely out of touch with the reasons why people undergo exorcism. In Tamilnadu, as in Sri Lanka, they do so because they have been diagnosed as suffering from demonic possession—a condition that can cause madness. It is because they are thought to have lost normal means of communication and to be trapped in "a state of isolation, of existential solitude in the world," as Kapferer also notices (1983: 70), that their demons are "made to run away." In other words, it is expected, indeed highly wished, that the exorcism will change them and return them to sociality. And the merit of Kapferer's analysis is that it precisely details the "logic" of such experiential transformations.

6. Of course, this was consistent with Dumont's theory of Indian society in general: "In the caste society, nothing is true by nature and everything by situation, there are no essences but only relations. To say caste is to say structure" (1970: 29). By structure this supremely logical Frenchman meant "systematic oppositions" between categories (1980: 39–42). The key principle of Hindu society was "the opposition of the pure and the impure," which in turn yielded the ideological rationale behind caste hierarchy: the "pure" stood in a relation of superiority to the "impure" (1980: 43). As Dumont repeatedly emphasized, "Everything is founded on the complementarity of the pure and the impure, of the superior and the inferior" (1970: 38).

7. A recent ethnographic study suggests how such persons might achieve a state of equilibrium in Tamilnadu. According to Valentine Daniel they do so by matching their bodily "substances" to that of their village, house, and sexual partner (1984). Something of such a "fluid" person is also captured in Margaret Trawick's description of a Tamil family (1990a). For all her attempts to individuate her consultants, and to account for their unique emotions and motivations, she nonetheless concludes that they are neither bounded nor quite complete.

8. The structure that emerges from my research on Tamil rituals is less radical than that applied by the French structuralist Claude Lévi-Strauss to the cross-cultural study of formal, communicative systems such as kinship, myth, and language. For one thing, it is intrinsically tied to empirical circumstances. Thus, whereas Lévi-Strauss explicitly contends that his use of the term *structure* has

"nothing to do with empirical reality but with models which are built up after it" (1963: 279), I regard structure as a reality that is given by processes and practices. Thus, I do not submit Tamil rituals to the kind of synchronic cutting and diachronic recutting that Lévi-Strauss applies to myth and its variants (1963). Instead my method of analysis consists in comparing phenomena—symbols, processes, and procedures—that for the most part are visible, emergent, and at the surface of reality. What I retain from French structuralism is this notion of "distinctive opposition," even if I express it for the most part in the language of oppositions of fact and of experience.

Chapter 1

1. The high percentage of male initiates in my sample (a ratio of six to one) reflects my focus on healers who served large constituencies from their homemade sanctuaries. Since in the Gingee area female initiates tended to restrict their practices to smaller circles of kin and immediate neighbors or to already established temples devoted to particular goddesses, most of the specialists I worked with were male.

2. Despite the undeniable prominence of these independent religious practitioners among Tamil villagers in the South Arcot district, South Indian scholarship in general has remained singularly vague on them. Michael Moffat, for instance, gives no hint as to the personal circumstances that caused a landless Untouchable (*Paṇṇaikkar*) man of the Chengelput district to "become possessed" by his lineage goddess and to conduct "foretelling" and "exorcist" rites (1979: 230). Margaret Trawick (1984) and Manuel Moreno (1985) do provide evidence that sickness and physical handicaps are at the origin of what Moreno terms, the "forceful call" (1985). But since each of their accounts concentrate on the testimony of a single individual, they miss the opportunity to ground their discussion in a broader cultural perspective. Moreover, they do not describe the spiritual application of their informants' gifts and therefore fail to investigate how their experiences of suffering shape the dynamics of their divining or healing practices. Finally, some ethnographers present transcriptlike excerpts of seances but formulate few interpretations (Montgomery 1974/75; Moffat 1979; Harper 1957). Save for Charles Nuckolls's research on divination among the Jalaris, a Telugu fishing community from Andhra Pradesh (1991a, 1991b, 1991c), and Lionel Caplan's study of Protestant charismatic prophets in Madras city (1988), nowhere have I found a comprehensive analysis of the role played by these practitioners in South Indian society.

This lack of systematic scholarship is particularly evident in the loose vocabulary used to identify them. The literature refers to them irregularly as "shaman" (Harper 1957), "oracle" (Dumont and Pocock 1959), "trance-therapist" (Montgomery 1974/75), and "possession-medium" (Nuckolls 1991b, 1991c). Tamil terms, such as *cāmiyāṭi*, which means "god dancer," have also been applied (Moffat 1979; Moreno 1985; Diehl 1956; Dumont 1986). All these glosses suggest that the defining feature of these specialists' practices is their capacity to enter altered states of consciousness (like trance and possession, or in Tamil "dance"). Yet as we will see in chapter 2, it is wrong to identify these initiates primarily on the basis of such characteristics, for some actually do not obtain nor communicate their supernatural knowledge by means of states of trance. Moreover, such terms reduce their seances to exotic and even irrational psychological dynamics when in reality many of these practitioners are consciously focused on manipulating dramatic, rhetorical, and performative effects. Finally, they lead us to expect that genuine "altered states of consciousness" are the authentic requirements for divining. But in point of fact, one of the *cāmis* I worked with actually appeared to despise trance-possession as a technique,

> Those people who claim that the goddess descends [*iṟaṅku*] on them are not telling the truth. Śakti is a kind of fire, an abstract thing [*uruvamillāta*: literally "without form"]. No one would be able to bear Śakti. She is the whole earth. How can an ordinary man support the whole earth on his head? If these people shake it is because something is wrong with their nervous system.

Instead, his mode of access to his goddess involved "meditation" (*yōkam*).

3. The recruits may also go by other names. When male initiates work with mantras or incantations, they are called *mantiravātirhal* ("they who say mantras"), or they may also be referred to simply as *vaittiyar*, or "healers."

4. Like the Protestant, charismatic prophets studied by Lionel Caplan in Madras, my consultants made a linguistic distinction between dreams (*kanavu*) and visions (*taricaṉam*) and indicated that visions of gods were "clearer in terms of their meaning" than religious dreams (1988: 12).

5. See Kolenda 1982; Nicholas 1981; Bang 1973; Marglin 1990; Dumont 1986: 431.

6. See Trawick 1984; Nuckolls 1991c.

7. Edgar Thurston, the superintendent of ethnography of the Madras Presidency, understood the *Tēnpaḷḷis* to be related to the tribals named *Irulas* of the Nilgiri Hills (1987 [1909] vol 2: 382–91).

8. As the noted South Indian scholar and translator, A. K. Ramanujan emphasizes, the translation of the Tamil term *Amma* as "mother" is misleading because "the Goddess . . . is not a mother, She has no children, in most of the myths" (1986: 57; also see Dumont 1986: 432 and Assayag 1992: 34).

9. This is a common endeavor in Tamil village festivals, which Eveline Meyer interprets as being motivated by the devotee's "desire to invite the goddess to take hold of him, to take possession of him" (1986: 260).

Chapter 2

1. When used to decode the future, the "interpretation of signs" often consists of disclosing the conditions that might avert unwanted results or achieve valued goals, delimiting, for example, the auspicious time and place for seeking a bride, resolving a conflict, or treating an illness. It yields such instructions as "Go East for marriage," "Go to court on the fifth day of next month," or "Observe a fast for seven days."

2. I want to thank Raja Shaker, the director of the Wisconsin Language Program in Madurai, for bringing this point to my attention.

3. Their seances begin between ten and twelve o'clock in the morning, the sacred time (*tirukkalam*) that, according to Fred Clothey, "virtually all [Saiva] temples observe" with a *pūjā* (1982: 159).

4. The *cāmis* tend to restrict their decoding seances to a particular time of the week and a particular place. However, many *cāmis* strive to liberate themselves from such spatio-temporal constraints. Nagaji, for example, explained to me that for years he could only reincorporate his goddess Śakti in the very spot where she

had first appeared, and where he founded his sanctuary and spiritual practice. This was a hindrance, he told me, "If you profess the word of the goddess in a particular place only, people begin to suspect that it is the place rather than the person that has the power." Over time he extracted from Śakti the boon (*varam*) of entering in communication with her at any time, anywhere.

5. Never again was I to see a Hindu goddess styled in such an old-fashioned, frilly Western dress, neither at village processions nor even at popular dramatizations of mythological plots. Since Murukan was not very talkative, I never found out where he had obtained that odd dress. But it appeared to be a late-nineteenth-century original and was completely out of style with what contemporary Christian women wore in cities. Moreover, the dress was faded, torn at a few seams, and clearly too tight on the *cāmi*.

6. In most scholarship the carrying of this pot is described for yearly ceremonial processions where it suffuses the "essence" of the goddess into the body of its carrier. As many ethnographers have documented, where you find these *karakam* processions you also usually see trance-possession as well (Whitehead 1988: 38, 101–4; Beck 1969: 564; Dumont 1986: 377, 433, 435; Moffat 1979: 227, 264; Hiltebeitel 1991: 448–57, 464–67, 465 footnote #58, 473–75; Frasca 1990; Meyer 1986: 238).

7. As the word *tāmpūlam* ("betel leaf") suggests, betrothal is ratified by the exchange of betel leaves and areca nuts between the two families. This exchange gives the assurance (*niccayam*) that the marriage will take place.

8. Nagaji's idea of love medicine effecting Gita's emotions was not exactly an original idea. From Sri Lanka, Nandadeva Wijesekera also noted that "if a girl or a boy makes their own [marriage] arrangements the parents suspect that *ina* (or black magic) medicine has been given to one or the other" (1989: 178).

9. Murukan's impersonation is reminiscent of the way in which *cāmi* Raghavan of the last chapter surrendered to the goddess by donning her costume and her emblems. In Tamil festivals this sort of identification is not unusual: devotees sometimes fulfill a vow by putting on their deity's customary attire (*vēṣam*) and undertaking processional circumambulations (also see Meyer 1986: 357). According to Eveline Meyer, such act is of a "devotional nature, it is a sacrifice, an offering to the goddess" (1986: 260). She also comments that when a temple priest (*pūcāri*) assumes the ceremonial task of personifying the goddess, he becomes the deity and is treated as such. Furthermore she observes that

> although it is desired that the person be possessed for his role, it is in fact not absolutely necessary. Whether the person is possessed or not has no bearing on the fact that he is considered to be the goddess while he acts her part, and since he *is* the goddess, he may as well be called possessed by her. (1986: 257)

This illuminates Murukan's performance. While he did not appear to be in a state of trance or possession, he was treated as if he incarnated the goddess.

10. The *karakam* pot, however, sometimes represents a male deity (see Meyer 1986: 235)

11. As George Park has discerned, "An important aspect of divination as institutionalized procedure is just this—that it provides 'resistance' in its own right to any client's proposal" (1963: 197).

Chapter 3

1. In anthropological terminology sorcery is usually defined as the acquired knowledge of specific spells and ritual procedures that enable a specialist (the sorcerer) to control mystical forces or spiritual agents for the deliberate purpose of harming or even eliminating another person (Evans-Pritchard (1937: 21). Tamils employ at least two terms that correspond roughly to this anthropological category. The first is *mantiratantiram*, which Reverend Diehl translated as "that which has to do with Mantras" (1956: 267). Mantras are syllables, words, formulas, names, curses, prayers, invocations, or songs that when properly uttered create power (Padoux 1989). That power can be used for benevolent or malevolent ends. On the one hand, mantras can help people secure a good marriage alliance, transfer to a better job, retrieve stolen property, and so on. We may recall how Basha, the Muslim recruit in chapter 1, learned mantras from the Koran in order to improve his school grades. On the other hand, mantras can also destroy property, cripple an enemy, or separate lovers. Although mantras can be learned by anyone from widely available handbooks sold in train stations and bus stands, they are, as Diehl also observed, generally "in the hands of professional people" (1956: 268).

The second Tamil gloss for sorcery is *pillicūṉiyam*, which Diehl translated as "black magic" (1956: 267). The word is actually a compound derived from two foreign words. *Pilli* is the Malayalese term for sorcery and literally means "embryo child" (Wijesekera 1989: 181), suggesting, as we will see, that the South Indian sorcerer's power derives not only from words or mantras but also from substances, such as the corpses of unborn babies or infants. As for the word *cūṉiyam*, it comes from the Sanskrit *śunya*, which means "destruction," confirming that the sorcerer's activities are indeed lethal.

2. Although the *cāmis* sometimes advised their clients to go back to the hospital or to change their doctor, I observed that they were prone to rule out medical explanations for physical ailments. Since these specialists were in constant rapport with the goddess it was not too surprising that they leaned toward supernatural interpretations of affliction.

3. Save for two dated studies—that of W. T. Elmore's description of an exorcist ceremony (1984: 47–51) and Carl Diehl's review of Tamil printed handbooks on mantras (1956: 267–334)—this topic of South Indian sorcery has gone virtually undocumented in the region's ethnography. Sorcery, however, has been widely discussed in the ethnography of nearby Sri Lanka. But Tamil and Sinhalese sorcery traditions differ in several important respects. Whereas Gananath Obeyesekere (1975; 1976) and Bruce Kapferer (1983, 1988, 1997) both present real evidence for the practice of sorcery in Sri Lanka, I was only able to record imputations of sorcery in Tamilnadu. I never encountered the songs known as *vaskavi*, which Obeyesekere describes as "the most deadly form of sorcery practice in Sri Lanka" (1975: 4). Nor did the key myths of Sinhalese sorcery seem to function as chartering narratives for Tamil sorcery (see Kapferer 1988, 1997). Instead, one of my consultants associated the origin of Tamil sorcery with a version of a well-known Sanskrit story that relates how King Dakṣa (or Takkaṉ in Tamil) excludes Lord Śiva from his sacrifice (see chapter 12).

4. This belief is so entrenched that the corpses of first-born sons are not buried, as is the case with most Tamil Hindus, but are cremated instead. However, early in the century Edgar Thurston observed that: "Among the Paraiyans [Untouchables], and some other castes, a first born child, if it is a male, is buried

near or even within the house, so that its corpse may not be carried away by a witch or sorcerer, to be used in magic rites" (1906: 271).

5. For instance, I was told that the sorcerer utters his commands at night while standing naked in a water tank. Edgar Thurston reported a similar practice among the Pulluvan caste of Malabar (1987: 231; for another reference to the standing position in water see Diehl 1956: 293).

6. These spells appear to derive from the Vedic tradition of sorcery known as *abhicāra* (Turstig 1985). According to A. MacDonell, Atharva-Veda hymns relate how "an image was frequently made and operated on for the purpose of producing a similar effect on the victim" (1958: 319). As he explains: "An enemy is destroyed by piercing the heart of his clay effigy with an arrow, or by transfixing his shadow. His death is also produced by melting a wax figure of him over the fire, or by killing or burning a chameleon as representing him" (ibid).

7. The *cāmis* said that sorcerers had at their disposal another category of spells, which corresponds to what James Frazer termed "contagious magic" (1965: 301). This operated on the principle that affliction could be transmitted via physical contact. Known in Tamil as *vaippu* ("deposit"), these spells involved infusing certain organic substances (egg, lime, copper foil) with sickness and secretly placing them in the houses of victims or at a nearby cross-road. When human targets came into contact with these objects, they absorbed their malevolent power. Apparently the result was a slow but steady decrease of their life-strength. A consultant, however, explained the mechanisms of such "deposits" without invoking this principle of contagion. He said that as these loaded objects begin to rot or rust, everything that the victim owned (in the form of wealth and health) would deteriorate. In any case, this method was said to work only for a limited period of time.

Although this procedure was by far the best known to lay people, I noted that it was almost never identified by the *cāmis* at their actual diagnosis of sorcery. It was the category of spells known as *ēval*, meaning "command," that was the most common sorcery technique identified by these specialists. It may be that the *cāmis* had some vested interest in underreporting the incidence of *vaippu*, for its neutralization did not require an elaborate intervention from their part. The *cāmis* simply advised their clients to bury certain substances imbued with the goddess's power (in particular, limes) in their homes or at particular cross-paths.

8. The *Tamil Lexicon* glosses *vaciyam* as "magic art of bringing under control a person, spirit or deity" (vol 6: 3461).

9. From nearby Sri Lanka where sorcery is openly practiced, Gananath Obeyesekere also observed that "in general, people who came to sorcery centers labor under a sense of felt injustice, and what they expect of the deity is that 'justice be done' " (1975: 17).

10. In a rare study of witchcraft beliefs in a South Indian village, Scarlett Epstein confirmed that

> not all tensions find expression in witchcraft accusation; only tensions which have no other outlet lead to such accusations. Wherever a judicial mechanism exists to settle quarrels between individuals or groups tensions in their social relations can be brought out into the open and therefore will not be channelled into witchcraft accusations. (1967: 153)

11. This also seems to apply to sorcery in Sri Lanka, see Obeyesekere 1975: 12–14; Kapferer 1983: 76, but see 25–51.

12. These various interpretive options are not mutually exclusive or contradictory. From Sri Lanka, Gananath Obeyesekere has noted: "My illness may be due to *preta dosa* [i.e., intrusion of a mean spirit]. However, the *preta* may have been put into my body by the action of a sorcerer, *huniyan dosa*. This in turn had a particularly strong effect because of my astrologically bad times, *graha dosa*, and this is surely due to my bad karma from a previous birth, *karma dosa*" (1976: 206).

13. When Nagaji listened to other family members describe his client's condition usually some extrapolation was required, for often they failed to list all the symptoms. In this case, Laksmi's mother never mentioned her daughter's convulsions and the deaths of her three children. But it was the duration of her condition that seemed to cue Nagaji that she was suffering from *ēval*. This also led him to conjecture correctly that her parents had already explored a number of therapeutic treatments without success.

14. *Kāṭṭēri* would seem to be the counterpart of the North Indian *Churail*, who is also the spirit of a woman that passed away while in the middle of her reproductive function (Fuller 1992: 230).

15. The distinctive expression of the spell that afflicted Kumar was wild entrancement. Kumar insisted that without the goddess's intervention he would have died of exhaustion, for these uncontrollable outbursts wasted him away. In this respect his predicament was quite different than that of Laksmi and many other sorcery victims, who appeared not so much "possessed" (in a sense of being penetrated and taken over by a spirit) as "dispossessed" of their most basic faculties—speaking, walking, and reproducing. What both conditions shared, however, was their victims' loss of the "command" over their minds and bodies—over their selves.

16. The basic ingredients cost one hundred rupees and Nagaji's fees took another twenty-five rupees.

Chapter 4

1. Nagaji asserted that on full moon (*paurṇamī*) nights, the goddess was particularly strong, explaining that the root for full moon (*paur*) stemmed from the word "power" (this English word is part of the Tamil lexicon and almost sounds like "paur"). His vernacular etymology was also consistent with Fred Clothey's analysis of the Tamil festival calendar when he writes, "The full moon . . . suggests the deity's attainment of full maturity and powers" (1982: 167).

2. However, *cāmi* Nagaji was not above supplementing the revelations of his goddess with mass-produced books that simplify for the general public the Sanskritic and Malayalese textual traditions of magic and sorcery. As he could not read, he would ask others to read him passages from these pamphlets.

3. The use of effigy symbolism in Tamil healing rituals appears to be quite old. According to Fred Clothey, the *Caṅkam* poets describe how the god Murukan's priest would "elevate a puppet designed to take the illness from the maiden" (1978: 27).

4. Each *cāmi* operated with his own semiotic system and what was true for one was not necessarily so for another. For example, the building materials for the dolls were invested with conflicting meanings. For Nagaji rice flour was associated with the transmission of violent stomach pains, to *cāmi* Murukan it caused head aches.

5. The fan is ceremonially crushed when the funeral procession reaches the village boundary. According to one village man, "This means that we want no

further connection with the dead. We don't even want him to rebirth in our lineage."

6. This is a metalinguistic phrase commonly used in Tamil grammar books; it literally means: "making a verb active."

7. In order to understand exactly what Nagaji meant, we must appreciate Hindu beliefs about human birth. Let me relate a chartering myth told to me by a villager:

> At birth, the god Brahmā draws a figure in the shape of a human body [*pāṇṭam*]. Without looking at the result, Brahmā holds the figure behind his back and writes some letters on its forehead. This determines its fate [*viti*], the number of children that it will have, the quality of its health, as well as the duration of its life. Brahmā then looks at the figure, thereby giving it life [*uyir*] and sends it to a man and a woman who have intercourse. When the man's semen flows into the woman's body the life that Brahmā created is transferred into her womb.

In other versions of this story that I recorded the figure was not drawn but was shaped out of clay or blood. And sometimes it was the god Śiva who infused Brahmā's creation with life. But the point made by each narrator was that the length of time that each human being would live was predetermined by Brahmā, and this was called *talai viti* (literally "head fate") or *talai eḻutu* ("headwriting"). When this divine mandate had been thwarted by a sorcerer's "command", it was Nagaji's job to restore the personal fate initially "written" for each of his patients. This was why he marked each ritual enclosure with letters or mantras.

8. The Fabricius dictionary does not gloss this word, but its root meaning *kumaṭṭu* means "to nauseate, and to vomit" (1972: 265).

9. In Tamil rituals these two substances are replete with auspicious, transformational meanings. In her study on the use of color in South Indian rituals, Brenda Beck discerns that their combination is often used to signify the potential revelation of auspicious power or spiritual force in a particular place, a tree, a pot, or a domestic sanctuary (1969: 559).

10. On another occasion I watched this cosmic repositioning accomplished by a different healer who did not use the *cakkaram*. In the rear of his sanctuary he wrapped patients several times in white, thin cotton string (*nūl*), which he fastened to an iron stick planted above the head of the goddess Aṅkāḷaparamēcuvari, who was represented by a twenty-five-foot-long, reclining mud effigy. When all were fastened together, the ritual musicians (*pampaikkārar*) proceeded to invoke the deity. "Through the conduit of the thread ladder [*nūl ēṇi*]," one musician explained, "the goddess's power [*śakti*] flows into the people and protects them." The string served the same purpose as the sacred enclosure, incorporating the victim within larger cosmic processes that possessed the power to end suffering (for similar uses of the string in Sinhalese exorcisms see Yalman 1964).

11. I never observed this prestation in contexts other than death, but I presume that the rice is cooked and eaten by the recipient.

12. At a real death, it is the barber who rips the *muṭitttunṭu* ("knot") that contains the ceremonial change (*kāl paṇam*). He then hands the knot to a washerman who passes it on to the village *tōṭṭi* or Untouchable funeral specialist.

13. This also fits with Sinhalese exorcist or *Bali* rites, which according to Nur Yalman, involve the "construction of elaborate painted clay images and figures

. . . which depict the planetary beings or particular demons" (1964: 122; also see Obeyesekere 1976; Kapferer 1983, 1988, 1997).

14. The fearsome power of "little Satan" also illustrated how the most threatening sorcery demons could be recruited from outside the Hindu pantheon.

15. Nagaji's exegesis also confirmed Margaret Trawick's recent argument that four of the main Tamil healing systems are rooted in the "idea . . . that there cannot be birth without death" (1992: 132).

16. However, according to Louis Dumont, among the *Piramalai Kallars* of Madurai it is a woman—either the widow or daughter of the deceased—who performs the "breaking of the trickling-pot" at the center of the village. The rite is repeated at the cemetery by the chief male mourner (in Good 1991: 162).

17. But I did observe that among low-castes, close female relatives (especially daughters) were allowed to follow the funeral procession up to the village's boundary.

18. The way Laksmi did this strikingly evoked the treatment accorded a missing person presumed to be dead in North India. According to Maurice Bloch and Jonathan Parry, "[His] effigy . . . will be cremated, and his subsequent mortuary rituals performed. If he then reappears, he does so as an intrusive ghost who has no place in the world of the living" (1982: 13).

19. Nagaji may have also predicated his healing rites on the model of the prototypical Hindu renouncer or *sannyasin*, who at the time of his initiation performs his own funeral service (Hopkins 1992: 151; Bloch and Parry 1982: 13).

Chapter 5

1. To the best of my knowledge the ritual that exorcises the untimely dead has received scant treatment in the South Indian ethnographic literature. In the Coimbatore district, for example, W. T. Elmore's meager account of such a ritual was not based on firsthand observation (1984: 51–53). From the Madurai district, Louis Dumont managed to record one exorcist ceremony, but offered little interpretation (1986: 450–52). And in a joint publication with Pocock he made it clear that he attached minimum significance to "the occasional possession of persons by evil spirits or 'demons' " (1959: 56). From Karnataka, Edward Harper acknowledged that in order "to remove the woman's spirit," "many hours" are spent in "negotiations," but he neither elaborated on the ritual nor explored the nature of the possessing spirits (1963). In the Chengelput district, Michael Moffat obtained from one healer his mode of handling *pēy* spirits, but he does not appear to have witnessed this healer in action (1979: 241–43), while from Madras, Lionel Caplan has recently described such exorcist rites, but only from a Christian (Pentecostal) perspective (1989: 64–68). Kalpana Ram has documented rituals of possession and healing at a Catholic shrine in the Kanyakumari district (1991: 94–105). And David Mosse has provided a full description of Catholic exorcism cults in the Ramnad district (1986: 478–87; 1994).

2. For example, Dumont 1986; Opler 1958; Harper 1963; Freed and Freed 1964, 1993; Kakar 1986; Gold 1988; Caplan 1989; Ram 1991.

3. This explanation drew upon I. M. Lewis' argument that possession by amoral spirits cross-culturally affords women and other marginal or subordinate individuals a safe outlet for protesting "status deprivation" (1966, 1971, 1986).

4. For example, Sinhalese women take part in polluting activities such as cooking, disposal of the dead, menstruation, and childbirth that expose them to impure and potentially malevolent forces. They also attract demons because they are

viewed, and view themselves, as sharing certain personality traits with such beings. Much like demons, women are more prone to "emotional disturbance and excess, attachment to persons and relationships born of this world, [and are seen] as being more engaged in the pursuit of worldly desires, and as being mentally weak" (Kapferer 1983: 140). And finally, women's mediating position between the Sinhalese Buddhist poles of nature and culture makes them structurally "weak and vulnerable to disorder" (Kapferer 1983: 147).

5. In the Madurai district, Louis Dumont also noted that relationships between *pēys* and their prey were "very clearly stated to be . . . love relationships" (1986: 450).

6. The predominance of male *pēys* in my sample appears to contradict the findings of David Mosse, who notes that "63% of the ghosts exorcised at the shrine of St. Anthony [in the Ramnad district] were female" (1986: 469). However, his statistics include minor deities who are often female (1986: 455).

7. In Sinhalese scholarship much has been written on what David Scott calls "the vulnerability to the possible consequences of 'being alone' [*taniyama*]" (1991: 96). Ethnographers argue over the specific connotations of this important concept but agree that, as Kapferer put it, being alone "is a precondition of demonic attack" (1983: 70; also see Obeyesekere 1969: 176).

8. David Mosse also notes that "beautification . . . increases vulnerability to attack" (1986: 470). It is because widows lose the privilege of wearing Tamil insignia of female beauty that they are not "caught" by the untimely dead.

9. For scholarship on termite mounds in South Indian temples see Meyer 1986: 58–59; Shulman 1980: 110–30.

10. A standard troupe consists of two *pampai* drummers and three other musicians who respectively play a small hour-glass shaped drum (*uṭukkai*), a pair of anklet-shaped, brass rattles (*cilampu*), and a bell (*maṇi*).

11. The *pampai* drum symbolically encodes the full representation of a possession through the hard (brass) male *pēy* on top of his absorbing (wood) female victim. It also captures meanings associated with the avowed purposes of the exorcism, which as we will see in the next chapter, is to nail the *pēy* on a tree. This is perhaps why, according to Marie-Louise Reiniche, in Tamil dictionaries the *pampai* is referred to as the "drum of forest tracts" (1979: 243, trans. mine).

12. Historical and ethnographic records somewhat conflict on the question as to whom did the goddess originally give this drum. In his monumental survey of *Castes and Tribes of Southern India* Edgar Thurston indicated that "pampaikkārar is an occupational name for Paraiyans [Untouchables], who play on a drum called pampai" (1987, Vol vi: 29). His record is consistent with recent work by Marie-Louise Reiniche, which suggests that, at least in the Tirunelveli district of southern Tamilnadu, the *Paṟaiyaṉs* do play the *pampai* drum at funerals of caste Hindus (1979: 243). Since the *Paṟaiyaṉs* already specialize in escorting the "departed" out of this world by beating drums continuously until the funeral procession reaches the cremation ground, it makes sense that they were the ones entrusted with the responsibility of drumming the untimely dead out of society. But in the South Arcot today, many *pampaikkārar* are neither *Paṟaiyaṉs* nor low-caste. Eveline Meyer observed that such musicians, "often belong to the hunter (*Vēṭar*) or inland-fishermen (*Cempaṭavar*) castes" (1986: 3). This was my impression too, but I also met *pampaikkārar* who belonged to *Kavuṇṭar* and *Nayakkar* castes. And while this defies the caste-specific functions that one usually expects from Hindu ritual specialists, I encountered numerous troupes, like that of Malaiyaṉūr, which brought together a cross-section of caste affiliations. Most of these musicians learned their

trade from their fathers, who, in turn, had inherited it through their paternal line. But quite a few musicians also told me that they had chosen this vocation because of its attractive performative aspects. Yet, all of them denied that there ever was an original caste of *pampaikkārar*. If Thurston was correct, then, it would seem that over the last hundred years the profession had expanded beyond its "traditional" ritual functions. Indeed, I noted one other indication of this development, namely the high fees that the musicians charged for their services. To be sure, a *pampaikkārar* performance mobilized five musicians and could be quite strenuous, but their revenues still exceeded that of other *mēḷams* ("drum," "a collection of musical instruments," and by extension "a band"). In a nearby village, members of the *mēḷam* that played all day at funerals earned only a meal and fifteen rupees collectively. By contrast, the Malaiyaṉūr musicians charged approximately five hundred rupees for a given exorcism.

13. This "warning" is consistent with Tamil ceremonial protocol, which prescribes that village deities be formally consulted before the performance of festivals and other such celebrations (Richard 1920; Beck 1981).

14. This is also done by inserting a lime in the mouth of the possessed woman.

15. The term was also used to address Europeans in colonial times.

16. The exception to this is the issue of caste. As Mosse points out, "Ghosts are of any caste except Brahman" (1986: 469). However, as he adds, *Pēys* tend to identify themselves as being members of communities that are "associated with the fringes of Tamil village society, or with the 'forest' " (ibid). Their low or marginal status might explain why some *pēys* (like Shankar) refuse to name their caste.

Chapter 6

1. This oath used to be common practice in trying Tamil court cases. It was said to be binding. Persons taking it were supposed to flutter out like the camphor flame they extinguished if they swore a false statement.

2. Many Hindu deities are associated with a specific number of heads: six for god Murukaṉ, five for Śiva, four for Brahmā, and one hundred for the goddess Kālī.

3. See Hiltebeitel's detailed analysis of myths and rituals associated with the goddess Draupadi 1988; 1991; also see Doniger 1980: 81–87; Beck 1981.

4. This is corroborated by Doctor C. R. Chandrashekar, associate professor of psychiatry in Bangalore, who relates in a mass-market booklet on possession and witchcraft: "Mani [a young man living in a small village of Karnataka] fell unconscious while *traveling in the bus*. From the bus stand he was taken straight to (a local) temple. He was declared to be . . . victim of . . . a female spirit [who had drowned herself in a local well because her husband was 'ill treating her']" (1991: 23–25, emphasis mine).

5. In Tamil cultural history such associations between a woman's demonic possession and her alleged desire for forbidden sexuality seem to run very deep. According to George Hart, almost two millennia ago the *Caṅkam* poets commonly used the experience of spirit possession as an idiom for speaking of "a girl's despondency at being in love with an unsuitable man" (1975: 23 also see Ramanujan 1967: 78). These meanings still prevail, for the *pēy* in today's social landscape is considered the "unsuitable" suitor par excellence.

6. My discussion of this ritual sequence contradicts Ram's interpretation of the symbolism of unbound female hair in Tamil demonic possession. I agree with

her when she writes that in day-to-day life women's loose hair signifies "disorder," "extreme passion," "sexual passion," and more generally improper femininity (1991: 88, 100–01). But I cannot endorse her argument that possessed women "are deliberately using hair as a symbolic weapon" to break loose from the daily restraints imposed on the female body (1991: 101). At the Hindu exorcisms I documented Tamil women were encouraged to loosen their hair and required to surrender a lock, which was then tied, cut, and nailed—a sequence of actions that aimed at curbing rather than freeing their sexuality.

7. This motif is especially highlighted in the well-known story of the goddess Reṇukā, also known as "Māriamma," that I will recount in the next chapter (also see Trawick 1984; Biardeau 1968; Beck 1981; Assayag 1992).

8. We also note that the *pēy* returns not to the modern wasteland of liminal bus stands and movie theaters, but to the older, barren, drought-ravaged landscape of stagnant pools and tamarind trees. This should come as no surprise. In Tamil culture, the two settings constitute interchangeable topographies, as female alienation must remain identified with whatever liminal spaces are associated with untamed eroticism, and barrenness.

9. In Hinduism fire is perhaps the most common medium by which devotees may experience direct physical contact with the divine. At temple worship, for instance, devotees pass their hands above the flame of a burning camphor, or oil lamp, that the priest extends to them. As the heat contains the deity's essence, worshipers quickly apply their warmed hands to their eyes so as to absorb the divine into their bodies (Fuller 1992: 73; Assayag 1992: 380).

10. The word *alaku* means "the blade of a sword." As for *pū* it means "flowers," but the word is often used as euphemism for "fire."

11. This confirms Howard Eilberg-Schwartz's recent interpretation of symbolism of female beheading in cross-cultural myths and religious traditions. "Removing the female head," he writes, "relieves woman of both identity and voice and reduces her to a mere sexual and reproductive body" (1995: 1). His further observation that "there are other, less obvious, forms of beheading" applies to the Tamil exorcism, which in making the woman's head swirl around unaware in a flurry of loose hair, also "turns [it] into an alluring and sexually provocative organ" (ibid).

12. That this "wild" behavior is a source of danger and disorder is also attested by the fact that, in contrast with life-giving, marital sexuality, this union remains unproductive. It is in this sense that the possessed woman shares the fate of the mythic Tamil prostitute who, according to David Shulman, is also a "symbol of barren eroticism" (1980: 262).

Chapter 7

1. Likewise, the characters of the Tamil narrative genre, known as *kolai chindu* ("ballads of suicide and murder") are not construed as demons (Vanamamalai 1981: 256–315). The well-known story of Nallataṅkāḷ ("Good Little Sister"), for instance, laments how this heroine was led to drown herself and her seven children because of the cruelty of her sister-in-law. At ritual occasions such as funerals, I often witnessed that the recitation of her sufferings brought women and children to tears. Her tragic fate exposed social inequalities and injustice that everyone deplored.

2. Such possessions were the most frequent, if not normative, religious "facts" I recorded. Of 78 people (33 women and 45 men) I interviewed in a South Arcot

village, 5 reported that they had at least once "seen" or "danced" the goddess, none had experienced *pēy* possession, 7 suspected that they had been on one occasion victimized by sorcery, but 10 (7 women and 3 men) said they had been (or were still) visited by their dead relatives.

3. Moreover, in the Hindu worldview dead kin (and especially dead parents) are held as purveyors of key benefits—health, fertility, and personal success. The dead are believed to be supremely solicitous of the welfare of their living family and are recipient of numerous rites of commemoration and ancestral worship (also see Jacob-Pandian 1975; Knipe 1977, 1990; Hanchett 1988: 191–228). At anniversaries of death (*titi*), new moon days (*amāvācai*), and virtually any festive day of the ritual calendar, they are presented with offerings of food and camphor by the eldest male or the married women of the family. As we will see in the next chapter, at times it is even expected that their involvement assumes tutelary proportions.

4. The *karumāti* also finalizes the period of pollution imposed by the death of a kin. Following the ceremony, relatives celebrate the resumption of their day-to-day lives by feasting on meat and other delicacies that are prohibited throughout the mourning phase.

5. The marriage necklace (*tāli*) is actually not "cut" but simply removed, a rite often performed by the widow's brother.

6. And she was not alone. Many Tamil women complained to me about their propensity for unpredictable and unrestrained trance-behavior [by the dead or even by the gods], which they regarded as a liability if not a curse. To the extent that they lost control, the outward predicament of these helpless dancers seemed not unlike that of people caught by demons. We recall how Kumar, a victim of sorcery, was regularly subjected to exhaustive entrancements (see chapter 3). But once again, the difference here, and it is a significant one, is that one did not separate from protective spirits, even though their bodily manifestations and claims might be disagreeable.

7. To Leila the medium's seance offered some logic behind recent unfortunate events, such as her son's sickness. It was not that she directly attributed their cause to Ramesh, but she came to feel that he had not prevented them. And she concluded that through "fluctuating happiness" her husband was indeed making sure that she would "remember" him.

8. This Māriamman narrative appears to be quite old, as evidenced by the fact that in 1709 the French priest, Jean-Jacques Tessier de Queralay, recorded a remarkably similar version (in Dharampal 1982: 130).

9. This goddess also controls the forces of "coolness." Another gloss for *māri* may be "rain" so that Māriamman, as Trawick pointed out, can also mean the "rain mother" (1984: 31). This was why when Māriamma entranced Leila at the Mēl Malaiyaṉūr temple, she was asked by the musicians to forecast the coming of rain. Since "rain, moisture, and coolness," according to Trawick, "are closely associated with concepts of love, pleasure, and compassion," this goddess also has a benevolent side (1984: 26).

10. Her bodily motions exemplified the sort of trances that Gilbert Rouget calls "figurative," in which the possessed clearly imitate the distinguishing behavior of the supernaturals who have taken them over (1985: 115). To Rouget such imitative trances clearly suggest a somewhat higher degree of identification with spirits than what trancers express in what he terms, "abstract" dances, which he sees as "pure physical expenditure" of the energy overpowering trancers (1985: 118). He specifies that trance adepts are more likely to realize "figurative" dances than

neophytes (1985: 117). However, in the case of Leila this point is debatable. Her very first trance episode indicated that even at this early stage she was prone to intense identificatory experiences. As we recall her hopping dance adopted the behavior of her husband as she had last seen it in the dream.

Chapter 8

1. According to Pier Vitebsky, the Soras, an aboriginal tribe of eastern India, also discriminate between "funeral shamans" (*sanatung*) who reincorporate the dead by means of trance so that they may "dialogue" with the living, and "divining/healing shamans" (*tedung*) (1993: 18, 60). It is my impression that in contrast with the Sora, however, Tamil practitioners who specialize in personifying gods and goddesses rank higher than those, like Padmini, who mediate on behalf of human spirits. I base this comment on a conversation I had once with a *Paṟaiyaṉ* diviner who was initiated by goddess Māriattai (a form of Māriamman) five days after his elder brother "had become cool," died of smallpox. To him it was critical that there was "no connection" between his Māriattai and his brother's spirit who had been recalled to join this goddess. When I asked what difference it made, he replied:

> If the spirit of my brother was on me I would not be able to help people. Only my family and myself would benefit from his advice. This is why I am telling you that it is the goddess herself who has descended upon me. How else would I be able to tell this lady how to cure her baby and this man how to remove the sorcery spell?

To this specialist the goddess stood above and beyond personal ties and was not only more powerful but also more "moral" than the spirits of the dead who symbolized fragmentary solidarity.

2. While I only worked with one such medium who could transact with the dead, in Vellore in the North Arcot district Edward Montgomery observed seven such "trance therapists"—four women and three men—who, he wrote, "serve in a regularized schedule on certain hours of certain days solely as mediums for their clients' communications with the spirits of deceased relatives" (1974/75: 112). The only specialist whom Montgomery profiled was a young woman whose career was launched unexpectedly by hosting the goddess (in this case Māriamma) when she was a girl. Later the goddess frustrated her marriage and, like Padmini, she devoted her life to incorporating the spirits of once-living people.

The high percentage of male mediums reported by Montgomery is somewhat surprising for it was my strong impression that in Tamilnadu women usually mediate communications between the living and the dead. We recall that victims of the untimely dead known as *pēys* are predominantly female. Moreover, women appear most likely to "dance" the spirits of dead relatives. This will be underscored in the next two chapters as I document that out of twenty-six instances of trance at ceremonial "invitations" to deceased relatives, nineteen were enacted by female members of the family.

In the adjacent state of Andhra Pradesh, women also appear to mediate contacts with the otherworld. Charles Nuckolls reports that among the Jalaris "possession-mediums" are female (1991b, 1991c). What is interesting is that in this case these mediums communicate with the spirits of their clients' dead relatives through the intermediary of "tutelary deities" who are "the spirits of their own male children . . . who died in infancy or early adolescence" (Nuckolls 1991b: 63). Also from Andhra Pradesh, David Knipe documents how during certain ceremonial nocturnal processions held during Mahashivaratri (Great Śiva's night), the spirits of deceased children often possess their mothers (1990).

The wide participation of women as corporal hosts for the dead seems connected with broader Hindu notions regarding female ritual roles. In Tamilnadu, it is women who are responsible for maintaining links between this world and the hereafter. At funerals of relatives, neighbors, and friends they sing laments. Many (like Rita) have dreams which alert them that a dead relative is in need of ceremonial attention. Even female ancestors maintain this mediation. We recall that when Leila was first possessed by her husband, two female spirits, envoys of the afterworld, came to claim his soul.

3. In Tamilnadu, such sicknesses are not merely understood to be caused by the goddess but *are* the goddess herself. As we have seen in chapter 1, despite their element of harmful contact these afflictions may thus be construed as a sign of divine election or, in Tamil, *aruḷ* ("grace") and may initiate a career of devoteeship or even divining or healing (also see Trawick-Egnor 1984; Meyer 1986: 67). What has been less appreciated is that those (especially children and teenagers) who "die" as a result of such sicknesses obtain permanent identification with the goddess and are eligible for deification. A recent study, however, has shown that in Andhra Pradesh all spirits of deceased infants and children regardless of the manner of their death are actually eligible for worship, either at home or in a nearby temple (Knipe 1990).

4. As we will see in the next chapter an investiture is expensive. As Rita explained, it can cost "as much as 600 rupees." She detailed some of the expenses, "The ritual musicians will charge as much as 250 rupees. We will need new clothes to wear that day. And our little sister will need a new skirt and special dishes."

5. Marie-Louise Reiniche's analysis of a similar case in a Tirunelveli village helps us understand this bond to which our spirit appealed. Reiniche explains that the dead virgin is "the symbol of an alliance which has not realized itself" (1979: 69, trans. mine). Unwed and without children, she is incapable of marrying her own offspring to those of her brother, as should be the case according to South Indian preferential marriage patterns. And this is why, Reiniche adds, in her case study the spirit of a dead virgin manifested herself to her brother's wife who had just given birth to a baby girl and asked for a cloth (1979: 69). The plea to be consecrated in her brother's household at that time was actually a demand to realize a deified alliance in place of the human alliance that had been thwarted by her own death. Reiniche's analysis appears correct, for as we will see in chapter 9, the investiture ceremony that our spirit insisted upon is richly encoded with bridal symbolism.

6. In Tamil folk taxonomy dirges are actually classified according to relational kinship categories. Those that deplore the loss of fathers, mothers, husbands, brothers, sisters, sons, and daughters are given special intensity.

7. In an attempt to explain the "intense attachment between brother and sister," Margaret Trawick has recently suggested that in Tamil childhood erotic feelings for the mother are transferred to those who share the same womb and likewise must remained repressed (1990a: 172). As she writes: "Never being fulfilled, the brother and sister's desire for each other will never be spent. It will remain chaste and eternal, but pervaded by pain. Each will feel sacrificed—the one a martyred protector, the other a martyred innocent. In quest of a cultural ideal

. . . each will seek to recover the other. But only in death, out of time and beyond the code, will they find this recovery possible" (1990a: 172; also see 170–78; 187–204). This is, of course, precisely what the spirit Mīṉāṭshi was now proposing to her brother.

8. Similarly Marie-Louise Reiniche reports that the newborn girl of her case study in Tirunelveli was named after the deceased little sister of the husband (1979: 69). To Reiniche this affirmed the common origin of the two girls in the same lineage. But since women ideally reproduce themselves by marrying their children to those of their brothers it is no wonder that spirits of dead little virgin sisters like Mīṉāṭshi (and her Tirunelveli counterpart) were granted the right to gain a second human life in the lines of descent of their brothers and to "possess," or become the persons (or names) of their nieces.

Chapter 9

1. This ceremony has received scant treatment in the South Indian ethnographic literature. In the Chengelput district, for example, Michael Moffat's brief account of such a ritual does not appear based on firsthand observation (1979: 227–28). E. T. Jacob-Pandian recorded the ceremony in a non-Brahmin household of high ritual status, but offers little interpretation (1975). None of the classic monographs on Tamil village life (Dumont 1986; Beck 1972; Reiniche 1979) contain any description of this ritual. For detailed ethnographic accounts of other South Indian ceremonial reincorporations of dead relatives into household devotions see Hanchett 1988 and Knipe 1990.

2. As Michael Moffat has written, "The family goddess, a being called *puvaaDai*, is the spirit of a deceased woman in the family, one who has died in an auspicious married state rather than in an inauspicious widowed state (1979: 226–27). And Margaret Trawick concurs, "Female house deities . . . are, minimally, those who have died unwidowed, 'still with flowers' (*pūvodakkāri*)" but she adds that girls "who die unmarried" also become family goddesses (1990a: 168; also see Elmore for Telugu worship of the married woman 1984: 27).

3. The few available reports on the ceremony that incorporates the newly dead into Tamil household devotions suggest that it is performed in times of crisis to counteract misfortune. This is how, for example, E. T. Jacob-Pandian describes the circumstances that led a Tamil family to hold this ritual:

> The head of the household was once a successful merchant but had suffered several financial setbacks. A few members of the household were sick, and a son's marriage and the ear-piercing ceremonies of the other children were postponed. All these misfortunes were attributed to the non-performance of appropriate mortuary rites for a daughter who had met with an untimely death. It was believed that her spirit did not have a resting place and that proper rituals would make the spirit function as a family deity and thus prevent any more misfortunes in the family. (1975: 76)

While in the South Arcot district this can also be the case, none of the fourteen investitures I recorded arose out of affliction. The closest I came to witnessing a prophylactic scenario was when the "cool" little sister of the last chapter's case study assured her brother and his wife that her deification would end their troubles. But by the end of my fieldwork, this spirit's "request to come home" was still not met, some eight months after her initial communication to her family through the medium.

4. These investiture rituals may also be conducted prior to the marriage of younger sons or first-born daughters who are orphaned. Of the fourteen "invitations" that I recorded, however, only one was held for the coming wedding of a first daughter.

5. Such "invitations" appear to be old in India. The Brahmanical rite, known as *Nandi Sraddha*, served to "request" paternal ancestors (*nandimukha pitrs*) to "utter benedictions" at the marriages of sons and daughters, the move to a new house, and the birth of a son (see Kane 1973: 527–28). And A. R. Kulkarni documents that as early as 1664 the Bhonsale (warrior) kings of Satara in Karnatakka hand-wrote formal letters to their deceased ancestors, "inviting [them] to a marriage and seeking their blessings" (1966: 193). Apparently these "requests" remained "in vogue at least till the end of the nineteenth century," upon which time the descendants of the Bhonsale kings only invoked the blessings of family deities at the time of a marriage (Kulkarni 1966: 193–194).

6. Except for garish posters of the great Hindu gods, the only other representation of a deity in this domestic sanctuary is usually three horizontal stripes in yellow turmeric paste on the wall, which are encircled and interspersed by vermillion dots.

7. This lamp is called *Kamakshiammaṉ viḷakku* and represents Laksmi, the goddess of fortune.

8. Symbolism of touching and physical contact is often exploited in Tamil rituals to seal an agreement between two or more parties. At a real betrothal (*paricam*: "touch," "contact"), for instance, bride givers sanction the coming engagement by placing their right hands over those of the groom's parents.

9. This order accords with Olivier Herrenschmidt's observation that in India processions exhibit three successive categories of ceremonial participants, in the following order: musicians, carriers of symbols, and those who occupy what he terms the "place of honor" (1982: 45–49; in Hiltebeitel 1991: 449). For this *pūjā* it appears that the groom is this designate, for he is usually last in line.

10. In most scholarship on Tamil folk worship, the icon of the flower-wrapped pot carried during ceremonial processions at yearly temple festivals is said to represent the goddess (Hiltebeitel 1991; Moffat 1979; Dumont 1986; Reiniche 1979; Meyer 1986). For instance in 1921, Henri Whitehead observed that during a village festival in the Trichinopoly district, this *karakam "is treated exactly like the goddess"* (1988: 38; emphasis mine). In the present context, however, this religious symbol embodies the wedding party's guest of honor, the *pūvāṭaikkāri*, or "the woman who wears flowers." For another material representation of the dead see David Knipe, who documented in the town of Rajahmundry in Andhra Pradesh how the spirits of deceased infants and children are worshiped, either at home or in a local temple, in the form of "ash-fruits" (*vibhuti-pandu*)—small cones made of cow dung ash mixed with gum (1990).

11. Among Harijan families the collection of the mud is highly ceremonialized. Once I witnessed that the entire procession stopped at the cremation grounds. Before the deceased's grave the musicians proceeded to invoke the spirit who responded by possessing one of her relatives. After she expressed her satisfaction with the coming *pūjā*, the cone-shaped rock that marked her grave was unearthed and three handfuls of soil were wrapped in a leaf. The stone was then replaced, a lump of camphor was lit on the grave and the procession with the precious mud moved on to the main ritual site.

12. The symbolism of the *karakam* pot is also consistent with broader, Tamil ritual representations of human death. In chapter 4 we have learned that at funeral rites the chief mourner performs what is called in Tamil "the breaking of the trickling pot" (*kalikuṭam uṭaittal*), an act that for one of my consultants meant "the end of life." But this symbolic destruction of the physical remains of a person also represents, as M. N. Srinivas noted among the Coorgs of South India, a termination of social bonds (1952: 151). So it seems fitting that in this ritual context a "remade" pot of water should represent both the dead's reembodiment and his reunification with kin. And since Tamil burial practices call for returning the corpse to earth, it also makes sense that mud from their grave would infuse the *karakam* with the personalized essence of the dead. The ceremonial pot thus becomes a perfect icon for the reincorporation of human spirits in the household.

13. When high castes (*Mutaliyār* and *Ceṭṭiyār*) perform such *pūjās*, instead of depositing mud in the pot they use the *nūlēṇi* ("thread ladder"). The groom is given a thread (*nūl*) to which is tied a cone-shaped bunch of margosa leaves. Standing at the edge of the nearby well (the *pūjā* is always performed near a water source), he lowers the leaves in the water while the thread's other end is wedged into the *karakam*. This thread is the "ladder" (*ēṇi*), the musicians explained to me, by which spirits of the dead "climb" into this world. Unlike the mud deposit, suggestive that the dead reside in the graveyard in their bodily remains and close to the living, the "thread ladder" hints that this world and the hereafter are positioned on different cosmological planes. To be sure, the dead do not dwell under water, but water is considered only the conduit between states of life and death. This notion appears influenced by Sanskrit conceptions of the afterlife, for funeral practices represent a pond as passage *to* the otherworld. On the last of the funeral cycle (*karumāti*) three small, iconic stones representing the deceased and two of his or her ancestors are ceremonially sunk in the village tank or a river.

By enabling the dead to return by way of the gate they have left, however, this "thread ladder" converts Sanskritized funeral practices, which actually aim at preventing the return of the dead (Malamoud 1982: 443). The procedure actually makes three concessions to this orthodox system of beliefs. The thread suggests that the means of communication between the social and spiritual worlds are fragile and man-made. The ladder emphasizes that the dead reside far. Their disembodied form is conveyed by the fact that in order to personalize the *karakam* with the unique life-force of spirits, their names are uttered as a camphor lump is lit on a betel leaf inside the pot. Their identities therefore are not invested in their bodies. Finally, the return to life is conceived as an ascent, a movement which folk Hinduism commonly associates with deification (Blackburn 1985: 36).

It would be wrong to infer that the two methods for activating the *karakam* are mutually incompatible. Middle-ranking castes, such as the *Kavuṇṭar* community, combine both the mud deposit and the "thread ladder." However, *Kavuṇṭar* families themselves do not collect the mud. Instead in the morning of the *pūjā* the village washerman, a funeral specialist, procures it on their behalf. Moreover, both procedures share (or there would not be a need for the *pūjā*) a common premise: the dead must return to their living kin.

14. The desired behavior of dead spirits was actually assumed to be directly proportional to the family affection and devotion extended to them. "If relatives have continuously worshiped the spirit since its death," a musician said, "the *pūvāṭaikkāri* will arrive fast." But he was highly dubious that if over ten or fifteen years elapsed since its death the spirit would heed the invitation, and the absence of any family member could also delay its arrival. But the same consultant believed

these problems could still be overcome, "if it is essential to the groom to receive the blessing of the *pūvāṭaikkāri*."

15. As Eveline Meyer also observed the trance is stopped by the application of sacred ash on the dancer's forehead (1986: 258).

16. Eveline Meyer also noted that in Tamilnadu "certain tests" are performed before a sacrifice (*pali*), a firewalk (*kuṇṭum iṟaṅkutal*), or making the sword stand upright on the *karakam* pot (*alaku niṟuttal*) (1986: 237–238). Their successful outcomes ensure that the goddess "accepts" the offerings, "gives her blessings" for the firewalk, or "simply proves [her] presence or grace in making the sword stand upright" (ibid). In the context of our marriage invitation it would appear that the "test" fulfills the same consecrative purpose. The idea is to verify that the spirit has truly elected and merged with its chosen medium.

17. If the spirits of a mother and father appear together they announce themselves as *orumuham*, meaning "one face."

18. As many ethnographers have observed in Tamilnadu, whenever there is *karakam* crowning there is trance (*āṭṭam*, "shaking") (Whitehead 1988: 101–4; Dumont 1986: 377, 433, 435; Moffat 1979: 227; Hiltebeitel 1991: 465, footnote 58). We may recall how in chapter 2 the *cāmi* Nagaji automatically entered into a state of trance by placing such *karakam* on his head.

19. The *karakam* bearer thus stands in structural opposition to the basket carrier. As the latter transports the raw elements (pot, flowers, turmeric, and vermillion powders, etc.) that would transform the dead into *pūvāṭaikkāri*, the former bears this "woman who wears flowers" back home. We understand why the basket carrier is preferably a married woman, such as a daughter-in-law, while the *karakam* bearer is always the groom. In Tamilnadu preparing the bride for her wedding is the ceremonial responsibility of auspicious, married women, but escorting her from the outskirts of the village to her new in-laws' home is always the duty of the groom. This was also the case at the one *pūjā* that I witnessed for the marriage of a young woman, the bride's younger, unmarried brother carried the pot back home.

20. Their order suggested a modification of the already mentioned, tripartite structure that Herrenschmidt discerned in Indian processions (1982: 45–49; in Hiltebeitel 1991: 449). Much as Alf Hiltebeitel has observed in other South Arcot *karakam* processions, the central position accorded these carriers of ceremonial pots suggests that they occupy "the place of honor" otherwise reserved, according to Herrenschmidt, to those who usually bring up the rear (1991: 449).

21. The *pūvāṭaikkāris* are, of course specifically invested in strengthening the *tāli* of their own families.

22. Among the Rajputs of Rajasthan, Lindsey Harlan also notes that however many *satimatas*, or spirits of "good women," a family may worship in the domestic sanctuary, "it generally collapses them into one personality and refers to them in the singular" (1992: 136).

23. That the crowning of the decorated pot symbolizes a "recapitation" is also suggested by a smallpox healing rite witnessed in 1709 by the French missionary, Jean-Jacques Tessier de Queralay, in Pondichery. Apparently this ritual was performed to placate Māriamma, the smallpox goddess who, as we heard in chapter 7, had her head chopped off by her son and reconnected to the body of an Untouchable woman. This is what Tessier observed:

> Carrying on her head a vase filled with water and margosa leaves, and holding in her right hand some leaves of that tree and a rattan cane, a

Paraiyan̲ (Untouchable) woman, a servant of this goddess, proceeds through town—accompanied of musicians and other persons in charge of receiving alms. Each time that she stops in front of a house, she dances, the vase on her head. (in Dharampal 1982: 130–31, translation mine)

The procession documented by the priest reenacted the ambiguous corporal predicament of this goddess whose head, here symbolized by the *karakam* pot, was attached to the body of a female Untouchable specialist. Does this not suggest that in the context of our "invitation" the crowning with the *karakam* represents the reconnection of the disembodied parents, "heads of the household" (*talaik-kaṭṭu*) to the bodies of their "headless" children?

Chapter 10

1. See Herdt's excellent discussion of this debate, 1981: 328–329; and Turner 1967).

2. From nearby Chengelput district Michael Moffat recorded the same folk etymology. One of his high-caste informants, a *Mutaliyār* man, told him that the term *puuvaaDai* "derived from the way the goddess was brought from a well in a flower pot: *puu* "flower" + *aDai* = "coming in contact with" (1979: 226, footnote #2).

3. This is in sharp contrast with most historical cases of incorporation by means of affinal ties. Usually the supernatural "bride" is an outsider—be "she" a northern deity, a female tutelary on the margins of the "orthodox" cult, or a previously unworshiped goddess.

4. I observed that women who were "born in" the house (*pir̲anta peṇhal*) were twice as likely to perform this task than women who "entered" it at marriage (*puhunta peṇhal*). This makes good sense, for paternal aunts and sisters stand in a direct structural equivalence with the *pūvāṭaikkāri*. Upon their marriage, they become guests in their natal households (*tāy vīṭu*) and depend on "invitations" or propositions to marry their children to those of their brothers to formally reenter the house in capacity of affines.

5. Unlike the Malaiyan̲ūr musicians who had conducted Shanti's exorcism in chapter 6, the *pampaikkārar* who officiated at this particular "invitation" were not attached to any temple. They performed at yearly village festivals, or at investiture ceremonies that were sponsored by families of the same caste (*Par̲aiyan̲*) and ceremonial status. Throughout the ritual season—from the Tamil month of *Māci* (February/March) until *Āṭi* (July/August)—they were constantly busy, but the rest of the year they complemented their income by working in the millet or peanut fields. Less flamboyant perhaps than the Malaiyan̲ūr musicians, these *pampaikkārar* were nonetheless talented and insightful and greatly facilitated my understanding of this system of familial worship that Saravana's family celebrated.

6. These "notification" rites have much to say about the unfinished business between the family and their current household deities. At the fourteen *pūjās* that I recorded, all five spirits who came inside the house had undergone this ceremonial investiture within the previous fifteen years. But when the last ritualized relationship with the *pūvāṭaikkāri* had taken place longer ago than that, the line of communication between the living and the dead might have been too weak to be renewed for no spirit showed up. In such case this formal preamble was skipped. When a family managed to maintain an active practice of conducting these functions, the spirits normally appeared quite rapidly. Sometimes there was not even

time to finish the formulaic praise (*kāppu*) to the gods who patronize ritual art before they "dance."

7. It was not uncommon for the goddess Aracāttā to appear to her devotees in the form of a snake. No sooner had they reached the family grove than the women anointed with holy substances the two young margosa trees in which, I was told, the goddess herself lay coiled.

8. It is David Shulman's reading of the *Brahmāṇa* narrative of Śunaḥśepa that elucidates this symbolism of incest. The story begins with an explanation of what a man finds in a son. The answer is similar to that of our ritual: the father finds a self in the son (1993: 88). But as Shulman points out, this explication also "builds up to the description of procreation as inherently incestuous" (1993: 92). As he elaborates: "The father enters his wife, who thereby becomes his mother; he is born again, renewed, as the child, who is thus little more than a replica of his father" (ibid). The same reasoning underlies these marriages with the dead.

Chapter 11

1. Until the beginning of the foundation of the Danish/German mission in Tranquebar, south of Pondichery in 1706, the Reformed Churches had little impact over the missionization of South India. However, British, Danish, and Dutch priests like Roger were dispatched to the so-called "Malabar Country" to serve the religious needs of their respective country fellows who were posted at trading stations such as Paliacat, the first Dutch *comptoir* in India.

2. The contrast between human or divine forces should not be understood as a sharp opposition; as Christopher Fuller points out, Hindu "religion is premised on the lack of any absolute divide between them" (1992: 32). Indeed, the myths of origin associated with lineage deities often relate how they too have once met death, and particularly an untimely death. Nonetheless, their ontological statuses distinguish them from family deities: while one comes and goes the other remains, while one is intimately related to the family the other is simply a familiar guest, and while one is fickle the other is entirely dependable.

3. Common genealogical ancestry sometimes defines the relationship between a *tēvam* ("deity") and its *kulam* ("lineage"). However, such ties are putative and cannot be demonstrated.

4. When the lineage deity is denied this "share," when the children's initiation is performed far from his or her temple and without any ceremony it is known as *tiruṭṭu kātukuttal*, meaning "stolen ear-piercing rite." That may prompt the lineage deity to take back his or her "gift" of "life."

5. Nor do Periyāṇṭavar's festivities follow the common protocol of Tamil lineage cults. These cults vary according to the identity of the lineage deities and the idiosyncratic relationships people have established with them (Reiniche 1979; Beck 1972; Moffat 1979; Dumont 1986). Yet as Louis Dumont also discerned in the Madurai district, lineage worship "can be reduced to a common formula. . . . a play in four acts" (1986: 417). First, members of the descent group gather inside the temple to "offer" (*kāṭṭu*) *pūjā*. Second, they settle on a spot outside the sanctuary where married women boil offerings of sweetened rice (*poṅkal*). Third, they engage in the "cutting" (*veṭṭal*) of a male goat, a rite often performed by a low-caste specialist. Last, they complete what Dumont calls the "distribution of honours [*mudalmei*, "primacy"]" or apportionment of the offerings to the various householders of the lineage (ibid).

6. The cost of the Periyāṇṭavar worship considerably exceeds the amount usually spent on household gods and other lineage deities. At the time of my fieldwork it approximated 4,000 rupees (about $180 at 1991 international exchanges rates, but closer to $4,000 in actual buying power). Part of this amount goes into the cost of building the god's icon and temporary sanctuary. Thus truck drivers must be paid to haul fresh clay for the effigy and the musicians who will actually mold and dress the god, give him life, and "invite" him to the "feast," will also need remuneration. Finally, the numerous vegetarian offerings, the sacrifice, and the actual "feast" are expensive.

7. Other ethnographers have noted that at Tamil temple festivals the tying of such protective wristlets officially inaugurates the ceremonial process (Hiltebeitel 1991: 88, 441; also see Beck 1981: 110).

8. For instance the god Śiva sits across a bull (Nanti) and Ganesh faces a mouse (Eli).

9. This rite is done in secrecy so that people's glances do not pollute it.

10. This impression is confirmed by Henri Whitehead's observation that in 1921, in a village of the Pudukkottai taluk, after sacrificing a goat to the goddess Pidari, "the *pujari* with the *kapu* on his wrist takes the earthen pot, with the blood of the black goat inside it . . . and runs to the boundary-stone on the extreme limit of the village land. About twenty or thirty villagers run with him, holding him by the arms, as he is out of his senses, being possessed with Pidari" (1988: 103–4).

Chapter 12

1. For Sanskrit versions, see Zimmer 1948; Doniger 1973; Kinsley 1987; for South Indian ritual enactments of the story see Beck 1981; Meyer 1986; Knipe 1990.

2. Shulman takes this king as a prime exemplar of a popular figure of Tamil Saivite myths, whom he terms the "demon devotee" (1980: 317). In brief, Shulman detects in South Indian tradition a "fascination" with demons who flaunt the intensity of their devotion, even competing on that score with the gods. Being demons (or like Takkaṉ, enemies of the gods), however, their *bhakti* is invariably "imperfect and self-centered" and masks a drive for "naked power" (1980: 319). So these figures must be executed and according to Shulman, their "death, however unwilling, at the hands of the god is a recommendation for self-sacrifice, for the loss of self that accompanies the recognition of an inner identity with the god" (1980: 320). This must have also been clear to my narrator, for when I asked him, "Why would your people want to worship this demon?" he answered, "Periyāṇṭavar's death, like that of Takkaṉ, taught us to have devotion for the god." We are thus a long way from the Dutch priest's explanation that blood sacrifice is a means to ward off a dreadful power. True Periyāṇṭavar *is* something of a demon. And true again when I asked my narrator why his people presented Periyāṇṭavar, with "lives," he replied, "because blood is what demons (*pēy*) like." But Periyāṇṭavar is hardly an object of fear. To the contrary, people trust, indeed expect, that he will look out for them.

3. Moreover, many vows are made to gods who dwell in brahmanical temples where, as Olivier Herrenschmidt has observed, each pilgrim "whatever his mother tongue, home state, or caste may be, is there for himself, in a private and individual capacity and not as a member of a collectivity" (1981: 139; trans. mine). We may recall that in chapter 2 I introduced a young woman who had pledged to

pay the god Vēṇkātesvara (Viṣṇu) in rupee coins seven months after the birth of a child at his famous abode at Tirupati in the state of Andhra Pradesh. To Herrenschmidt, the pilgrimages that result from such vows express what he calls, "la 'religion de l'individu' " (1981: 138; Dumont makes the same point 1986: 456).

4. As Michael Moffat noticed among Harijans of the Chengelput district, "a person might exhaust the powers of available local gods, and be referred to the power of a new god, some distance away" (1979: 224). If that "power" proves efficacious, people then might adopt this "desired" or "chosen" deity (*iṣta tēvam*) as a personal tutelary (ibid). This was the case for Perumal who, after being granted a vow by Murukan, had walked barefoot on pilgrimage to this god's famous hilltop abode in the town of Paḻaṉi.

5. But this climax to the ceremony was delayed by an inauspicious astrological intervention. It was now near 4:30 P.M., and the malevolent influence of the asterism, Irāku kālam, began on Sunday at that particular hour. During this unfavorable interval (*Irāku kālam*), which falls every day of the week at different times, no ceremonial activity (especially none honoring a deity) could be undertaken (Clothey 1982: 160). Not until 6:00 P.M. were the musicians free to prepare the sacrificial grounds.

6. As Marie-Louise Reiniche points out, however, it is not as much marriage but conception that is then prohibited. Throughout the month of *Āṭi* young couples are separated in order to prevent birth nine months later during the Tamil month of *Cittirai*—an inauspicious month for coming into this world (1979: 46; footnote # 8).

7. However, the *pūvāṭaikkāri* has precedence in the ceremonial complex described in this chapter, for "she" must authorize the sacrifice and be presented with vegetarian offerings before the lineage god. This etiquette may suggest a concession made to the value of marriage, women, and their birth-giving potential. In this world marital fertility cannot be entirely denied, for without it there can be no life at all. This is perhaps why the "woman who wears flowers" must sanction the "life" obtained from lineage cults.

8. Olivier Herrenschmidt has also observed that in the state of Andhra Pradesh, "the [bloody] sacrifice serves first to satisfy the needs of the collectivity and, second, those of the individual" (1981: 140; trans. mine).

9. According to J. C. Heesterman, this was also the case for Vedic sacrifice, which was an arena of conflict, a world so fraught with tension and rivalry, that it was "broken at its very center and forever balanced on the brink of collapse" (1993: 44).

Conclusion

1. Only once, in the case of exorcism, did I make my own connection between myth and ritual. It was not the narrative of Śiva's Brahmanicide recited to me by one of the musician-exorcists that allowed me to see that at the end of this ritual the demon's severed head was attached to the tamarind tree, but the apparently unrelated story of Māriamma's "recapitation" on to the body of an Untouchable woman. There seems justification for placing the Tamil exorcism into two, rather than one, mythic contexts. In her analysis of a Māriyamman festival in the Coimbatore District of Tamilnadu, Brenda Beck notes that "the ceremonies . . . do not reenact any one myth . . . Instead, they serve to combine and merge scraps of stories from many sources into a locally distinctive whole" (1981: 128).

2. Once freed from their demons, women may be thereafter linked up to the goddess through an initiation that may even turn into a vocation of "sign-decoding." Nothing prevents them from switching specializations and embodying the dead spirits related to their consultants. Or a woman may first be visited by her deceased husband's spirit and come to host the goddess and mediate between the living and the dead. And those who fall under a sorcerer's "command" may commence a new cycle of trance experiences. De Heusch's comment that "the amazing variety of African forms of possession truly constitutes a field of transformations" applies in abundance to Tamilnadu (1981: 175).

REFERENCES

Appadurai, Arjun. 1986. "Is Homo Hierarchicus?" *American Ethnologist* 13: 745–761.

———. 1990. "Topographies of the Self: Praise and Emotion in Hindu India." In *Language and the Politics of Emotion*. Eds. Catherine A. Lutz and Lila Abu-Lughod, 92–112. Cambridge: Cambridge University Press.

Appadurai, Arjun, and Carol Breckenridge. 1976. "The South Indian Temple: Authority, Honor, and Redistribution." *Contributions to Indian Sociology*, n.s. 10: 187–209.

Assayag, Jackie. 1992. *La Colère de la déesse decapitée. Traditions, cultes et pouvoir dans le sud de l'Inde*. Paris. CNRS editions.

Babb, Lawrence A. 1975. *The Divine Hierarchy. Popular Hinduism in Central India*. New York. Columbia University Press.

———. 1981. "Glancing: Visual Interaction in Hinduism." *Journal of Anthropological Research* 37: 387–401.

Bang, B.G. 1973. "Current Concepts of the Smallpox Goddess Sitala in Parts of West Bengal." *Man in India* 53 (1): 79–104.

Barnett, Steve A. 1976. "Coconuts and Gold: Relational Identity in a South Indian Caste." *Contributions to Indian Sociology* (n.s.) 10: 133–156.

Bayly, Susan. 1989. *Saints, Goddesses and Kings. Muslims and Christians in South Indian Society 1700–1900*. Cambridge: Cambridge University Press.

Beattie, John. 1963. "Sorcery in Bunyoro." In *Witchcraft and Sorcery in East Africa*. Eds. John Middleton and E. H. Winter, 27–56. London: Routledge & Kegan Paul.

Beck, Brenda E. F. 1969. "Colour and Heat in South Indian Rituals." *Man* 4 (4): 553–572.

———. 1972. *Peasant Society in Konku : A Study of Right and Left Sub-castes in South India*. Vancouver: University of British Columbia Press.

———. 1979. "Body Imagery in the Tamil Proverbs of South India." *Western Folklore* 38 (1): 21–41.

———. 1981. "The Goddess and the Demon. A Local South Indian Festival and its Wider Context." In *Autour de la Déesse hindoue*. Ed. Madeleine Biardeau. *Puruṣārtha* 5: 85–136.

Bell, Catherine. 1997. *Ritual. Perspectives and Dimensions*. New York: Oxford University Press.

Berreman, Gerald, 1971. "The Brahmanical View of Caste." *Contributions to Indian Sociology*, n.s. 5: 16–23.

Béteille, André. 1986. "Individualism and Equality." *Current Anthropology* 27 (2): 121–134.

Bharathi, B.S. 1993. "Spirit Possession and Healing Practices in a South Indian Fishing Community." *Man in India* 73(4): 343–352.

Biardeau, Madeleine. 1968. "La décapitation de Renuka dans le mythe de Parasurama." In *Pratidanam: Indian, Iranian and Indo-European Studies presented to Franciscus Bernardus Jacobus Kuiper on his Sixtieth Birthday*. Eds. J. C. Heesterman, G. H. Schokker, and V. I. Subramoniam, 563–572. The Hague: Mouton.

———. 1989. *Histoires de poteaux: Variations védiques autour de la Déesse hindoue*. Paris: École française d'Extrême-Orient, Vol. 154.

Blackburn, Stuart. H. 1985. "Death and Deification: Folk Cults in Hinduism." *History of Religions* 24 (3): 255–274.

———. 1988. *Singing of Birth and Death: Texts in Performance*. Philadelphia. University of Pennsylvania Press.

Bloch, Maurice. 1988. "Introduction: Death and the Concept of a Person." In *On the Meaning of Death. Essays on Mortuary Rituals and Eschatological Beliefs*. Eds. S. Cederroth, C. Corlin, and J. Lindstrom, 11–30. Uppsala: Almqvist & Wiksell International.

———. 1989. "Symbols, Song, Dance and Features of Articulation: Is Religion an Extreme Form of Traditional Authority?" In *Ritual, History and Power: Selected Papers in Anthropology*. Ed. M. Bloch, 19–45. Atlantic Highlands, N.J.: The Athlone Press.

———. 1992. *Prey into Hunter: The Politics of Religious Experience*. Cambridge: Cambridge University Press.

Bloch, Maurice and Jonathan Parry. 1982. "Introduction: Death and the Regeneration of Life." In *Death and the Regeneration of Life*. Eds. Maurice Bloch and Jonathan Parry, 1–44. Cambridge: Cambridge University Press.

Boddy, Janice. 1994. "Spirit Possession Revisited: Beyond Instrumentality." *Annual Review of Anthropology* 23: 407–434.

Brubaker, Richard Lee. 1977. "Lustful Woman, Chaste Wife, Ambivalent Goddess: A South Indian Myth." *Anima* 3: 59–62.

Burkert, Walter. 1972. *Homo Necans: The Anthropology of Ancient Greek Sacrificial Ritual and Myth*. Trans. P. Bing. Berkeley: University of California Press.

Burkhart, Geoffrey. 1987. "Family Deity Temples and Spatial Variance among Udayars of Northern Tamil Nadu." In *Religion and Society in South India (A Volume in Honour of Prof. N. Subba Reddy)*. Eds. V. Sudarsen, G. Prakash Reddy, and M. Suryanarayana, 3–20. Delhi: B. R. Publishing Corporation.

Caldwell, Robert. 1984 [1849]. "Religion of the Shanars." In *Genealogy of the South-Indian Gods*, by Bartholameus Ziegenbalg. New Delhi: Unity Book Service.

Caplan, Lionel. 1988. "Visions of God: Prophecy and Agency in Christian South India." *South Asian Social Scientist* 4(1): 1–23.

———. 1989. "The Popular Culture of Evil in South India." In (his) *Religion and Power: Essays on the Christian Community in Madras*, 51–71. Madras: The Christian Literature Society.

Carstairs, G. M. and R. L. Kapur. 1976. *The Great Universe of Kota. Stress, Change and Mental Disorder in an Indian Village*. London: The Hogarth Press.

Chandrashekar, C. R. 1991. *Gods, Ghosts, Witchcraft and the Mind.* Bangalore: Navakarnataka Publications.

Claus, Peter J. 1973. "Possession, Protection, and Punishment as Attributes of the Deities in a South Indian Village." *Man in India* 53: 231–242.

Clothey, Fred. W. 1978. *The Many Faces of Murukan̲. The History and Meaning of a South Indian God.* The Hague/New York: Mouton Publishers.

———. 1982. "Chronometry, Cosmology, and the Festival Calendar in the Murukan̲ Cult." In *Religious Festivals in South India and Sri Lanka.* Eds. Guy R. Welbon and Glenn E. Yocum, 157–188. New Delhi: Manohar Publications.

———. 1986. "Tamil Religions." In *The Encyclopedia of Religions.* Ed. Mircea Eliade, Vol. 14: 260–268. New York: Macmillan Publishing Company.

Comaroff, Jean. 1985. *Body of Power. Spirit of Resistance.* Chicago: University of Chicago Press.

Crick, Malcolm. 1976. *Explorations in Language and Meaning: Towards a Semantic Anthropology.* London: Malaby Press.

Csordas, Thomas J. 1983. "The Rhetoric of Transformation in Ritual Healing." *Culture, Medicine, and Psychiatry* 7: 333–375.

———. 1994. *The Sacred Self: A Cultural Phenomenology of Charismatic Healing.* Berkeley: University of California Press.

Daniel, Valentine E. 1984. *Fluid Signs. Being a Person in the Tamil Way.* Berkeley: University of California Press.

de Heusch, Luc. 1981. *Why Marry Her? Society and Symbolic Structures.* Trans. Janet Lloyd. Cambridge/ Paris: Cambridge University Press and Éditions de la Maison des Sciences de L'Homme.

———. 1985. *Sacrifice in Africa. A Structuralist Approach.* Manchester: Manchester University Press.

Desjarlais, Robert R. 1992. *Body and Emotion: The Aesthetics of Illness and Healing in the Nepal Himalayas.* Philadephia: University of Pennsylvania Press.

———. 1996. "Presence." In *The Performance of Healing.* Eds. Carol Laderman and Marina Roseman, 143–164. New York: Routledge.

Dharampal, Gita. 1982. *La Religion des Malabars: Tessier de Quéralay et la contribution des missionnaires européens à la naissance de l'indianisme.* Immensée, Switzerland: Nouvelle Revue de Science Missionnaire.

Dickey, Sarah. 1993. *Cinema and the Urban Poor in South India.* Cambridge: Cambridge University Press.

Diehl, Carl Gustav. 1956. *Instrument and Purpose: Studies on Rites and Rituals in South India.* Lund: CWK Gleerup.

Dikshitar, Ramachandra V. R. 1930. *Studies in Tamil Literature and History.* London: Luzac & Co.

Doniger, Wendy O'Flaherty. 1973. *Asceticism and Eroticism in the Mythology of Siva.* Oxford: Oxford University Press.

———. 1976. *The Origins of Evil in Hindu Mythology.* Delhi: Motilal Banarsidass.

———. 1980. *Women, Androgynes, and Other Mythical Beasts.* Chicago: University of Chicago Press.

———. 1995. " 'Put a Bag over Her Head' ": Beheading Mythological Women. In *Off with Her Head! The Denial of Women's Identity in Myth, Religion, and Culture.* Eds. Howard Eilberg-Schwartz and Wendy Doniger, 15–31. Berkeley: University of California Press.

Douglas, Mary (ed.). 1970. *Witchcraft Confessions and Accusations.* Association of Social Anthropologists Monograph 9. London: Tavistock Publications.

Dow, James. 1986. "Universal Aspects of Symbolic Healing: A Theoretical Synthesis." *American Anthropologist* 88(1): 56–69.

Dumont, Louis. 1970. *Religion/Politics and History in India. Collected Papers in Sociology*. Paris/The Hague: Mouton Publishers.

———. 1980 [1966]. *Homo Hierarchicus. The Caste System and Its Implications.* Chicago: University of Chicago Press.

———. 1983. *Affinity as a Value. Marriage Alliance in South India, with Comparative Essays on Australia.* Chicago: University of Chicago Press.

———. 1986. [1957]. *A South Indian Subcaste. Social Organization and Religion of the Pramalai Kallar.* Trans. M. Moffat and A. Morton. Delhi: Oxford University Press.

Dumont, Louis and D. F. Pocock. 1959. "Possession and Priesthood." *Contributions to Indian Sociology* 3: 55–75.

Durkheim, Emile. 1965 [1915]. *The Elementary Forms of the Religious Life*. Trans. Joseph Ward Swain. New York: Free Press.

Eck, Diana L. 1981. *Darśan. Seeing the Divine Image in India*. Chambersburg, Penn.: Anima Books.

Egnor, Margaret T. 1986. [also see Trawick] "Internal Iconicity in Paraiyars' 'Crying Songs.'" In *Another Harmony: New Essays on the Folklore of India.* Eds. Stuart H. Blackburn and A. K. Ramanujan, 294–344. Berkeley: University of California Press.

Eilberg-Schwartz Howard, 1995. "Introduction: The Spectacle of the Female Head. In *Off with Her Head! The Denial of Women's Identity in Myth, Religion, and Culture*. Eds. Howard Eilberg-Schwartz and Wendy Doniger, 1–14. Berkeley: University of California Press.

Eliade, Mircea. 1964. *Shamanism. Archaic Techniques of Ecstasy*. Trans. Williard R. Trask. Princeton, N.J.: Princeton University Press: Bollingen Series 76.

Elmore, W. T. 1984 [1913]. *Dravidian Gods in Modern Hinduism.* New Delhi: Asian Educational Services.

Epstein Scarlett. 1967. "A Sociological Analysis of Witch Beliefs in a Mysore Village." In *Magic, Witchcraft, and Curing*. Ed. John Middleton, 135–154. American Museum Sourcebooks in Anthropology. Garden City, N.Y.: The Natural History Press.

Evans-Pritchard, E. E. 1937. *Witchcraft, Oracles, and Magic among the Azande.* Oxford: Clarendon Press.

———. 1965. *Theories of Primitive Religion.* Oxford: Clarendon Press.

Ewing, Katherine Pratt. 1984. "The Sufi as Saint, Curer, and Exorcist in Modern Pakistan." In *South Asian Systems of Healing*. Eds. E. Valentine Daniel and Judy F. Pugh. *Contributions to Asian Studies* 18: 106–114. Leiden: E. J. Brill.

———. 1997. *Arguing Sainthood. Modernity, Psychoanalysis, and Islam*. Durham, N.C.: Duke University Press.

Fabricius, J. P. 1972 [1779]. *Tamil and English Dictionary.* Tranquebar: Evangelical Lutheran Mission Publishing House.

Fortes, Meyer. 1987. *Religion, Morality and the Person. Essays on Tallensi Religion.* Cambridge: Cambridge University Press.

Frasca, Richard. 1990. *The Theatre of the Mahābhārata: Terukkuttu Performances in South India.* Honolulu: University of Hawaii Press.

Frazer, James G. 1965 [1911–1915]. "Sympathetic Magic." Reprinted in abridged form in *Reader in Comparative Religion. An Anthropological Approach.* 2nd ed. Eds. William A. Lessa and Evon Z. Vogt, 300–315. New York: Harper and Row, Publishers.

Freed, Stanley A., and Ruth S. Freed. 1964. "Spirit Possession as illness in a north Indian village." *Ethnology* 3(2): 152–171.
Freed, Ruth S., and Stanley A. Freed. 1993. *Ghosts: Life and Death in North India.* Anthropological Papers of the American Museum of Natural History, Vol. 72. Seattle: University of Washington Press.
Freud, Sigmund. 1957. [1917]. "Mourning and Melancholia." In *The Standard Edition of the Complete Psychological Works of Sigmund Freud.* Vol. 14. Trans. J. Strachey, et al., 239–258. London: Hogarth Press.
Fuller, Christopher J. 1984. *Servants of the Goddess. The Priests of a South Indian Temple.* Cambridge: Cambridge University Press.
———. 1987. "Sacrifice (*Bali*) in the South Indian Temple." In *Religion and Society in South India (A Volume in Honour of Prof. N. Subba Reddy).* Eds. V. Sudarsen, G. Prakash Reddy, and M. Suryanarayana, 21–36. Delhi: B. R. Publishing Corporation.
———. 1992. *The Camphor Flame. Popular Hinduism and Society in India.* Princeton, N.J.: Princeton University Press.
Gandhi, Maneka. 1989. *On the Mythology of Indian Plants.* Calcutta: Rupa & Co.
Geertz, Clifford. 1979. "From the Native's Point of View: On the Nature of Anthropological Understanding." In *Interpretive Social Science. A Reader.* Eds. Paul Rabinow and William Sullivan, 225–242. Berkeley: University of California Press.
Geertz, Hildred. 1995. "The Sakti Conjecture: New Views on Balinese 'Religion.'" Unpublished manuscript.
Gibbal, Jean-Marie. 1994. *Genii of the River Niger.* Trans. Beth G. Raps. Chicago: University of Chicago Press.
Girard, René. 1972. *La Violence et le Sacré.* Paris: Editions Bernard Grasset.
Gold, Ann Grodzins. 1988. "Spirit Possession Perceived and Performed in Rural Rajasthan." *Contributions to Indian Sociology* (n.s.) 22: 35–63.
Good, Anthony. 1983. "A Symbolic Type and its Transformations: the Case of South Indian *Poṅkal.*" *Contributions to Indian Sociology* (NS) 17: 223–244.
———. 1991. *The Female Bridegroom. A Comparative Study of Life-Crisis Rituals in South India and Sri Lanka.* Oxford: Clarendon Press.
Hanchett, Suzanne. 1988. *Coloured Rice. Symbolic Structure in Hindu Family Festivals.* Delhi: Hindustan Publishing Corporation.
Hardy, Friedhelm. 1983. *Viraha Bhakti: The Early History of Kṛṣṇa Devotion in South India.* Delhi: Oxford University Press.
Harlan, Lindsey. 1992. *Religion and Rajput Women. The Ethic of Protection in Contemporary Narratives.* Berkeley: University of California Press.
Harman, William P. 1989. *The Sacred Marriage of a Hindu Goddess.* Bloomington: Indiana University Press.
Harper, Edward B. 1957. "Shamanism in South India." *Southwestern Journal of Anthropology* 13: 267–287.
———. 1963. "Spirit Possession and Social Structure." In *Anthropology on the March.* Ed. Bala Ratnam, 165–177. Madras: The Book Centre.
Hart, George L., III. 1975. *The Poems of Ancient Tamil: Their Milieu and Their Sanskrit Counterparts.* Berkeley: University of California Press.
———. 1979. *The Poets of the Tamil Anthologies.* Princeton, N.J.: Princeton University Press.
———. 1983. "The Theory of Reincarnation among the Tamils." In *Karma and Rebirth in Classical Indian Traditions.* Ed. Wendy Doniger O'Flaherty, 116–133. Delhi: Motilal Banarsidass.

Heesterman, J. C. 1993. *The Broken World of Sacrifice. An Essay in Ancient Indian Ritual.* Chicago: University of Chicago Press.

Herdt, Gilbert. 1981. *Guardians of the Flutes. Idioms of Masculinity*. Chicago: University of Chicago Press.

Herrenschmidt, Olivier. 1981. "Le sacrifice du buffle en Andhra côtier. Le 'culte de village' confronté aux notions de sacrifiant et d'unité de culte." *Puruṣārtha* 5: 137–177.

———. 1982. "Quelles fêtes pour quelles castes?" *L' Homme* 22: 31–56.

Hertz, Robert. 1960. *Death and the Right Hand.* Trans. R. and C. Needham. London: Cohen and West.

Hiebert, Paul G. 1983. "Karma and Other Explanation Traditions in a South Indian Village." In *Karma. An Anthropological Inquiry*. Eds. Charles F. Keyes and E. Valentine Daniel, 119–130. Berkeley: University of California Press.

Hiltebeitel, Alf. 1988. Director. *Lady of Gingee: South Indian Draupadī festivals*, parts 1 and 2. Videotape. Washington, D.C.: George Washington University. Distributed through University of Wisconsin South Asia Center.

———. 1988. *The Cult of Draupadī.* Vol 1. *Mythologies: From Gingee to Kuruksetra.* Chicago: University of Chicago Press.

———. 1991. *The Cult of Drapaudī.* Vol 2. *On Hindu Ritual and the Goddess.* Chicago: University of Chicago Press.

Hopkins, Thomas J. 1992. "Hindu Views of Death and Afterlife." In *Death and Afterlife. Perspectives of World Religions.* Ed. Hiroshi Obayashi, 143–156. New York: Greenwood Press.

Hubert, Henri, and Marcel Mauss. 1964. *Sacrifice: Its Nature and Function.* Trans. W. D. Halls. Chicago: University of Chicago Press.

Hudson, Dennis. 1982. "Two Citras Festivals in Madurai." *Religious Festivals in South India and Sri Lanka.* Eds. Guy R. Welbon and Glenn E. Yocum, 101–156. New Delhi: Manohar Publications.

Huntington, Richard, and Peter Metcalf. 1979. *Celebrations of Death. The Anthropology of Mortuary Ritual.* Cambridge: Cambridge University Press.

Inden, Ronald B. 1976. *Marriage and Rank in Bengali Culture.* Berkeley: University of California Press.

Inglis, Stephen. 1985. "Possession and Pottery: Serving the Divine in a South Indian Community." In *Gods of Flesh. Gods of Stone. The Embodiement of Divinity in India.* Eds. Joanne Punzo Waghorne and Norman Cutler, 89–102. Chambersburg Penn.: Anima Books.

Jacob-Pandian, E.T. 1975. "Nadu Veedu Rituals and Family Shamanisn in Tamil Society: a Cult Institution of Hinduism." *Man in India* 55(1): 67–78.

James, William. 1961. [1902]. *The Varieties of Religious Experience: A Study in Human Nature.* New York: Collier Books, Macmillan Publishing Company.

Kailasapathy. K. 1968. *Tamil Heroic Poetry*. Oxford: The Clarendon Press.

Kakar, Sudhir. 1982. *Shamans, Mystics and Doctors. A Psychological Inquiry into India and Its Healing Traditions.* New York: Alfred A. Knopf.

———. 1986. Psychotherapy and Culture: Healing in the Indian Tradition. In *The Cultural Transition. Human Experience and Social Transformation in the Third World and Japan.* Eds. Merry I. White and Susan Pollak, 9–23. Boston: Routledge & Kegan Paul.

Kane, Pandurang Vaman. 1973. *History of Dharmasastra. Ancient and Medieval Religious and Civil Law.* Vol. 4, 2nd ed. Poona: Bhandarkar Oriental Research Institute. Goverment Oriental Series, No: 6.

Kapferer, Bruce. 1979a. "Introduction: Ritual Process and the Transformation of Context." *Social Analysis* 1: 3–19.

———. 1979b. "Emotion and Feeling in Sinhalese Healing Rites." *Social Analysis* 1: 153–176.

———. 1983. *A Celebration of Demons. Exorcism and the Aesthetics of Healing in Sri Lanka*. Bloomington: Indiana University Press.

———. 1988. *Legends of People, Myths of State. Violence, Intolerance, and Political Culture in Sri Lanka and Australia*. Washington: Smithsonian Institution Press.

———. 1995. "From the Edge of Death. Sorcery and the Motion of Consciousness." In *Questions of Consciouness*. Eds. Anthony P. Cohen and Nigel Rapport, 134–152. New York: Routledge.

———. 1997. *The Feast of the Sorcerer. Practices of Consciousness and Power*. Chicago: University of Chicago Press.

Kaushik, Meena. 1976. "The Symbolic Representation of Death." *Contributions to Indian Sociology* (n.s.) 10 (2): 265–292.

Kendall, Laurel. 1988. *The Life and Hard Times of a Korean Shaman*. Honolulu: University of Hawaii Press.

Kersenboom, Saskia. 1995. *Word, Sound, Image. The Life of a Tamil Text*. Washington D.C: Berg Publishers.

Kinsley, David. 1987. *Hindu Goddesses. Visions of the Divine Feminine in the Hindu Religious Tradition*. Delhi: Motilal Banarsidass.

Kjaerholm, Lars. 1984. "Aiyanar and Aiyappan in Tamilnadu: Change and Continuity in South Indian Hinduism." Folk 26 (Copenhagen).

———. 1990. "Kula Teyvam Worship in Tamilnadu: A Link between Past and Present." In *Rites and Beliefs in Modern India*. Ed., Gabriella Eichinger Ferro-Luzzi, 67–88. New Delhi: Manohar Publications.

Knipe, David M. 1977. "Sapiṇḍikaraṇa: the Hindu Rite of Entry in Heaven." In *Religious Encounters with Death: Insights from the History and Anthropology of Religion*. Eds. E. Reynolds and E. H. Waugh, 111–124. University Park, Penn.: Pennsylvania State University Press.

———. 1990. "Night of the Growing Dead: A Cult of Vīrabhadra in Coastal Andhra." In *Criminal Gods and Demon Devotees. Essays on the Guardians of Popular Hinduism*. Ed. Alf Hiltebeitel, 123–156. New Delhi: Manohar Publications.

Kolenda, Pauline. 1982. "Pox and the Terror of Childlessness: Images and Ideas of the Smallpox Goddess in a North Indian Village." In *Mother Worship. Themes and Variations*. Ed. James J. Preston, 227–250. Chapel Hill: University of North Carolina Press.

Kulkarni, A.R. 1966. "Marriage Invitations to the Dead." Poona: *Bulletin of the Deccan College Research Institute* 25: 191–194.

Kurtz, Stanley N. 1992. *All the Mothers are One. Hindu India and the Cultural Reshaping of Psychoanalayis*. New York: Columbia University Press.

Laderman, Carol. 1983. *Wives and Midwives. Childbirth and Nutrition in Rural Malaysia*. Berkeley: University of California Press.

———. 1987. "The Ambiguity of Symbols in the Structure of Healing." *Social Science and Medicine* 24 (4): 293–301.

Lambek, Michael. 1993. *Knowledge and Practice in Mayotte. Local Discourses of Islam, Sorcery, and Spirit Possession*. Toronto: University of Toronto Press.

Lévi-Strauss, Claude. 1963. *Structural Anthropology*. Trans. Claire Jacobson and Brooke Grundfest Schoepf. New York: Basic Books.

———. 1981 [1971]. *The Naked Man. Introduction to a Science of Mythology: 4*. Trans. John and Doreen Weightman. London: Jonathan Cape.

Lewis, I. M. 1966. "Spirit Possession and Deprivation Cults." *Man* 1(3): 307–329.

———. 1971. *Ecstatic Religion. An Anthropological Study of Spirit Possession and Shamanism*. Harmondsworth: Penguin Books.

———. 1986. *Religion in Context.Cults and Charisma*. Cambridge: Cambridge University Press.

Macdonell. A. A. 1958. "Magic." In *Encyclopaedia of Religion and Ethics*. Vol 8. Ed. James Hastings, 311–321. New York: Charles Scribner's Sons.

Malamoud, Charles. 1982. "Les morts sans visage. Remarques sur l'idéologie funéraire dans le brâhmanisme." In *La mort, les morts dans les sociétes anciennes*. Eds. Gherardo Gnoli and Jean-Pierre Vernant, 441–453. Cambridge and London: Cambridge University Press & Editions de la Maison des Sciences de l'Homme.

Malinowski, Bronislaw. 1984 [1922]. *Argonauts of the Western Pacific*. New York: Dutton.

Maloney, Clarence. 1976. "Don't Say 'Pretty Baby' Lest You Zap It with Your Eye—The Evil Eye in South Asia." In *The Evil Eye*. Ed. Clarence Maloney, 102–148. New York: Columbia University Press.

Marglin, Frederique Apffel. 1990. "Smallpox in Two Systems of Knowledge." In *Dominating Knowledge: Development, Culture, and Resistance*. Eds. Frederique Apffel Marglin and Stephen A. Marglin, 102–144. Oxford: Clarendon Press.

Marriott, McKim. 1976. "Hindu Transactions: Diversity without Dualism." In *Transaction and Meaning*. Ed. Bruce Kapferer, 109–142. Philadelphia: Institute for the Study of Human Issues.

Marriott, McKim, and Ronald Inden. 1977. "Toward an Ethnosociology of South Asian Caste Systems." In *The New Wind: Changing Identities in South Asia*. Ed. Ken David, 227–238. The Hague: Mouton.

Marwick, Max. 1982 [1970]. "Witchcraft as a Social Strain-Gauge." In *Witchcraft and Sorcery: Selected Readings*. Ed. Max Marwick, 300–313. New York: Penguin Books.

Mauss, Marcel. 1979 [1938]. "A Category of the Human Mind: The Notion of Person; the Notion of 'Self.' " In (his) *Sociology and Psychology. Essays*, 59–94. London: Routledge & Kegan Paul.

Meyer, Eveline. 1986. *Aṅkāḷaparamēcuvari: A Goddess of Tamilnadu, her Myths and Cult*. Weisbaden: Franz Steiner Verlag.

Mines, Mattison. 1994. *Public Faces, Private Voices. Community and Individuality in South India*. Berkeley: University of California Press.

Moffat, Michael. 1979. *An Untouchable Community in South India. Structure and Consensus*. Princeton, N.J.: Princeton University Press.

Montgomery, Edward. 1974/75. "Trance Mediumship Therapy in Southern India: A Transcript of a Session." *Ethnomedizin*. 3 (1/2): 111–125.

———. 1976. "Systems and the Medical Practitioners of a Tamil Town." In *Asian Medical Systems: A Comparative Survey*. Ed. Charles Leslie, 272–284. Berkeley: University of California Press.

Moreno, Manuel. 1981. "An Untouchable Funeral in a Village of South India." *Chicago Anthropology Exchange* 14 (1, 2): 152–163.

———. 1985. "God's Forceful Call: Possession as a Divine Strategy." In *Gods of Flesh. Gods of Stone. The Embodiement of Divinity in India*. Eds. Joanne Punzo Waghorne and Norman Cutler, 103–122. Chambersburg PA: Anima Books.

Mosse, David. 1986. Caste, Christianity and Hinduism: a study of social organization and religion in rural Ramnad. Thesis, Oxford University.

———. 1994. "Catholic saints and the Hindu village pantheon in rural Tamil Nadu, India." *Man* (n.s) 29 (2): 301–332.
Nabokov, Isabelle. 1995. "Who Are You?": Spirit Discourse in a Tamil World. Ph.D diss., University of California, Berkeley.
———. 1996. "When the Dead Become Brides, Gods, and Gold: Marriage Symbolism in a Tamil Household Ritual." *Journal of Ritual Studies* 10(1): 113–133.
———. 1997. "Expel the Lover, Recover the Wife: Symbolic Analysis of a South Indian Exorcism." *The Journal of the Royal Anthropological Institute* (N.S.) 3 (2): 297–316.
Nicholas, Ralph W. 1981. "The Goddess Sitala and Epidemic Smallpox in Bengal." *Journal of Asian Studies*, 41 (1): 21–44.
———. 1995. "The Effectiveness of the Hindu Sacrament (*Samskara*): Caste, Marriage, and Divorce in Bengali Culture." In *From the Margins of Hindu Marriage. Essays on Gender, Religion, and Culture*. Eds. Lindsey Harlan and Paul B.Courtright, 137–159. New York: Oxford University Press.
Noll, Richard. 1985. "Mental Imagery Cultivation as a Cultural Phenomenon: The Role of Visions in Shamanism." *Current Anthropology* 26(4): 443–460.
Nuckolls, Charles W. 1991a. "Culture and Causal Thinking: Diagnosis and Prediction in a South Indian Fishing Village." *Ethos* 19(1): 3–51.
———. 1991b. "Deciding How to Decide: Possession-Mediumship in Jalari Culture." In *Recent Trends in Ethnomedicine*. Ed. Mark Nichter. *Medical Anthropology* 13 (1–2): 57–82.
———. 1991c. Becoming a Possession-Medium in South India: A Psychocultural Account. *Medical Anthropology Quarterly* 5 (1): 63–77.
———. 1993. *Siblings in South Asia: Brothers and Sisters in Cultural Context*. New York: Guilford.
———. 1996. *The Cultural Dialectics of Knowledge and Desire*. Madison: University of Wisconsin Press.
Obeyesekere, Gananath. 1969. "The Ritual Drama of the *Sanni* Demons: Collective Representations of Disease in Ceylon." *Comparative Studies in Society and History* 11: 175–216.
———. 1970."The Idiom of Demonic Possession: A Case Study." *Social Science and Medicine* 4: 97–111.
———. 1975. "Sorcery, Premeditated Murder, and the Canalization of Aggression in Sri Lanka." *Ethnology* 14(1): 1–23.
———. 1976. "The Impact of Ayurvedic Ideas on the Culture and the Individual in Sri Lanka." In *Asian Medical Systems: A Comparative Study*. Ed. Charles Leslie, 201–226. Berkeley: University of California Press.
———. 1977. "Psychocultural Exegesis of a Case of Spirit Possession in Sri Lanka." In *Cases Studies in Possession*. Eds. Vincent Crapanzano and Vivian Garrison, 235–294. New York: Wiley and Sons.
———. 1981. *Medusa's Hair. An Essay on Personal Symbols and Religious Experience*. Chicago: University of Chicago Press.
———. 1990. *The Work of Culture*. Chicago: University of Chicago Press.
Olivier de Sardan, Jean-Pierre. 1986. "Possession, Exotisme, Anthropologie." In *Transe, Chamanisme, Possession*. Actes des Deuxièmes Rencontres Internationales sur la Fête et la Communication, 149–155. Nice: Éditions Serre.
Opler, Morris E. 1958. "Spirit possession in a rural area of north India." In *Reader in Comparative Religion*. 1st ed. Eds. William A. Lessa and Evon Z. Vogt, 553–566. White Plains, N.Y.: Row, Peterson and Company.

Oppert, Gustav. 1893. *On the Original Inhabitants of Bharatavarsa or India.* Westminter: Constable.

Ostor, Akos. 1980. *The Play of the Gods: Locality, Ideology, Structure, and Time in the Festivals of a Bengali Town.* Chicago: University of Chicago Press.

Padoux, André. 1989. "Mantras—What Are They?" In *Mantra.* Ed. Harvey P. Alper, 295–318. Albany: State University of New York Press.

Park, George K. 1963. "Divination and its Social Contexts." *The Journal of the Royal Anthropological Institute* 93 (2): 195–209.

Parry, Jonathan P. 1994. *Death in Banaras.* Cambridge: Cambridge University Press.

Peterson, Indira Viswanathan. In press. "The Drama of the Kuṟavañci Fortuneteller: Land, landscape, and Social Relations in and 18th Century Tamil Genre." In *Tamil Geographies: Cultural Constructions of Space and Place in Tamil South India.* Eds. Martha Ann Selby and Indira Viswanathan Peterson. Albany: SUNY Press.

———. 1988. "The Tie that Binds: Brothers and Sisters in North and South India." *South Asian Social Scientist* 4 (1): 25–52.

Pocock, D. F. 1973. *Mind, Body and Wealth. A Study of Belief and Practice in an Indian Village.* Oxford: Basil Blackwell.

Preston, James J. 1985. "Creation of the Sacred Image: Apotheosis and Destruction in Hinduism." In *Gods of Flesh. Gods of Stone. The Embodiement of Divinity in India.* Eds. Joanne Punzo-Waghorne and Norman Cutler, 9–32. Chambersburg, Penn.: Anima Books.

Raheja, Gloria Goodwin. 1988. *The Poison in the Gift. Ritual, Prestration, and the Dominant Caste in a North Indian Village.* Chicago: University of Chicago Press.

Ram, Kalpana. 1991. *Mukkuvar Women. Gender, Hegemony and Capitalist Transformation in a South Indian Fishing Comunity.* North Sydney: Allen & Unwin.

Ramanujan, A.K. 1967. *The Interior Landscape. Love Poems from a Classical Tamil Anthology.* Bloomington: Indiana University Press.

———. 1981. *Hymns for the Drowning: Poems for Viṣṇu̱ by Nammalvar.* Princeton, N.J.: Princeton University Press.

———. 1986. "Two Realms of Kannada Folklore." In *Another Harmony. New Essays on the Folklore of India.* Eds. Stuart Blackburn and A.K. Ramanujan, 41–75. Delhi: Oxford University Press.

Redfield, Robert. 1941. *The Folk Culture of Yucatan.* Chicago: University of Chicago Press.

Reiniche, Marie-Louise. 1975. "Les 'démons' et leur culte dans la structure du panthéon d'un village du Tirunelveli." *Puruṣārtha* 2: 173–203.

———. 1979. *Les Dieux et les hommes. Études des cultes d'un village du Tirunelveli, Inde du Sud.* Paris/ La Haye: Mouton.

Reynolds, Holly Baker. 1980. "The Auspicious Married Woman." *The Powers of Tamil Women.* Ed. Susan Wadley, 35–60. Maxwell School Foreign and Comparative Studies, South Asian Series, no. 6, Syracuse University.

Richard, F. J. 1920. "The Village Deities in Vellore Taluk, North Arcot District." *Quaterly Journal of the Mythic Society* 10 (2): 109–120.

Roger, Abraham. 1670. *Le théatre de l'idolatrie, ou la porte ouverte, pour parvenir 'a la cognoissance du paganisme caché, et la vraye representation de la vie, des moeurs, de la religion, et du service divin des Bramines, qui demeurent sur les costes de Chormandel, & aux pays circonvoisins.* Translated by Thomas la Grue. Amsterdam: Jean Schipper.

Roland, Alan. 1988. In *Search of Self in India and Japan: Toward a Cross-Cultural Psychology.* Princeton, N.J.: Princeton University Press.

Rosaldo, Michelle. 1984. "Toward an Anthropology of Self and Feeling." In *Culture Theory; Essays on Mind, Self, and Emotion.* Eds. Richard A. Shweder and Robert Levine, 137–157. Cambridge: Cambridge University Press.

Rosaldo, Renato. 1984. "Grief and a Headhunter's Rage: On the Cultural Force of Emotions." In *Text, Play, and Story: The Construction and Reconstruction of Self and Society.* Ed. Edward M. Bruner, 178–195. Washinghton, D.C.: *1983 Proceedings of the American Ethnological Society.*

Rouget, Gilbert. 1985. *Music and Trance: A Theory of the Relations Between Music and Possession.* Translation revised by Brunhilde Biebuyck. Chicago: University of Chicago Press.

Russell, Jeffrey Burton. 1977. *The Devil: Perceptions of Evil from Antiquity to Primitive Christianity.* Ithaca, N.Y.: Cornell University Press.

Sahlins, Marshall. 1985. *Islands of History.* Chicago: The University of Chicago Press.

Sax, William S. 1991. *Mountain Goddess. Gender and Politics in a Himalayan Pilgrimage.* New York: Oxford University Press.

Schieffelin, Edward L. 1985. "Performance and the Cultural Construction of Reality." *American Ethnologist* 12(4): 707–724.

———. 1993. "Performance and the Cultural Construction of Reality: A New Guinea Example." In *Creativity/ Anthropology.* Eds., Smadar Lavie, Kirin Narayan, and Renato Rosaldo, 270–295. Ithaca, N.Y.: Cornell University Press.

———. 1996. "On Failure and Performance: Throwing the Medium Out of the Seance." In *The Performance of Healing.* Eds. Carol Laderman and Marina Roseman, 59–90. New York: Routledge.

Scott, David. 1991. "The Cultural Poetics of Eyesight in Sri Lanka: Composure, Vulnerability, and the Sinhala Concept of Distiya." *Dialectical Anthropology* 16: 85–102.

———. 1994. *Formations of Ritual. Colonial and Anthropological Discourses on the Sinhala Yaktovil.* Minneapolis: University of Minnesota Press.

Shanmugam Pillai M., and David E. Ludden. 1976. *Kuṟuntokai. An Anthology of Classical Tamil Love Poetry.* Madurai: Koodal Publishers.

Shulman, David Dean. 1978. "The Serpent and the Sacrifice: An Anthill Myth from Tiruvarur." *History of Religions* 18 (2): 107–137.

———. 1980. *Tamil Temple Myths: Sacrifice and Divine Marriage in the South Indian Saiva Tradition.* Princeton, N.J.: Princeton University Press.

———. 1993. *The Hungry God. Hindu Tales of Filicide and Devotion.* Chicago: University of Chicago Press.

Shweder, Richard A., and E. J. Bourne. 1984. "Does the Concept of Person Vary Cross-culturally?" In *Culture Theory: Essays on Mind, Self, and Emotion.* Eds. R. A. Shweder and R. A. LeVine, 158–199. Cambridge: Cambridge University Press.

Skultans, V. 1987. "The Management of Mental Illness Among Maharashtrian Families: A Case Study of a Mahanubhav Healing Temple." *Man* (N.S.) 22: 661–679.

Sopher, D. E. 1986. "Place and Landscape in Indian Tradition." *Landscape* 29 (2): 1–9.

Srinivas, M. N. 1952. *Religion and Society among the Coorgs of South India.* Bombay: Asia Publishing House.

———. 1969. "Sanskritization." In *Social Change in Modern India*, Ed. M. N. Srinivas. 1–45. Berkeley: University of California Press.

Stanley, John M. 1977. "Special Time, Special Power: The Fluidity of Power in a Popular Hindu Festival." *Journal of Asian Studies* 37 (1): 27–43.

Stein, Burton. 1980. *Peasant State and Society in Medieval South India.* Delhi: Oxford University Press.

Stirrat, R. L. 1977. "Demonic Possession in Roman Catholic Sri Lanka." *Journal of Anthropological Research* 33 (2): 133–157.

———. 1992. *Power and Religiosity in a Post-Colonial Setting. Sinhala Catholics in contemporary Sri Lanka.* Cambridge: Cambridge University Press.

Thurston, Edgar. 1906. *Ethnographic Notes in Southern India.* Madras: Superintendent, Government Press.

———. 1987 [1909]. *Castes and Tribes of Southern India.* Vols. 1–7. New Delhi: Asian Educational Services.

Torrance, Robert M. 1994. *The Spiritual Quest. Transcendence in Myth, Religion, and Science.* Berkeley: University of California Press.

Trawick, Margaret. 1984. "The Changed Mother, or what the Smallpox Goddess did when there was no more smallpox." In *South Asian Systems of Healing.* Eds. E. V. Daniel and J. F. Pugh. *Contributions to Asian Studies* 18: 24–45. Leiden: E. J Brill.

———. 1990a. *Notes on Love in a Tamil Family.* Berkeley: University of California Press.

———. 1990b. "Untouchability and the Fear of Death in a Tamil Song." In *Language and the Politics of Emotion.* Eds. Catherine A. Lutz and Lila Abu-Lughod, 186–206. Cambridge: Cambridge University Press.

———. 1992. "Death and Nurturance in Indian Systems of Healing." In *Paths to Asian Medical Knowledge.* Eds. Charles Leslie and Allan Young, 129–159. Berkeley: University of California Press.

Turner, Victor. 1957. *Schism and Continuity in an African Society: A Study of Ndembu Village Life.* Manchester: Manchester University Press.

———. 1964. "Betwixt and Between: The Liminal Period in *Rites of Passage.*" In *The Proceedings of the American Ethnological Society* 4–20. Symposium on New Approaches to the Study of Religion. Seattle: The University of Washington Press.

———. 1967. *The Forest of Symbols.* Ithaca, N.Y.: Cornell University Press.

———. 1968. *The Drums of Affliction: A Study of Religious Processes among the Ndembu of Zambia.* Oxford: Clarendon.

———. 1969. *The Ritual Process. Structure and Anti-Structure.* Ithaca, N.Y.: Cornell University Press.

———. 1974. *Dramas, Fields, and Metaphors: Symbolic Action in Human Society.* Ithaca, N.Y.: Cornell University Press.

Turstig, Hans-Georg. 1985. "The Indian Sorcery Called *Abhicāra.*" In *Wiener Zeitschrift fur die Kunde Sudasiens.* Ed. G. Oberhammer, 69–117. Leiden: E. J. Brill.

Tylor, Edward Burnett. 1871. *Primitive Culture: Researches into the Development of Mythology, Philosophy, Religion, Language, Art and Custom.* 2 Vols. London: Murray.

Valeri, Valerio. 1985. *Kingship and Sacrifice. Ritual and Society in Ancient Hawaii.* Trans. Paula Wissing. Chicago: University of Chicago Press.

Vanamamalai, N. 1981. *Interpretation of Tamil Folk Creations.* Trivandrum (Kerala): Dravidian Linguistics Association.

Van Gennep, Arnold. 1909. *Les Rites de Passage.* Paris: Emile Nourry.

Vitebsky, Piers. 1993. *Dialogues with the Dead. The Discussion of Mortality among the Sora of Eastern India.* Cambridge. Cambridge University Press.

Wadley, Susan Snow. 1975. *Shakti. Power in the Conceptual Structure of Karimpur Religion.* Chicago: The University of Chicago Studies in Anthropology, Series in Social, Cultural, and Linguistic Anthropology, No. 2.

Wallace, Anthony F. C. 1956. "Revitalization Movements." *American Anthropologist* 58: 264–281.

Whitehead, Henry. 1988. [1921]. *The Villages Gods of South India*. New Delhi: Asian Educational Services.

Wijesekera, Nandadeva. 1989. *Deities and Demons. Magic and Masks.* Part 2. Colombo, Sri Lanka: M.D. Gunasena & Company Limited.

Yalman, Nur. 1964. "The Structure of Sinhalese Healing Rituals." In *Religion in South Asia*. Ed. Edward B. Harper, 115–150. Seattle: University of Washington Press.

Yocum, Glenn E. 1973. "Shrines, Shamanism, and Love Poetry: Elements in the Emergence of Popular Tamil Bhakti." *Journal of the American Academy of Religion* 41(1): 3–17.

Ziegenbalg, Bartholameus. 1984 [1867]. *Genealogy of the South-Indian Gods*. Trans. G. J. Metzger. New Delhi: Unity Book Service. Zimmer, Heinrich. 1948. *The King and the Corpse. Tales of the Soul's Conquest of Evil.* Washington D. C.: Pantheon Books, The Bollingen Series 11.

Zvelebil, K.V. 1973. "The Beginnings of Bhakti in South India." *Temenos* 13: 223–257.

INDEX

Aham, 8, 9, 10, 25, 26, 29, 73, 74, 128, 136, 156. *See also* pu<u>r</u>am

Aloneness, 73–74, 91, 104, 140, 186 n.5, 195 n.7

Aṅkāḷaparamēcuvari, 3, 21, 47, 77, 79, 80, 82, 87, 95–96, 107, 110, 111, 115, 174, 193 n.10

- myth of, 89–91. *See also* Mēl Malaiyan̲ūr temple; Meyer, Eveline

Beck, Brenda, 95, 157, 193 n.9

Bhakti, 16, 207 n. 2

Bloch, Maurice, 11, 12, 97, 98, 165, 176

Blood, 46, 87, 91, 152, 160. *See also* sacrifice

Cakkaram, 57, 59, 80. *See also* effigy; nūl ēn̲i

Cāmi Nagaji

- countersorcery ritual for Laksmi, 55–59
- diagnosis of Laksmi's problems, 50–52, 192 n.13
- initiatic vision, 20–21, 36
- interpretation of countersorcery, 61–62, 68
- séance for Gita, 36–40

Cāmis, 4, 5, 20, 188 n.3

- initiatic dreams and visions, 19–30, 115, 140, 183
- knowledge of sorcery, 45–48
- medium for the dead compared to, 115–116, 121–124
- pampaikkārar compared to, 78–79, 80
- profession of ku<u>r</u>i, 31–33, 75, 76, 116, 188–189 n.4, 190 n. 2. *See also* fruit
- scholarship on, 187–188 n. 2
- trance, 19, 187–188 n.2, 189 n.9

Camphor, 87, 105–106, 108, 115, 117, 118, 128, 131, 132, 135, 144, 158, 160, 166, 174, 196 n.1, 197 n.9, 198 n.3

Caplan, Lionel, 23, 33, 34, 72, 78, 187 n.2, 188 n.4, 194 n.1

Clothey, Fred, 32, 185 n.1, 188 n.3, 192 nn.1–2

Cosmology and personal investments, 9–10, 12, 17, 26–27, 49, 66–68, 84–86, 97, 184. *See also* love

Countersorcery, 5, 7, 16, 49, 52, 54, 55–63, 66–69, 86

- exorcism compared to, 86, 95, 97–98
- funeral symbolism in, 56, 58–63, 67–69, 114, 123

Cumaṅkali, 72, 102, 103, 109, 112, 126, 135, 143

Daniel, Valentine, 26, 137, 186 n.7

Death

- deifying, 116–117, 126, 200 n.3
- dream of, 104

Inden, Ronald, 13, 14, 15
Inglis, Stephen, 31
Investiture of the household deity. *See* pūvāṭaikkāri pūjā
Invitation to feast, 154, 156–161, 169–178. *See also* Periyāṇṭavar; sacrifice
  exclusion of women at, 172, 175–176
  exorcism and pūvāṭaikkāri pūjā compared to, 154, 161–163, 175, 176
  myth of, 165–169
  trance-possession at, 159, 160, 174, 175, 176
Invitation to marriage, 6, 10, 127, 138, 139, 142, 202 n.4. *See also* pūvāṭaikkāri pūjā

Jacob-Pandian, E. T., 106, 108, 201 n.3

Kakar, Sudhir, 26, 64–65, 183
Kālī, 23, 33, 34, 36, 42
  in sorcery and countersorcery, 46, 47, 55, 58, 59
Kaṉṉiyamma, 20, 28
Kapferer, Bruce, 11, 12, 48, 63, 65–66, 68–69, 70, 71, 165, 178, 186 n.5, 190 n.3
Kāppu, 80, 156, 159, 171–172, 207 n.7
Karakam, 37, 129, 130, 131, 134, 135, 136, 143, 147, 148, 155, 189 n.10, 202 n.10, 203 nn.12, 13
  crowning with, 135, 137, 138, 148, 149, 204 n.23. *See also* decapitation; head; recapitation
  myth of, 140–141
  trance and, 135, 189 n.6, 204 n.18
Kāṭṭēri, 51, 52, 61, 66, 87, 192 n.14
Kersenboom, Saskia, 99, 137
Knipe, David, 199–200 n.2
Kōvintā, 96, 119, 132, 135, 147, 158, 159, 172, 174
Kuṟi, 19, 20, 22, 31–32, 33–40, 40–44, 54, 75, 76, 79, 116, 188–189 n.4, 190 n.2. *See also* camis; fruit; medium for the dead

Lament, 60, 63, 119, 122, 123, 168, 199–200 nn.2, 6
Lévi-Strauss, Claude, 11, 64, 186–187 n.8
Lewis, I. M., 24, 194 n.3
Life
  activation of religious icons, 45, 60, 86. *See also* karakam; nūl ēṉi; seeing
  coming back to, 61–62, 140
  death and, 157, 161, 175
  offering of, 46, 80, 84, 87, 88, 95, 134, 153 *See also* blood; sacrifice
  wanting, 80, 84, 87, 88, 184
Lineage deities, 147, 151, 154–156, 159, 206 nn.3, 5. *See also* Periyāṇṭavar
  demon-pēys compared to, 175
  pūvāṭaikkāri, 154–156, 159–160, 175
Love (role of)
  in possession by demon-pēys, 72, 74, 195 n.5, 196 n.5
  in possession by spirits of the dead, 116, 183
  in prevention against sorcery, 47
  in pūvāṭaikkāri puja, 132, 138, 144, 145, 146, 147, 149–150, 183, 203–204 n.14

Margosa tree and foliage, 36, 37, 52, 76, 82, 96, 120, 129, 135, 147
Māriamma, 23, 95, 104, 108, 110, 111–113, 117, 198 n.9, 199 n.2
  myth of, 110–112, 197 n.7, 198 n.8, 204–205 n.23
  smallpox as, 23, 111, 199 n.1
Marriage, 37, 141, 142, 144, 145, 166–169, 202 n.8
  myth of Śakti's, 140–141
  sacrifice compared to, 168, 175, 177
Marriage symbolism in
  exorcism, 93–94, 136
  pūvāṭaikkāri pūjā, 124, 126, 129, 136, 138, 139, 141, 142–145, 150, 177, 200 n.5
  representations of demonic possession, 72, 84
  village cults, 27, 151, 205 n.3

role of women in, 142–145, 148, 149, 205 n.4
scholarship on, 201 n.1, 201–202 n.3

Ram, Kalpana, 48, 70, 71, 194 n.1, 196–197 n.6
Ramanujan, A. K., 8, 9, 73, 74, 188 n.8
Recapitation, symbolism of, 94, 111, 137, 138, 162, 169, 204–205 n.23. *See also* decapitation; head
Reiniche, Marie-Louise, 200 n.5, 201 n.8
Representation of spirits and deities, 8, 155, 202 n.10. *See also* cāmis; effigy; karakam; medium for the dead; trance-possession
Ritual process (exorcism, investiture, and sacrifice), 7–10, 10–13, 136–137, 161–163
Roger, Abraham, 151–152, 206 n.1
Running (the role of)
in exorcism, 70, 74, 87, 91, 93, 134, 136, 162. *See also* exorcism
in initiatiory experiences, 29
in sacrifice, 160, 162, 177, 182, 207 n.10. *See also* sacrifice

Sacrifice
anthropological interpretations of, 164–165
consecration of victims, 157, 172, 173
in exorcism, 80, 87, 88
interpretations of Tamil sacrifice, 151–154, 207 n.2
in lineage cults, 17, 151, 154, 155, 156, 157, 160, 161, 169, 178, 206 n.5
personal investments in, 164, 169, 176, 177
sacrificial trance, 160, 162, 207 n.10
in sorcery, 46
in structural perspectives, 17, 89, 154, 161–163, 168, 175, 177
Sahlins, Marshall, 12
Śakti, 21, 28, 36, 37, 42, 52, 55, 59, 82, 188 n.2, 188–189 n.4
myth of, 140–141
See also margosa tree and foliage
Sax, William, 31–32
Schieffelin, Edward, 11, 41, 43, 65, 121
Scott David, 186 n.5, 195 n.7
Seeing
the dead, 104, 108, 114, 115, 118–119, 121. *See also* medium for the dead
with an evil eye, 46, 56, 74, 92, 102, 135
the goddess, 8, 9, 20, 23, 25, 40, 41, 43, 78, 111. *See also* camis
as healing, 54, 56–57, 65, 67
as mode of incorporation, 57, 86, 158, 207 n.9. *See also* effigy
with a third eye, 140–141
Shulman, David, 8, 29, 42, 77, 123, 149, 166, 168, 172, 197 n.12, 206 n.8, 207 n.2
Śiva, 34, 35, 36, 77, 168
myth of brahmanicide, 89–91
myth of fight with Takkaṉ (Dakṣa), 166–169
myth of marriage to Śakti, 140–141
Smallpox, 22–23, 28, 116–117. *See also* Māriamma
Sorcery, 21, 44, 45–47, 48, 51, 54, 66, 67, 109, 190 nn.1, 2, 191, nn.6, 7, 194 n.14. *See also* cahaṭai; ēval
Laksmi's case study, 49–53, 55, 62–63, 68. *See also* cāmi Nagaji
role of subjectivity in, 49, 66–67
Spirits of the dead, 16, 17, 112, 116, 198 n.3. *See also* demon-pēys; medium for the dead; pūvāṭaikkāri, 17, 117, 122. *See also* death (deifying); pūvāṭaikkāri; smallpox
entrancement or possession by, 16, 70, 74–76, 105, 106–107, 109, 116, 119–120, 197–198 n.2
timely and untimely, 17, 66, 70, 72, 91, 100–102, 106, 110, 113, 172, 197 n.1
Stirrat, R. L., 72, 75, 76, 85

Takkan (Dakṣa), 166–169, 175, 190 n.3, 207 nn.1, 2
Talai viti, 193 n.7
Tamarind tree, 73, 87, 91, 94, 95, 134
Test (pariṭcai), 134, 160, 204 n.16
Trance-possession, 9, 19, 78, 79, 80, 81, 82, 96, 99, 101, 114, 112, 115, 180, 187–188 n.2, 192 n.15, 198 n.6, 204 n.15. *See also* cāmis; demon-pēys; exorcism, medium for the dead; Periyāṇṭavar; pūvāṭaikkāri; sacrifice; spirits of the dead
  role of emotion in, 108, 132, 144, 149, 195 n.5, 196 n.5
  snake dance, 107, 112, 147, 148, 149
Trawick, Margaret, 28, 46, 145, 181, 182, 186 n.7, 187 n.2, 194 n.15, 200–201 n.7, 201 n.2
Trident, 19, 28, 37, 96, 98, 99, 158
Turner, Victor, 5, 7, 8, 10, 11, 12, 25, 94, 139, 181, 185–186 n.3

Vaciyam, 46, 47, 167, 168, 191 n.8. *See also* sacrifice; sorcery
Van Gennep, Arnold, 7, 8, 9
Vow, 34, 35, 36, 42, 43, 165–169, 170, 173, 174, 189 n.9, 207–208 n.3

Wallace, Anthony, 23, 29–30
Warning (eccarikkai), 8, 12, 80, 88, 128, 129, 136, 143, 147, 156, 157, 161, 183, 196 n.13, 205 n.6. *See also* exorcism; investiture; sacrifice
Widow, 102, 103, 112, 195 n.8
  widow making rite, 105, 108, 109, 198 n.5
Winnowing fan, 57, 59, 86, 192–193 n.5